55

50¢

This book may be kept

FOURTEEN DAYS

A fine will be charged for each day the book is kept overtime.

NB 9-31-76			
FEB 28 '77			
MAR 12 78			
MAR 16 79			
OCT 18 79			
MAR 19 '86			
OCT 08 '87			

THE FUTURE OF MARRIAGE

It may no longer be a lifetime contract, demand
sexual fidelity, or even involve sharing the same
household . . . It may disavow parenthood, recognize the autonomy of women, and pledge an even
deeper commitment between partners than it does
now . . .

Jessie Bernard, the renowned sociologist and author of *American Family Behavior, Academic
Women,* and *The Sex Game,* offers well-docu-
mented and highly controversial new views on the
survival of marriage—for better or for worse.

the
future
of marriage

jessie ^{shirley} bernard, 1903 –

This low-priced Bantam Book
has been completely reset in a type face
designed for easy reading, and was printed
from new plates. It contains the complete
text of the original hard-cover edition.
NOT ONE WORD HAS BEEN OMITTED.

THE FUTURE OF MARRIAGE
*A Bantam Book / published by arrangement with
World Publishing Company*

PRINTING HISTORY
World Publishing edition published May 1972
*A condensation entitled "Marriage: Hers and His"
appeared in* MS *magazine, December 1972*

Bantam edition published May 1973
2nd printing

Published simultaneously in the United States and Canada

---

*Bantam Books are published by Bantam Books, Inc., a National
General company. Its trade-mark, consisting of the words "Bantam
Books" and the portrayal of a bantam, is registered in the United
States Patent Office and in other countries. Marca Registrada.
Bantam Books, Inc., 666 Fifth Avenue, New York, N.Y. 10019.*

PRINTED IN THE UNITED STATES OF AMERICA

contents

4 / as i see it

introduction

what to look for in the future of marriage

The interest of some people in the future of marriage is really an interest in the future of sexual mores. When they ask, as many of them do, whether marriage is going to survive, their follow-up questions show that they are asking about the future of the controls on sexual behavior. Are the mores going to become so permissive that there will be no need for marriage at all?

The control of sexual behavior is, in fact, one of the major concerns of all societies, and, lenient or strict, they all have such controls. The topic has engaged the dedicated attention of the most serious scholars and scientists, including not only theologians but also Sigmund Freud himself and, more recently, Herbert Marcuse. They see an intrinsic relationship between such controls and the stability of the whole social structure. Freud told us that, in effect, we pay for civilization with our sexuality, and Marcuse now tells us that this bill has been paid and is no longer demanded of us. I am not at all deprecating this approach to the future of marriage when I say that the topic is of only tangential concern in this discussion. The subject here is not primarily marriage as part of a system of controls of sexual behavior, but rather the commitment which men and women make to each other—including the sexual commitment but not restricted to it—that constitutes their marriage.

The interest of others in the future of marriage has to do with the future of life styles. Their follow-up questions have to do with communes and other alternatives to the modern, isolated, privatized household inhabited exclusively by one nuclear family. And life styles are also fundamental, not at all irrelevant for the future of marriage. It is one of the major assumptions of the discussion here that the nature of the household in which a marriage functions is a powerful determinant of the nature of the relationship itself. We know that marriage was one thing when people lived in large rural households, and that it is quite a different thing when they live in small suburban or inner-city apartments.

There are still other reasons why there is interest in the future of marriage. Industry, for example, wants to know how many wedding rings and bridal gowns to produce, how many appliances and other household furnishings to manufacture, how many dwelling units to build. Communities want to know how many schoolrooms and playgrounds to provide. All of these are legitimate interests, but of no concern here.

The direction of this inquiry is twofold: first, the nature and probable future of the commitment which transforms a relationship into a marriage and, second, the nature of the life styles that are going to accompany it.

where to look for the future of marriage

I look for the future of marriage primarily, although not exclusively, among the young. For what young people think and do really is the future. So it is to them that one must turn for clues. The clues are not infallible, though. For we know that—at least until now —young people have tended to become more conservative with age. Still, the direction they move in is toward the future.

The clues do not come from all of the young, however—not, for instance, from the blue-collar or working-class young. Marriages among them tend to be traditional, as a spate of research studies by Mirra Komarovsky, Helena Lopata, Lee Rainwater, and even A. C. Kinsey and his associates have shown. They retain the old patterns of husband-wife relations long after the white-collar classes have changed. Although they count heavily in cross-sectional surveys based on random samples because there are so many of them, their numbers do not indicate that they will determine future trends. They constitute a rear guard rather than an advance guard. They do change, though, and when they do, it is in the middle-class direction.[1]

With respect to the lower classes as clues to the future, some fine distinctions have to be made. A clever —but I do not believe valid—case can be made for the proposition that the lower classes are now offering models for the future. Research, or rather investigation, of such families for well over a century, both here and abroad, has shown remarkable consistency. Unsanctioned liaisons, female-headed families, and out-of-wedlock births—regardless of race—have characterized the slums as far back as the research records go.

How do these forms of relationships differ from those now being advocated by the more radical young? it might well be asked. How, for example, does the young woman who demands the privilege of bearing a child outside of marriage and rearing it without involving the child's father differ from the unwed mother of the slums? How do the liaisons with which young people are now experimenting differ from those long characteristic among the poor?

It was once taken for granted that fashions in clothing originated in the upper classes and trickled down. Kinsey and his associates showed that there was an analogous imitation of higher-class patterns in the area of sexual behavior also. They found that young men who had moved up the class ladder resembled men in the class they finally arrived at rather than the men in the class they started from. Somehow or other, even before they had arrived at their class destination, they had taken over its sexual patterns.

Tom Wolfe tells us that fashions now move upward rather than downward. Is it legitimate to ask about marriage if the same reversal is in process? Are the lower-class patterns the wave of the future? Should we look for the future of marriage in the slums?

I do not think so. The patterns in the slums have resulted from necessity, not choice. Even in the Caribbean, where they are not rejected, they are viewed as inferior to middle-class ones; where the conditions are propitious, conventional marriage is preferred. If there is convergence between the radical young of the upper middle class and the slums, it will not be one imposed on them but one achieved—on ideological grounds, in fact. In concluding that the two are not the same, I do not deny a superficial similarity. But it is primarily to the form the patterns take among the upper middle-class young that I look for clues about the future of marriage.

how to look for the future of marriage

Aside from crystal-ball gazing, horoscope studying, and tea-leaf or palm reading—all of which tell us mainly about our personal futures—there are not many ways of looking for answers about the future. There are a few though, and at least three warrant our attention: (1) prediction based on historical trends (chapters 5–7); (2) projection based on statistical curves (chapter 8); and (3) "prophecy" based on human wishes and desires (chapters 9 and 10).

"Time present and time past / Are both perhaps present in time future, / And time future contained in time past," T. S. Eliot tells us in "Burnt Norton," in the *Four Quartets*. He saw the present, as, actually, the future to which the past had led. We need not think of this as implying a telic or predetermined or predestined course of history, as the Victorian view used to imply. For the past has been as varied as the present, with a meandering course and scores of tributaries, large and small, and many potential futures. Not all of them are even remotely relevant to our present or to our future, especially as regards marriage. Still, although a look backward may not tell us much specifically about the future of marriage tomorrow or even next week, it does offer a perspective that tempers expectations. The most distant past that has relevance for today, and therefore tomorrow, is the past of the preindustrial seventeenth and eighteenth centuries—in the years, that is, just before so much industrial production moved out of the household and before people picked themselves up to move to the cities in large numbers. In our exploration of possible clues for the future from history we will not go much farther back than that. But we will ask: How have the contents of the commitment which constitutes a marriage changed over time (chapter 5)? What has been the historical trend in the democratization of marriage, in the sense both of making it available to more and more people (chapter 6) and of achieving egalitarianism within the relationship itself (chapter 7)?

Another way to look for the future—perhaps the safest, and certainly the one used by the soberest researchers—is by way of projecting statistical trends. It is based on the persistence of massive forms, on the assumption that the conditions and circumstances which have been shaping the past will continue to shape the future. It tells us what—ceteris paribus—we can reasonably expect if (and a most perverse *if* this is) past and present trends continue. Since projections in the past have been wrong so often, nowadays we are sometimes given a choice. This is what to expect under such-and-such assumptions; this under other assumptions. These weasel words are absolutely essential to protect ourselves from the possible havoc wreakable on our curves, for there is always an ineffable *if* between the present and the future (chapter 8).

There are, in fact, some who deny that we can learn anything from the past or forecast anything from the present. "The present is *not* big with the future," an outstanding sociologist, Robert Nisbet, insists. "Nor, let it be well understood, was the past ever big with what is now the present. . . . 'Trends' are particularly suspect." They are always vulnerable to change. After we have milked history and statistics for all that they can tell us about the future of marriage, we still have to take into account a variety of "change agents." Robert Nisbet specifies four kinds: the maniac, the prophet, the genius, and the random event.

We shall have little to say of the maniac. Hitler was the archetype, but the madman we all fear today is the one who may give the signal to send the nuclear warhead. Even now, his shadow is influencing trends in ways not reducible to statistics, graphs, or projections. At least much of the thinking of the avant-garde young about the future, including marriage, reflects his influence. When asked about the future of marriage, they sometimes reply, "What future?" And they make decisions in that frame of mind.

Having thus, however briefly, paid our respects to the possible impact of the madman on the future of marriage, we now dismiss him. We cannot, however, be so cavalier about the other three.

the prophet and the future of marriage

In Nisbet's use of the term, *prophet* means reformer, in the sociological sense of "change agent." In sociological analysis, following Max Weber, the prophet is contrasted with the priest, whose function it is to support the status quo, to enforce the rules and rituals. It is the function of prophets, on the other hand, to tell us what is wrong with the status quo; they are social critics par excellence, and they usually beam their messages to the oppressed. "The prophets," C. Wright Mills notes, aim to master "the course of historical events by the power of the word." They preach. Unlike the scientists and scholars who, on the basis of historical and statistical trends tell us what they think is probable in the future, prophets tell us what they believe ought to be the future. Their "prophecy or commandment" is, Weber says, intended to "systematize and rationalize the way of life, either in particular points or totally." Male prophets (chapter 9) are quite different from female prophets (chapter 10) in their blueprints for the future, especially in the "particular points" they emphasize, as we shall see in part three of this book. Historical and statistical trends seem to favor at least one of the blueprints of the female prophets—a marriage in which the partners share domestic and provider roles—and, barring madmen and random events, it seems to have a propitious future (chapter 11).

the genius and the future of marriage

Nisbet uses the term *genius* to symbolize technology. We shall not pay special attention to his impact on trends, although the enormous impact of technology is recognized throughout, specifically in chapter 12.

Compared with the madman, the genius is an innocent. He may not even know what he is doing, but, as scientist or technician, he is, wittingly or not, the true revolutionary. The geniuses who invented the power-driven machines around which the factories were built at the end of the eighteenth century, for example, had no idea what they were going to do to marriage. Nor did Henry Ford have much in mind beyond profit when he introduced the mass production methods which finally deluged us with automobiles and transformed the courting and living habits of millions.

Laboratory scientists pursue their goals around the

world, generating revolutions by the score. They are learning how to give us control over our heredity, to "engineer" it so that in time we may be able to breed to specifications, including rendering the sex of children a matter of choice. When the sex ratio becomes subject to control, a form of market interaction could change the whole nature of the relations between the sexes as, in fact, it tended to do when the sex ratio was influenced by infanticide, especially of females, and by contraception, which permitted parents to cut off the number of children they produced when they had a son. If parental preferences glut the "market" with boys, girls will acquire "scarcity value," and if they "overproduce" girls, polygyny may come to look appealing. Or there will be daily reports, as in the stock market, announcing the current sex ratio so that parents can make their decisions with respect to sex more knowledgeably. Since either a "bear" or a "bull" market in one sex would tend to correct itself, however, the sex ratio would undoubtedly continue to be pretty much the same as now.

Geneticists and cytologists, as well as the chemists who are preparing the ideal contraceptive which will definitively divorce sexual relations from reproduction, are profoundly influencing the future of marriage. Assured immunity to conception undercuts the rationale and justification for a millennial insistence on female virginity and chastity, with repercussions on the relations between the sexes as yet not completely charted.

The genius-as-scientist is learning how to do many other things that can alter the course of human events. He is increasing the length of life of more and more people so that they have time to learn that they are unhappy in their marriages, as they did not when death came early. The genius-as-scientist is learning how to conquer the degenerative diseases so that sexuality lasts longer; and he is learning about the nutrition that brings sexual maturity on earlier so that we are sexual beings a larger proportion of our life span—and sexually attractive into later years, so that the hormone-supplied postmenopausal woman need no longer deteriorate into a sexless cipher.

The genius-as-scientist and his fellows are learning about the nature of sex and gender, and how to unscramble or prevent the confusion which sometimes mixes them. They are learning how to transplant not only vital organs but also fetuses, so that in time surrogate females may gestate the infants of other females —or how to create a mechanical surrogate womb which would liberate any woman from nine months of gestating babies—or how to store sperm so that men could undergo vasectomy without relinquishing fatherhood forever. All these scientific achievements are changing the very bodies of the men and women who will be involved in marriage in the future.

There are other kinds of scientists, too. They research the relationships between and among people. The social scientists have been researching marriage for well over a generation—ever since it became respectable in the 1920s—and by now they have accumulated a considerable body of data, not necessarily as "hard" as chemical or biological data, but not so "soft" as to be denied serious attention. Their way of influencing the future is indirect. By making us aware of the nature of the present, they give us a chance to form an opinion about it; by putting the profane hands of science on what is taken for granted, they deprive it of its sacred character and open it up to challenge.

the random event: a classic case

The random event—usually not so random after we study it—is something that happens outside of the expected course of events. We do not always know what hit our projections to throw them so badly out of kilter. All we know is that something has done so—a sit-in, for example, which sets in motion a vast social movement that transforms a silent generation into a revolutionary one.

A classic illustration of misprojection, or of a projection fouled up by a random event, occurred between about 1947 and 1957, the decade of the so-called feminine mystique or marital togetherness. All of a sudden—it wasn't, of course, but it seemed so—the statistical curves began to change their direction, or at least their slant. The birthrate, which, with fluctuations due to wars and depressions, had been declining for as long as records had been kept, was showing surprising resistance to the resumption of the longtime downward trend after the expected postwar spurt. It even began to go up. It remained high until late in the 1950s. Nor were these simply delayed or anticipated babies, as at first they were believed to be; they were additional babies—third, fourth, fifth, and sixth babies. Women first married in the 1950s were not only having their babies sooner after marriage than women married any time earlier in the twentieth century—only 1.3 years after marriage—but the total number of babies they would ever have was also estimated by Paul C. Glick to be higher than that of any generation of women born since 1890. Women left college to get married earlier than ever before, families engaged in an orgy of togetherness. Women cooked and baked and wove and made a career of being homebodies. They accepted wholeheartedly the feminine mystique: a woman validated her femaleness by having babies.

A wide gamut of explanations has been invoked to explain this random event or strange deviation from expectations—for example, a reaction against the trauma of depression and war; affluence; or the full impact of Freudianism, which had now filtered down from the academy to the man in the street, setting the cause of women back half a century and convincing them they could fulfill themselves only in domesticity. It is not essential for our purposes here to delve into the causes of this interesting aberration; whatever it was due to, it changed the nature of marriage for that generation; produced a bumper crop of babies; set the stage for a second emancipation of women; and, in general, discredited old projections. For this reason, everyone is now more cautious than ever before about projections. A sudden random event can make the soberest predictions and projections look ridiculous—or the most ridiculous, plausible. The importance attached to the random event thus supplies a caveat behind which anyone talking about the future can hide if what he says proves too wide of the mark.

Before we can take off for the future, however, we have to start from the present (chapters 1–4). What is marriage like today? Part one tries to supply the answer.

1

where we are today

chapter one

the two marriages

the future of whose marriage?

Both Uncle Honoré and Gigi's grandmother remembered it well, according to Alan Jay Lerner's lyric. And this is what it had been like according to Uncle Honoré: "it was a lovely moonlit evening in May. You arrived at nine o'clock in your gold dress only a little late for our dinner engagement with friends. Afterwards there was that delightful carriage ride when we were so engrossed in one another that we didn't notice you had lost your glove." Ah, yes, Uncle Honoré remembered it well indeed, down to the last detail.

Or, come to think of it, did he? For Gigi's grandmother remembered it too, but not at all the same way. "There was no moon that rainy June evening. For once I was on time when we met at eight o'clock at the restaurant where we dined alone. You complimented me on my pretty blue dress. Afterwards we took a long walk and we were so engrossed in one another that we didn't notice I had lost my comb until my hair came tumbling down."

The Japanese motion picture *Rashomon* was built on the same idea—four different versions of the same

3

events. So, also, was Robert Gover's story of the college boy and the black prostitute in his *One Hundred Dollar Misunderstanding*. Also in this category is the old talmudic story of the learned rabbi called upon to render a decision in a marital situation. After listening carefully to the first spouse's story, he shook his head, saying, "You are absolutely right"; and, after listening equally carefully to the other spouse's story, he again shook his head, saying, "You are absolutely right."

There is no question in any of these examples of deliberate deceit or prevarication or insincerity or dishonesty. Both Uncle Honoré and Grandmamma are equally sincere, equally honest, equally "right." The discrepancies in their stories make a charming duet in *Gigi*. And even the happiest of mates can match such differences in their own memories.

In the case of Uncle Honoré and Grandmamma, we can explain the differences in the pictures they had in their heads of that evening half a century earlier: memories play strange tricks on all of us. But the same differences in the accounts of what happened show up also among modern couples even immediately after the event. In one study, for example, half of all the partners gave differing replies to questions about what had happened in a laboratory decision-making session they had just left. Other couples give different responses to questions about ordinary day-by-day events like lawn mowing as well as about romantic events. Once our attention has been called to the fact that both mates are equally sincere, equally honest, equally "right," the presence of two marriages in every marital union becomes clear—even obvious, as artists and wise persons have been telling us for so long.

Anyone, therefore, discussing the future of marriage has to specify whose marriage he is talking about: the husband's or the wife's. For there is by now a very considerable body of well-authenticated research to show that there really are two marriages in every marital union, and that they do not always coincide.

"his" and "her" marriages

Under the jargon "discrepant responses," the differences in the marriages of husbands and wives have come under the careful scrutiny of a score of researchers. They have found that when they ask husbands and wives identical questions about the union, they often get quite different replies. There is usually agreement on the number of children they have and a few other such verifiable items, although not, for example, on length of premarital acquaintance and of engagement, on age at marriage and interval between marriage and birth of first child. Indeed, with respect to even such basic components of the marriage as frequency of sexual relations, social interaction, household tasks, and decision making, they seem to be reporting on different marriages. As, I think, they are.

In the area of sexual relations, for example, Kinsey and his associates found different responses in from one- to two-thirds of the couples they studied. Kinsey interpreted these differences in terms of selective perception. In the generation he was studying, husbands wanted sexual relations oftener than the wives did, thus "the females may be overestimating the actual frequencies" and "the husbands . . . are probably underestimating the frequencies." The differences might also have been vestiges of the probable situation earlier in the marriage when the desired frequency of sexual relations was about six to seven times greater among husbands than among wives. This difference may have become so impressed on the spouses that it remained in their minds even after the difference itself had disappeared or even been reversed. In a sample of happily married, middle-class couples a generation later, Harold Feldman found that both spouses attributed to their mates more influence in the area of sex than they did to themselves.

Companionship, as reflected in talking together, he found, was another area where differences showed up.

Replies differed on three-fourths of all the items studied, including the topics talked about, the amount of time spent talking with each other, and which partner initiated conversation. Both partners claimed that whereas they talked more about topics of interest to their mates, their mates initiated conversations about topics primarily of interest to themselves. Harold Feldman concluded that projection in terms of needs was distorting even simple, everyday events, and lack of communication was permitting the distortions to continue.[1] It seemed to him that "if these sex differences can occur so often among these generally well satisfied couples, it would not be surprising to find even less consensus and more distortion in other less satisfied couples."

Although, by and large, husbands and wives tend to become more alike with age, in this study of middle-class couples, differences increased with length of marriage rather than decreased, as one might logically have expected. More couples in the later than in the earlier years, for example, had differing pictures in their heads about how often they laughed together, discussed together, exchanged ideas, or worked together on projects, and about how well things were going between them.

The special nature of sex and the amorphousness of social interaction help to explain why differences in response might occur. But household tasks? They are fairly objective and clear-cut and not all that emotion-laden. Yet even here there are his-and-her versions. Since the division of labor in the household is becoming increasingly an issue in marriage, the uncovering of differing replies in this area is especially relevant. Hard as it is to believe, Granbois and Willett tell us that more than half of the partners in one sample disagreed on who kept track of money and bills. On the question, who mows the lawn? more than a fourth disagreed. Even family income was not universally agreed on.

These differences about sexual relations, companionship, and domestic duties tell us a great deal about the two marriages. But power or decision making can cover all aspects of a relationship. The question of who makes decisions or who exercises power has therefore attracted a great deal of research attention. If we were interested in who really had the power or who really made the decisions, the research would be hopeless. Would it be possible to draw any conclusion from a situation in which both partners agree that the husband ordered the wife to make all the decisions? Still, an enormous literature documents the quest of researchers for answers to the question of marital power. The major contribution it has made has been to reveal the existence of differences in replies between husbands and wives.

The presence of such inconsistent replies did not at first cause much concern. The researchers apologized for them but interpreted them as due to methodological inadequacies; if only they could find a better way to approach the problem, the differences would disappear. Alternatively, the use of only the wife's responses, which were more easily available, was justified on the grounds that differences in one direction between the partners in one marriage compensated for differences in another direction between the partners in another marriage and thus canceled them out. As, indeed, they did. For when Granbois and Willett, two market researchers, analyzed the replies of husbands and wives separately, the overall picture was in fact the same for both wives and husbands. Such canceling out of differences in the total sample, however, concealed almost as much as it revealed about the individual couples who composed it. Granbois and Willett concluded, as Kinsey had earlier, that the "discrepancies . . . reflect differing perceptions on the part of responding partners." And this was the heart of the matter.

Differing reactions to common situations, it should be noted, are not at all uncommon. They are recognized in the folk wisdom embedded in the story of the blind men all giving different replies to questions on the nature of the elephant. One of the oldest experiments in juridical psychology demonstrates how different the statements of witnesses of the same act can be. Even in laboratory studies, it takes intensive training of raters to make it possible for them to arrive at agreement on the behavior they observe.

It has long been known that people with different backgrounds see things differently. We know, for example, that poor children perceive coins as larger than do children from more affluent homes. Boys and girls perceive differently. A good deal of the foundation for projective tests rests on the different ways in which individuals see identical stimuli. And this perception—or, as the sociologists put it, definition of the situation—is reality for them. In this sense, the realities of the husband's marriage are different from those of the wife's.

Finally, one of the most perceptive of the researchers, Constantina Safilios-Rothschild, asked the crucial question: Was what they were getting, even with the best research techniques, family sociology or wives' family sociology? She answered her own question: What the researchers who relied on wives' replies exclusively were reporting on was the wife's marriage. The husband's was not necessarily the same. There were, in fact, two marriages present:

One explanation of discrepancies between the responses of husbands and wives may be the possibility of two "realities," the husband's subjective reality and the wife's subjective reality —two perspectives which do not always coincide. Each spouse perceives "facts" and situations differently according to his own needs, values, attitudes, and beliefs. An "objective" reality could possibly exist only in the trained observer's evaluation, if it does exist at all.

Interpreting the different replies of husbands and wives in terms of selective perception, projection of needs, values, attitudes, and beliefs, or different definitions of the situation, by no means renders them trivial or incidental or justifies dismissing or ignoring them.

They are, rather, fundamental for an understanding of the two marriages, his and hers, and we ignore them at the peril of serious misunderstanding of marriage, present as well as future.

is there an objective reality in marriage?

Whether or not husbands and wives perceive differently or define situations differently, still sexual relations are taking place, companionship is or is not occurring, tasks about the house are being performed, and decisions are being made every day by someone. In this sense, some sort of "reality" does exist. David Olson went to the laboratory to see if he could uncover it.

He first asked young couples expecting babies such questions as these: Which one of them would decide whether to buy insurance for the newborn child? Which one would decide the husband's part in diaper changing? Which one would decide whether the new mother would return to work or to school? When there were differences in the answers each gave individually on the questionnaire, he set up a situation in which together they had to arrive at a decision in his laboratory. He could then compare the results of the questionnaire with the results in the simulated situation. He found neither spouse's questionnaire response any more accurate than the other's; that is, neither conformed better to the behavioral "reality" of the laboratory than the other did.

The most interesting thing, however, was that husbands, as shown on their questionnaire response, perceived themselves as having more power than they actually did have in the laboratory "reality," and wives perceived that they had less. Thus, whereas three-fourths (73 percent) of the husbands overestimated their power in decision making, 70 percent of the wives underestimated theirs. Turk and Bell found similar results in Canada. Both spouses tend to attribute decision-making power to the one who has the "right" to make the decision. Their replies, that is, conform to the model of marriage that has characterized civilized mankind for millennia. It is this model rather than their own actual behavior that husbands and wives tend to perceive.

We are now zeroing in on the basic reality. We can remove the quotation marks. For there is, in fact, an objective reality in marriage. It is a reality that resides in the cultural—legal, moral, and conventional—prescriptions and proscriptions and, hence, expectations that constitute marriage. It is the reality that is reflected in the minds of the spouses themselves. The differences between the marriages of husbands and of wives are structural realities, and it is these structural differences that constitute the basis for the different psychological realities.

the authority structure of marriage

Authority is an institutional phenomenon; it is strongly bound up with faith. It must be believed in; it cannot be enforced unless it also has power. Authority resides not in the person on whom it is conferred by the group or society, but in the recognition and acceptance it elicits in others. Power, on the other hand, may dispense with the prop of authority. It may take the form of the ability to coerce or to veto; it is often personal, charismatic, not institutional. This kind of personal power is self-enforcing. It does not require shoring up by access to force. In fact, it may even operate subversively. A woman with this kind of power may or may not know that she possesses it. If she does know she has it, she will probably disguise her exercise of it.

In the West, the institutional structure of marriage has invested the husband with authority and backed it by the power of church and state. The marriages of wives have thus been officially dominated by the husband. Hebrew, Christian, and Islamic versions of deity were in complete accord on this matter. The laws, written or unwritten, religious or civil, which have defined the marital union have been based on male conceptions, and they have undergirded male authority.

Adam came first. Eve was created to supply him with companionship, not vice versa. And God himself had told her that Adam would rule over her; her wishes had to conform to his. The New Testament authors agreed. Women were created for men, not men for women; women were therefore commanded to be obedient. If they wanted to learn anything, let them ask their husbands in private, for it was shameful for them to talk in the church. They should submit themselves to their husbands, because husbands were superior to wives; and wives should be as subject to their husbands as the church was to Christ. Timothy wrapped it all up: "Let the woman learn in silence with all subjection. But I suffer not a woman to teach, nor to usurp authority over the man, but to be in silence." Male Jews continued for millennia to thank God three times a day that they were not women. And the Koran teaches women that men are naturally their superiors because God made them that way; naturally, their own status is one of subordination.

The state as well as the church had the same conception of marriage, assigning to the husband and father control over his dependents, including his wife. Sometimes this power was well-nigh absolute, as in the case of the Roman patria potestas—or the English common law, which flatly said, "The husband and wife are as one and that one is the husband." There are rules still lingering today with the same, though less extreme, slant. Diane B. Schulder has summarized the legal framework of the wife's marriage as laid down in the common law.

The legal responsibilities of a wife are to live in the home established by her husband; to perform the domestic chores (cleaning, cooking, washing, etc.) necessary to help maintain that home; to care for her husband and children. . . . A husband may force his wife to have sexual relations as long as his demands are reasonable and her health is not endangered. . . . The law allows a wife to take a job if she wishes. However, she must see that her domestic chores are completed, and, if there are children, that they receive proper care during her absence.

A wife is not entitled to payment for household work; and some jurisdictions in the United States expressly deny payment for it. In some states, the wife's earnings are under the control of her husband, and in four, special court approval and in some cases husband's consent are required if a wife wishes to start a business of her own.

The male counterpart to these obligations includes that of supporting his wife. He may not disinherit her. She has a third interest in property owned by him, even if it is held in his name only. Her name is required when he sells property.

Not only divine and civil law but also rules of etiquette have defined authority as a husband's prerogative. One of the first books published in England was a *Boke of Good Manners,* translated from the French of Jacques Le Grand in 1487, which included a chapter on "How Wymmen Ought to Be Gouerned." The thirty-third rule of Plutarch's *Rules for Husbands and Wives* was that women should obey their husbands; if they "try to rule over their husbands they make a worse mistake than the husbands do who let themselves be ruled." The husband's rule should not, of course, be brutal; he should not rule his wife "as a master does his chattel, but as the soul governs the body, by feeling with her and being linked to her by affection." Wives, according to Richard Baxter, a seventeenth-century English divine, had to obey even a wicked husband, the only exception being that a wife need not obey a husband if he ordered her to change her religion. But, again, like Plutarch, Baxter warned that the husband should love his wife; his authority should not be so coercive or so harsh as to destroy love. Among his twelve rules for carrying out the duties of conjugal love, however, was one to the effect that love must not be so imprudent as to destroy authority.

As late as the nineteenth century, Tocqueville noted that in the United States the ideals of democracy did not apply between husbands and wives:

Nor have the Americans ever supposed that one consequence of democratic principles is the subversion of marital power, or the confusion of the natural authorities in families. They hold that every association must have a head in order to accomplish its objective, and that the natural head of the conjugal association is man. They do not therefore deny him the right of directing his partner; and they maintain, that in the smaller association of husband and wife, as well as in the great social community, the object of democracy is to regulate and legalize the powers which are necessary, not to subvert all power.

This opinion is not peculiar to men and contested by women; I never observed that the women of America consider conjugal authority as an unfortunate usurpation [by men] of their rights, nor that they thought themselves degraded by submitting to it. It appears to me, on the contrary, that they attach a sort of pride to the voluntary surrender of their own will, and make it their boast to bend themselves to the yoke, not to shake it off.

The point here is not to document once more the specific ways (religious, legal, moral, traditional) in which male authority has been built into the marital union—that has been done a great many times—but merely to illustrate how different (structurally or "objectively" as well as perceptually or "subjectively") the wife's marriage has actually been from the husband's throughout history.

the subversiveness of nature

The rationale for male authority rested not only on biblical grounds but also on nature or natural law, on the generally accepted natural superiority of men. For nothing could be more self-evident than that the patriarchal conception of marriage, in which the husband was unequivocally the boss, was natural, resting as it did on the unchallenged superiority of males.

Actually, nature, if not deity, is subversive. Power, or the ability to coerce or to veto, is widely distributed in both sexes, among women as well as among men. And whatever the theoretical or conceptual picture may have been, the actual, day-by-day relationships between husbands and wives have been determined by the men and women themselves. All that the institutional machinery could do was to confer authority; it could not create personal power, for such power cannot be conferred, and women can generate it as well as men, a matter examined in greater detail in chapter 7. Thus, keeping women in their place has been a universal problem, in spite of the fact that almost without exception institutional patterns give men positions of superiority over them.

If the sexes were, in fact, categorically distinct, with no overlapping, so that no man was inferior to any woman or any woman superior to any man, or vice versa, marriage would have been a great deal simpler. But there is no such sharp cleavage between the sexes except with respect to the presence or absence of certain organs. With all the other characteristics of each sex, there is greater or less overlapping, some men being more "feminine" than the average woman and some women more "masculine" than the average man. The structure of families and societies reflects the positions assigned to men and women. The bottom stratum includes children, slaves, servants, and outcasts of all kinds, males as well as females. As one ascends the structural hierarchy, the proportion of males increases, so that at the apex there are only males.

When societies fall back on the lazy expedient—as all societies everywhere have done—of allocating the rewards and punishments of life on the basis of sex, they are bound to create a host of anomalies, square pegs in round holes, societal misfits. Roles have been allocated on the basis of sex which did not fit a sizable number of both sexes—women, for example, who chafed at subordinate status and men who could not master superordinate status. The history of the relations of the sexes is replete with examples of such misfits. Unless a modus vivendi is arrived at, unhappy marriages are the result.

There is, though, a difference between the exercise of power by husbands and by wives. When women exert power, they are not rewarded; they may even be punished. They are "deviant." Turk and Bell note that "wives who . . . have the greater influence in decision making may experience guilt over this fact." They must therefore dissemble to maintain the illusion, even to themselves, that they are subservient. They tend to feel less powerful than they are because they *ought* to be.

When men exert power, on the other hand, they are rewarded; it is the natural expression of authority. They feel no guilt about it. The prestige of authority goes to the husband whether or not he is actually the one who exercises it. It is not often even noticed when the wife does so. She sees to it that it is not.

There are two marriages, then, in every marital union, his and hers. And his, as we shall see in the following chapters, is better than hers. The questions, therefore, are these: In what direction will they change in the future? Will one change more than the other? Will they tend to converge or to diverge? Will the future continue to favor the husband's marriage? And if the wife's marriage is improved, will it cost the husband's anything, or will his benefit along with hers?

chapter two

the husband's marriage

marriage has had a bad press among men

Despite the insistence of theologians that marriage is a holy estate, divinely instituted, it has had a bad press among men. Writers of the Middle Ages were already inveighing against it, invoking tales of domestic discord to support their complaints that wives were impossible. Not until the middle of the sixteenth century were there books on *The Prayse of All Women* (1541) and *The Defence of Women*. But even then we learn from *The Schole-howse of Women* that women were fastidious, sharp-tongued, quick-tempered, disputatious, fond of double-dealing, and, when married, querulous and gossipy, not willing to mind the house.

Thus, for centuries men have been told—by other men—that marriage is: no bed of roses, a necessary evil, a noose, a desperate thing, a field of battle, a curse, a school of sincere pretense. Robert Louis Stevenson commented on the dread of marriage that men professed. There was an aphorism attributed to Oscar Wilde that marriage was a wonderful institution; every woman should be married, but no man. Another, attributed to H. L. Mencken, is to the effect that since it

16

was to man's interest to avoid marriage as long as possible and to woman's to marry as favorably as possible, the sexes were pursuing diametrically antagonistic ends in this major life concern.

Even today, it is the rare stand-up comedian who omits from his repertoire half a dozen references to the unholy state of matrimony, its fetters, its frustrations. And Russell V. Lee, a physician with forty-four years of clinical experience, tells us, for reasons spelled out below, that, "men really suffer more in marriage than do women"; that "the state is less natural for the male; . . . [that] he contributes more and gets less out of marriage than the female."[1]

Men, in brief, have been railing against marriage for centuries. If marriage were actually as bad for men as it has been painted by them, it would long since have lost any future it may ever have had. In the face of all the attacks againt it, the vitality of marriage has been quite stupendous. Men have cursed it, aimed barbed witticisms at it, denigrated it, bemoaned it—and never ceased to want and need it or to profit from it.

The male clichés could hardly have been more wrong. However horrendous the inner picture of the husbands' marriage might be, the measurable evidence against that image is overwhelming. For, contrary to all the charges leveled against it, the husbands' marriage, whether they like it or not (and they do), is awfully good for them.

marriage is good for men

There are few findings more consistent, less equivocal, more convincing than the sometimes spectacular and always impressive superiority on almost every index—demographic, psychological, or social—of married over never-married men. Despite all the jokes about marriage in which men indulge, all the complaints they lodge against it, it is one of the greatest boons of their sex.

Employers, bankers, and insurance companies have long since known this. And whether they know it or not, men need marriage more than women do. As Samuel Johnson said, marriage is, indeed "the best state for man in general; and every man is a worse man in proportion as he is unfit for the married state."

The research evidence is overwhelmingly convincing. (See tables 1 through 9.)* Although the physical health of married men is no better than that of never-married men until middle age, their mental health is far better, fewer show serious symptoms of psychological distress, and fewer of them suffer mental health impairments. Married men, Otto Pollak tells us, seem also to be preserved from lives of crime. Blau and Duncan, Melita Odin, and William H. Whyte have shown that marriage is an asset in a man's career, including his earning power. The value of marriage for sheer male survival is itself remarkable. It does, indeed, pay men to be married. "Most men," Paul C. Glick notes, "profit greatly from having a wife to help them to take care of their health."

A great sociologist, Emile Durkheim, was one of the first to point out the salvaging effect of marriage on men in connection with a classic study of suicide.[2] He computed what he called a "coefficient of preservation"—the ratio of the suicide rate of the unmarried to that of the married—and found it higher for men than for women. The differential still holds. In the United States, the suicide rate for single men is almost twice as high as for married men, less than one-and-a-half times greater for single than for married women.

Marriage is so demonstrably good for men that when social scientists were asked to come up with a set of social indicators that would tell us how our society was operating, as the economic indicators told us how our economy was operating, one such index proposed by

---

* All tables appear in a separate section following the Afterword.

Paul C. Glick as a favorable sign was the proportion of adult males who were married. The statistical underpinning for this rationale was convincing. Compared with never-married men, the lot of married men is a providential one.

. . . and they know it

The actions of men with respect to marriage speak far louder than words; they speak, in fact, with a deafening roar. Once men have known marriage, they can hardly live without it. Most divorced and widowed men remarry. At every age, the marriage rate for both divorced and widowed men is higher than the rate for single men. Half of all divorced white men who remarry do so within three years after divorce. Indeed, it might not be far-fetched to conclude that the verbal assaults on marriage indulged in by men are a kind of compensatory reaction to their dependence on it.

but does marriage deserve all the credit?

Statistically speaking, there seems to be no doubt about the value of marriage for men, but a statistical view is not enough. There are selective factors involved that can distort the picture, and hence cannot be ignored. We are never sure how much of the good showing of married men as compared with never-married men is related to the beneficent effects of marriage itself, and how much to the selective processes that weed poor prospects out of marriage in the first place. It should be made clear that, when we speak of selective factors, we include not only conscious choices among both sexes but also the impersonal factors that influence who marries and who does not. A man may be "selected out" of marriage not by any decision on his part but by such factors as residence, occupation, and so on.

Some men do not marry because they do not want to, for whatever reason, and some because no one wants to marry them. In either case, we are faced with the irrepressible, inevitable, and—most researchers concede—insoluble chicken-and-egg, cause-and-effect question. Do the married men look so much better than the never-married because marriage is good for them or because the less good prospects were selected out of the married population in the first place? All the thoughtful researchers who tackle this problem end up by admitting that they cannot solve it. Short of a controlled experiment—unthinkable this side of 1984—we have to pick and choose our way around and through the data. At least two lines of evidence are helpful; one "controls" the selective factor by comparing the married with the widowed, and one by comparing men of the same general status and occupation who have and who have not married.

By comparing the married with the widowed we minimize, though we do not entirely eliminate, the selective factor,[3] for the widowed did once choose marriage or were chosen by someone. Such comparisons give us an indication of the value of marriage by showing what happens to men who are deprived of it by death. They are miserable. They show more than expected frequencies of psychological distress, and their deathrate is high. Men deprived of the benefits of marriage by bereavement show the effects in high mortality rates. That it is the deprivation itself which produces such a result can be seen in the fact that during the first half year after bereavement, one study found an increase of 40 percent in mortality. Five years after bereavement, the survival rate of married or remarried men in a sample of forty-seven men with an average age of seventy-six was higher than that of the never-married, the separated, the unremarried divorced, or the unremarried widowed. And although a fifth of widowed women in another study showed some deterioration of health in the year following bereavement, death resulted twice as often among widowed men as among widowed women. The suicide rate of the widowed man is high, too. In fact, suicide is the third-ranking cause of death among widowed men.[4]

The other, and less macabre, way to minimize the selective factor in measuring the benefits of marriage is to compare men of the same general background who have and who have not married. For one profession, the clergy, this has been done. A spate of studies in Germany, Austria, England, and Wales over a century, comparing the mortality of priests and that of clergy of other denominations does, indeed, as a summary by King and Bailar indicates, show that the married had greater longevity than the unmarried.[5]

who is selected into marriage? who out?

Even if one wants to give due recognition to the selective factor, it is not easy to determine what qualities or types are being strained into or out of marriage. Take health, for example. Because of the higher death-rate among the never-married men, one would expect poor health to characterize the single more than the married. Still, as measured in terms of the absence of chronic conditions or conditions that restrict activity, the never-married seem to show no inferiority to the married, at least in the years seventeen to forty-four, when most men marry.

Yet the higher mortality rates for the unmarried as compared with the married must have some explanation. The man who is not well, Paul Glick suggests, may be withdrawn and therefore not exposed to marriage-able women. Or, if he is, he may feel that he cannot add to the stresses of his life by assuming marital responsibilities, or subject a wife to infection. In either case he selects himself out of marriage; he thus remains in the unmarried population and raises its mortality figures. Conversely, Paul Glick continues, it may be the especially ebullient who, whether by temperament or habit, "are prone to take more chances that endanger their lives" who raise the mortality rates of the unmarried.

Quite aside from selective factors related to longevity, one would expect the unmarried to be the "easy riders," the men who cannot tolerate the restrictions of conventionality but seek to satisfy a wide gamut of desires. Veroff and Feld did, indeed, find that the unmarried more than the married felt marriage to be restrictive. It was, however, a more negative kind of reaction than one would expect on the basis of the "easy rider" hypothesis —that is, the single men "seemed to be avoiding the burdens of marriage and . . . the responsibilities to children" involved in marriage. It was, apparently, a passive avoidance of the difficulties of marriage rather than unlimited wants, desires, or aspirations that motivated them. A recessive, constricted, limited orientation rather than an aggressive, expansive one seemed to have selected these men out of marriage.

There are other hints that suggest a recessive rather than an aggressive selectivity at work. Veroff and Feld, for example, found that single men showed less desire than married men to avoid being alone. The National Center for Health Statistics reported inertia and passivity also more common among the single than among the married men.

Antisocial tendencies and greater moral laxness were found by Genevieve Knupfer to be more common among single than among married men, as was also a stressful childhood. All of these must be viewed as selective factors helping to explain the bad showing of the unmarried.

I have given so much attention to the selectivity factor because it is undoubtedly part of the explanation of the superiority married men show over the unmarried, and cannot therefore be ignored in evaluating the impact of marriage. But the weight of the evidence explaining differences by marital status seems to me to be overwhelmingly on the side of the beneficent effects which marriage has on men rather than on the initial superiority of the married men.

does it just seem longer? are they happier?

Survival might not be such a desideratum if a man's married life were miserable. A short and happy life outside of marriage might seem preferable to an infinitely longer one within it. Actually, life is not only longer among the married; it is also happier.[6] Despite all the protestations of men to the contrary, married life makes them happy. (See tables 6 through 9.) In fact, Norman M. Bradburn found that almost twice as many married as never-married men reported themselves as very happy, and, conversely, more than twice as many never-married men as married men reported themselves as not too happy. John Milton was right: "the main benefits of conjugal society . . . are happiness and peace," especially for men. For most husbands' marriages are, in fact, very happy.

It will be noted that only the documentable, research-based evidence of the benefits of marriage have been emphasized here. Every happily married man will be able to add a dozen more. Marriage is more comfortable than bachelorhood; sex is always available; responsibility is a rewarding experience. It is reassuring to have a confidante. And then there is love, friendship, companionship. . . . But the misogynists cited earlier in this chapter can shoot them all down. Marriage hasn't meant all that to *them!* It is difficult, however—indeed, impossible—for them to controvert the hard evidence from mental health, criminality, career success, and sheer survival that is cited here.

costs as benefits: the ineluctable conflict in marriage

The benefits of marriage for men do not come without costs. Some freedoms must be surrendered. The young man applying for a marriage license is not likely to ask what costs—in the form, for example, of limits on his freedom—marriage will impose. To be sure, the bachelor party that used to be popular the night before the marriage was a recognition that hereafter there would indeed be sacrifices—no more carousing, no more irresponsible fun.

Durkheim pointed out that there were no limits to man's desires, that unless limits were imposed on men they would dash themselves to pieces, for "man aspires to everything and is satisfied with nothing. This morbid desire for the infinite . . . everywhere accompanies anomie." There is thus an intrinsic conflict between the unlimited freedom of men to satisfy their wants and the restrictions that marriage imposes on them. Naturally, they chafe at these restrictions, but it is the very restrictions that save them.

The conflict is even deeper, and it is ineradicable. The discrepancy between the husband's horrendous inner picture of his marriage and its actual, observable, beneficent effects on him is a measure of the ineluctable conflict built into marriage. Human beings want dramatically opposite things: stability and adventure; security and variety, excitement and thrills—but also a quiet haven to retreat to when the fun and games are over.

the future of the husband's marriage

Two major "costs" or grievances of men against marriage have been the sexual restrictiveness it imposes on them and the economic responsibilities it demands of them. The clinician referred to earlier specified among other "agonies" of marriage for men, "the violence that marriage does to the biologically ingrained instinct for promiscuity." And the desire on the part of husbands for extramarital partners has been reported in a wide variety of studies by Burgess and Wallin, Kinsey, Terman, and myself. Another of the clinician's bill of particulars against marriage was that the husband's responsibilities were greater than those of the wife. There seem to be two major ways, then, in which the marriages of husbands could be improved. One would be to relieve them from the responsibility for the entire support of wives and children, and the other would be to make sexual varietism more feasible. Both seem to be in process of realization.

Relief from exclusive responsibility for support of the family is well along the way. The increase in the proportion of wives and mothers who share the provider role has been one of the most outstanding trends in the second half of the twentieth century. Between 1940 and 1950, the Women's Bureau tells us, the proportion of marriages including working wives doubled, and by 1967 it had more than tripled, reaching 34 percent in that year. In a third of all husbands' marriages, in brief, husbands were receiving help in supporting the family, and the proportion was increasing with great rapidity. In marriages where there were school-age children, the proportion of marriages which had help from the wives was as high as 53 percent in income brackets from $3,000 to $5,000. The proportion was less in higher-income families, but even among them it was not negligible; in fact, a considerable proportion of all middle- and upper-middle-class families depend on the wife's contribution to family income for their comfortable, not to say, affluent, style of living. Many would not even be in the upper middle class without the wife's contribution.[7] This "shared-role" pattern will undoubtedly increase in the future. (We add parenthetically here, anticipating fuller discussion later, that the benefits of "shared roles" are not exclusively on the husband's side. Women who work show fewer symptoms of psychological distress.)

With respect to the second grievance of men against marriage, the need for greater sexual freedom, the data are less hard—and, for that reason, quite puzzling. Kinsey and his associates were least satisfied with their data on extramarital relations; such data were most difficult to get. They concluded, therefore, that about 10 to 20 percent more men than they had reported (about half of their male respondents) had had extramarital relations. Since data on extramarital relations were so difficult to come by, there is no real bench mark, and a re-survey in our more permissive ambience might be expected only to bring out what was formerly unreported.

Actually, in a study reported in 1970, a generation after Kinsey's work, no increase was discovered. Kinsey had found that among men with high school and at least some college education, the proportion who had had extramarital sexual relations was about 40 percent. And that was precisely the proportion found in a similar sample by *Psychology Today* in 1970.[8]

Whether or not such relations are more frequent, however, the way is being prepared for their growing acceptance, for such a trend toward acceptance is unmistakable. I have shown elsewhere that a conception of marriage which tolerates, if it is not actually sympathetic with, extramarital relations is on its way, and as we shall see, provision for sexual varietism is almost standard in male blueprints for the future. The time is not far off when this desideratum of husbands' marriages may also be achieved.

At the present time, at least, if not in the future, there is no better guarantor of long life, health, and happiness for men than a wife well socialized to perform the "duties of a wife," willing to devote her life to taking care of him, providing, even enforcing, the regularity and security of a well-ordered home. And as the trends just noted become implemented—that is, as the wife shares increasingly the provider role and as there

develops greater tolerance for extramarital relations—
the pluses of marriage for men will be increased.

Like the annals of the poor, the story of the husband's marriage can be short and simple; not so, however, the story of the wife's. If, as Paul Glick tells us,
"being married is about twice as advantageous to men
as to women in terms of continued survival," being
married is only half as good for wives as for husbands,
not only in terms of survival but in other terms as well.

chapter three

the wife's marriage

Because we are so accustomed to the way in which marriage is structured in our society, it is hard for us to see how different the wife's marriage really is from the husband's, and how much worse. But, in fact, it is. There is a very considerable research literature reaching back over a generation which shows that: more wives than husbands report marital frustration and dissatisfaction; more report negative feelings; more wives than husbands report marital problems; more wives than husbands consider their marriages unhappy, have considered separation or divorce, have regretted their marriages; and fewer report positive companionship. Only about half as many wives (25 percent) as husbands (45 percent) say that there is nothing about their marriage that is not as nice as they would like. And twice as many wives (about a fourth) as husbands (about 12 percent) in a Canadian sample say that they would not remarry the same partner or have doubts about it. Understandably, therefore, more wives than husbands seek marriage counseling; and more wives than husbands initiate divorce proceedings.

In a population of couples undergoing counseling, the wives were found by Emile McMillan to be more discontent than the husbands. More of the wives than of the husbands rated themselves as unhappy during the first year of marriage, and also during the next several years. The wives saw the problems as having started sooner and lasting longer. ... They saw a greater density of problem areas. ... They showed less desire to save their marriage, and gave more negative reasons and fewer positive reasons for saving their marriage.

Even among happily married couples, Harvey J. Locke found, fewer wives than husbands report agreement on such family problems as finances, recreation, religion, affection, friends, sex, inlaws, time together, and life aims and goals; and more report serious marital difficulties. The proportions were not great in most cases, but the proportion of these happily married wives who reported no difficulties at all was considerably lower than the proportion of happily married men who reported none. The wives reported problems in more than twice as many areas as did husbands.

The evidence for the destructive nature of the wife's marriage does not, however, rest on this bill of particulars, impressive as it is. For, despite the dissatisfactions catalogued above, a very large proportion of married women, inconsistently enough, consider themselves and their marriages to be happy, a paradox to be commented on in greater detail below. It is not, therefore, the complaints of wives that demonstrate how bad the wife's marriage is, but rather the poor mental and emotional health of married women as compared not only to married men's but also to unmarried women's.

husbands and wives

Although the physical health of married women, as measured by absence of chronic conditions or restricted activity, is as good as, and in the ages beyond sixty-five even better than, that of married men, they suffer far greater mental-health hazards and present a far worse clinical picture. Gurin, Veroff, and Feld, for example, found that more married women than married men have felt they were about to have a nervous breakdown; more experience psychological and physical anxiety; more have feelings of inadequacy in their marriages and blame themselves for their own lack of general adjustment. Other studies report that more married women than married men show phobic reactions, depression, and passivity; greater than expected frequency of symptoms of psychological distress; and mental-health impairment. (See tables 11 through 13.)

Although marriage protects both marital partners against suicide as compared with single men and women, it protects husbands more than wives. Only about half as many white married as single men commit suicide; almost three-fourths as many married as single women do. And although women in general live longer than men, marriage is relatively better for men than it is for women in terms of sheer survival, quite aside from suicide. That is, the difference in deathrates between married and unmarried women is less than that between married and unmarried men (30 percent as compared to 48 percent).

Considerably less documentable but not to be ignored is Otto Pollak's interpretation of the different effect of marriage on the crime rate of men and women. He asks "whether in our culture marriage may help men to settle down while it may cause women to become disturbed and on occasions violators of the law."

The psychological costs of marriage, in brief, seem to be considerably greater for wives than for husbands and the benefits considerably fewer.

merely a sex difference?

If the mental and emotional health of wives—anxious, depressed, psychologically distressed—is so dismal, perhaps we are dealing with a sex difference quite unrelated to marriage. Perhaps, that is, what we find are not husband-wife but male-female differences. Perhaps the mental and emotional health of wives shows up so poorly simply because they are women? Perhaps it is just the nature of the beast.

This interpretation is one version of the perennial charge against women: it's their own fault. For it has been standard operating procedure among psychiatrists and counselors to place the blame for the psychological symptoms of wives on the women themselves. When or if a woman takes her problems to a psychiatrist, the response of the therapist has all too often taken the form, Robert Stoller reminds us, of convincing her that her misery was self-generated and could be relieved only by learning to come to terms with her position, even though, as Gurin, Veroff, and Feld reported, both husbands and wives believe that the husband is usually the source of problems in the marriage.

It is true that the costs of social change in terms of mental distress may be greater for women than for men. A comparison by Rice and Kepecs of patients in a university medical center in 1958 and in 1969, for example, showed that the young women in 1969 were sicker than those of 1958 had been, whereas the young men were not. But the disparities in mental health we are discussing here are of longer duration than just the last decade.

Even so, does this "it's-merely-a-sex-difference" interpretation really explain the wife's dismal mental and emotional health? This is an answerable question, and the answer is no. For the mental-health picture of wives shows up just as unfavorably when compared with unmarried women. Thus, for example, a study by R. R. Willoughby a generation ago found that married more than unmarried women were troubled by ideas that people were watching them on the street, were fearful of falling when on high places, had their feelings easily hurt, were happy and sad by turns without apparent reason, regretted impulsive statements, cried easily, felt hurt by criticism, sometimes felt miserable, found it hard to make up their minds, sometimes felt grouchy, were burdened by a sense of remorse, worried over possible misfortune, changed interests quickly, were bothered when people watched them perform a task, would cross the street to avoid meeting people, were upset when people crowded ahead of them in line, would rather stand than take a front seat when late, were self-conscious about their appearance, and felt prevented from giving help at the scene of an accident. Moreover, more recent studies tend to confirm such differences. Genevieve Knupfer found that more married than unmarried women tend to be bothered by feelings of depression, unhappy most of the time, disliking their present jobs, sometimes feeling they are about to go to pieces, afraid of death, terrified by windstorms, worried about catching diseases, sometimes thinking of things too bad to talk about, and bothered by pains and ailments in different parts of the body. Overall, more of the wives than of the single women she found to be passive, phobic, and depressed; and although the total number who showed severe neurotic symptoms was small, these were evident in almost three times as many married as single women. And, except in the menopausal decade, more married than single women, Leo Srole found, show mental-health impairment. Many symptoms of psychological distress show up more frequently than expected among married women: nervous breakdowns, nervousness, inertia, insomnia, trembling hands, nightmares, perspiring hands, fainting, headaches, dizziness, and heart palpitations. They show up less frequently than expected among unmarried women.[1] (See tables 14, 15, and 16.)

Related to these findings is Pollak's conclusion that "at least in the culture of Western civilization, the amount of crime committed by married women—independent of age—seems to be higher than the amount of crime committed by single women," suggesting again that something other than sex per se is needed to explain the relatively poor mental and emotional health of married women.

So far, we have held marital status constant and varied sex, as they say in laboratory experiments, and then we have held sex constant and varied marital status. Now again we hold marital status constant and vary sex by comparing single men and women. The sex differences that show up in this "design" are enormous —but quite opposite to those that show up when we compare married men and women. Now it is the women who show up well and the men poorly. Unless one has actually examined the evidence it is hard to realize what a poor showing unmarried men make and what a good showing the unmarried women make. (See tables 17 through 20.)

In Manhattan, for example, about twice as many never-married men as never-married women show mental-health impairments. Single women in this country, Gurin, Veroff, and Feld report, experience "less discomfort than do single men: they report greater happiness, are more active in . . . working through the problems they face, and appear in most ways stronger in meeting the challenges of their positions than men." Single women show far less than expected frequency of symptoms of psychological distress as compared with single men. And, as though further corroboration were necessary, single women suffer far less than single men from neurotic and antisocial tendencies. More single men than single women are depressed and passive. In 1960, about 10 percent of the never-married men thirty-five years of age and over, as compared with only half that proportion of single women thirty years of age and over "resided involuntarily in institutions," and over half were in mental institutions.

Like almost everyone else who researches this seemingly anomalous situation, even seasoned psychologists like Gerald Gurin, Joseph Veroff, and Sheila Feld were surprised to find results so "contrary to the popular stereotypes of the frustrated old maid and the free and unencumbered bachelor life." Now it is the superiority, not the inferiority, of the women that has to be explained. These researchers explored the possibility that age was a factor; perhaps the unmarried men were older and hence more demoralized. But, no; quite the opposite. The single men were younger than the single women. The psychologists then invoked a sex difference to explain the disparity: "perhaps it is in an ability to form and maintain meaningful personal attachments that we may find a clue to these differences we have seen—that single women are less distressed than single men."

This is not likely in view of the fact, reported by R. R. Willoughby, that more unmarried than married women lack self-confidence, feel inferior, prefer quiet amusements, avoid crowds, express themselves better in writing than in speech, keep in the background at social occasions, feel shy, like to be alone, avoid meeting the important people at a tea, hesitate to express themselves in a group, and feel self-conscious before superiors. True, this description tells us nothing about how unmarried women compare with unmarried men in such interpersonal relations, but it does not necessarily suggest a person with great "ability to form and maintain meaningful personal attachments."

Education, occupation, and income all tell the same story of the relative superiority of unmarried women over unmarried men. At every age level, the average single women surpass the average single men. At the earlier ages, say twenty-five to thirty-four, the single men and women are not very different in education, occupation, or income; the marriageables are still mixed in with the nonmarriageables. But as the marriageable men drop out of the single population, those who are left show up worse and worse as compared with their feminine counterparts, so that twenty years later, at ages forty-five to fifty-four, the gap between them is a veritable chasm. The single women are more educated, have higher average incomes, and are in higher occupations.[2]

When, finally, we vary both marital status and sex, by comparing married men and unmarried women, we find relatively little overall difference so far as mental health is concerned, superiorities and inferiorities tending to cancel out. But the women are spectacularly better off so far as psychological distress symptoms are concerned, suggesting that women start out with an inital advantage which marriage reverses. (See tables 21 through 23.)

All we have done so far is to show that we cannot explain the poor picture of the married woman's mental and emotional health on the basis of sex alone. But dismissing that explanation does not imply that we can explain it exclusively by marriage alone either. There is always that elusive "chicken-and-egg" problem, the selective factor. Do married women show up so poorly as compared to both married men and unmarried women because a certain type of woman prefers to marry? Or because men prefer to marry a certain type of woman?

Before we attempt to answer these questions, though, an interesting difference between the selective process among men and women has to be looked at, for it operates differently in the two sexes and hence produces different results.

the marriage gradient

In our society, the husband is assigned a superior status. It helps if he actually *is* somewhat superior in ways—in height, for example, or age or education or occupation—for such superiority, however slight, makes it easier for both partners to conform to the structural imperatives. The girl wants to be able to "look up" to her husband, and he, of course, wants her to. The result is a situation known sociologically as the marriage gradient.

By and large, both men and women tend to marry mates with the same general class and cultural background; there is "homogamy." But within that common background, men tend to marry women slightly below them in such measurable items as age, education, and occupation, and, presumably, in other as yet unmeasurable items as well. The result is that there is no one for the men at the bottom to marry, no one to look up to them. Conversely, there is no one for the women at the top to look up to; there are no men who are superior to them. The result, as shown in figure 1, is that the never-married men (B) tend to be "bottom-of-the-barrel" and the women (A) "cream-of-the-crop."

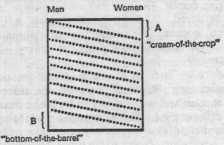

Figure 1 The Marriage Gradient

When we speak of "bottom-of-the-barrel," we have to extend the idea beyond measurable qualities, and recognize that we are talking only about qualities related to marriage. A man might be a poor prospect as a marriage partner but extremely attractive in practically every other way. He might make a pleasant escort. He might be a superb host at parties. He might be a good companion, a good tennis player. He might surpass in all these ways yet lack what Terman and Wallin called "marital aptitude." Suitability for marriage is only one human quality, though admittedly basic in the context of our discussion here.

The marriage gradient is the result of quite abstract sociological processes. But it tells us little about the specific boys and girls, men and women, whose lives are involved in it. For that kind of information we have to turn elsewhere.

what kinds of women are selected into and out of marriage?

A generation ago, Raymond R. Willoughby, in a study of the differences between married and unmarried women, raised this very question, and concluded that either "a calm type of woman remains unmarried or . . . marriage has disturbing effects upon women." Evidence for the first of these alternatives shows up at a fairly young age.

Thus, for example, Floyd M. Martinson, a sociologist, studying high school girls in 1955, concluded that in these early years marriage had its strongest appeal to the less mature and less well-adjusted girls. And, of course, once selected into marriage, many of these young women remained in the married population despite the high divorce rate for teen-age marriages. The high school girls who remained single showed better health, better emotional adjustment, greater self-reliance, a greater sense of personal freedom, and fewer withdrawal tendencies. They were also better adjusted to their families. They showed more social aggressiveness, participated in activities more, got better grades, accepted social standards more, and showed fewer antisocial tendencies. "The overall adjustment of the single girls," Martinson concluded, "was decidedly better than that of the married girls."

Girls who marry early tend to drop out of school. And Paul C. Glick has found that marital instability tends to be highest for women who drop out of school, either high school or college. He has posited "certain predisposing factors in the social background and psychological orientation of these persons that affect their persistence in education and also affect their persistence in marriage." The "predisposing factors" tend to be premarital pregnancies. It is not so much the mere fact of dropping out of school that is crucial as the reason for dropping out.

Very few girls are selected out of marriage because they do not want to marry, as in the case of some men. Practically all girls want to marry, want to very badly—too badly, some think. If, therefore, they are selected out of marriage, the reason is likely to lie in the behavior of men. What men select into or out of marriage reflects what men want or do not want in wives.

Especially suggestive in this connection, illustrating what men do not want in wives, is the evidence from a study by Richard Klemer which shows that the never-married women tend to be upwardly mobile; they, more than the married women, had started life in lower socio-economic levels and pulled themselves up educationally and professionally. The implication is that they must have been "aggressive" and had, more than most women, strong "achievement motivation." Along the same general line is the evidence from the relationship between income and marriage rates. Left to themselves, unpressured, a considerable number of young women might not want to marry, for at every age bracket, the more income a girl or woman has, the lower the rate of marriage, a situation just the reverse of that of men. Similarly, the better her job, the lower the rate of marriage. A good job that pays well is a strong competitor to marriage for many women. (See tables 24 and 25.) And the girl who has the well-paying job may be too achievement-motivated to attract men. For the talents it takes to achieve the best paying jobs—including competitiveness, aggressiveness, drive, and will to succeed—are precisely those not wanted by most men in wives, at least in the years when mates are being selected.

Another kind of woman is also selected out as well, and for quite different qualities. Contrary to the cliché that though men may play around with the freewheeling girl they marry the more conventional one, it is the conventional girl who is less likely to be chosen. That is, fewer unmarried than married women, Knupfer found, have engaged in unconventional heterosexual activities; fewer show antisocial behavior. On the other hand, Klemer reported that more are morally strict. More are conscientious. And, finally, more are scrupulous about family obligations.

What it all adds up to is that, although marriage may have "disturbing" effects on women, some women are more anxious than others to subject themselves to this disturbance, and men are more interested in marrying some types of women than others. The unfavorable mental-health showing of married women may be due at least in part to a perverse preference on the part of men.

We have gone out of our way to pay our respects to the selective factors in explaining the grim mental-health picture of wives precisely because we do not consider them of great importance. For, actually, they have slight weight compared to marriage itself since, sooner or later, practically everyone marries. We are now free, therefore, to explore whatever it might be about marriage itself that could also contribute to an explanation.

parenthetical interjection

Strictly speaking, we cannot speak of marriage as the "cause" of the dismal mental-health status of wives, for the evidence is not clinical but statistical in nature. The two are not identical. The statistical approach tries to discover relationships and associations among factors. If these relationships and associations are close, some kind of causal pattern is inferred even though it cannot be demonstrated in each individual case.

A classic illustration of the difference between the

clinical and the statistical or epidemiological approach is that of cigarette smoking. Most of the scientific evidence on the pathogenic effects was statistical or epidemiological rather than clinical. And for the layman such evidence is often confusing. Here is John Doe who has been smoking cigarettes for seventy years, still hale and hearty at eighty-five. So what's wrong with cigarettes? All right, says the epidemiologist, John Doe is lucky, a "deviant case," "a chance error" who represents the one case in a thousand that escapes the pathological effects. Similarly, not everyone exposed to plagues or epidemics dies. Not everyone in tuberculosis areas contracts the disease. Nor do all women exposed to the destructive aspects of marriage as now structured become depressed or develop mental-health impairments or show symptoms of psychological distress. Still, it is worthwhile to inaugurate public-health programs even though not everyone is susceptible to the pathogenic factor; and it is worthwhile to see what can be done about the wife's marriage even though not all wives are vulnerable to its depredations.

It is not necessarily the magnitude of the statistical differences between the mental health of married and single women or between married men and married women that is so convincing; it is, rather, the consistency of the differences. No one difference or even set of differences by itself would be definitive; but the cumulative effect of so many is. The poor mental health of wives is like a low-grade infection that shows itself in a number of scattered symptoms, no one of which is critical enough to cause an acute episode. And so, therefore, it is easy to ignore. Or to dismiss. Or to blame on women themselves. There must be something wrong with them if they are psychologically so distressed.

But even those who blame women themselves for their psychological malaise and see it as an inability on their part to cope with the demands of marriage or to come to terms with their destiny finally have to concede that the way the social world is organized may have something to do with their plight.

a shock theory of marriage

A generation ago, I propounded what I then called a shock theory of marriage. In simple form, it stated that marriage introduced such profound discontinuities into the lives of women as to constitute genuine emotional health hazards.

There are some standardized "shocks" that are almost taken for granted. Mirra Komarovsky, for example, has analyzed the conflict the bride experiences between her attachment to her parental family and her attachment to her husband. There is, too, the end of the romantic idealization that terminates the "honeymoon," known in the research literature as "disenchantment." The transition from the always-on-good-behavior presentation of the self during courtship to the daily lack of privacy in marriage, symbolized in the media by hair curlers and the unshaved face, presents its own kind of shock. So also does the change that occurs when the wife ceases to be the catered-to and becomes the caterer-to. These and related discontinuities have to do with redefinition of the self, with the assumption of new role obligations.

Another type of shock, not commonly recognized in the research literature, has to do with a different kind of disenchantment. Girls are reared to accept themselves as naturally dependent, entitled to lean on the greater strength of men; and they enter marriage fully confident that these expectations will be fulfilled. They are therefore shaken when they come to realize that their husbands are not really so strong, so protective, so superior. Like children who come to realize that their parents are not really omniscient or, actually, all that powerful, wives learn with a shock that their husbands are not truly such sturdy oaks. They can no longer take it for granted that their husbands are stronger than they. Like everyone else, they have been fooled by the stereotypes and by the structural imperatives. For some it becomes a full-time career to keep the self-image of husbands intact.

Some of the shocks that marriage may produce have to do with the lowering of status that it brings to women. For, despite all of the clichés about the high status of marriage, it is for women a downward status step. The legal status of wives, for example, is lower not only than that of husbands but also than that of unmarried women. A woman, Diane Schulder reminds us, loses a considerable number of legal rights when she marries. But that is relatively minor compared to other forms of status loss, to be documented presently, as Congreve's Mrs. Millamant in *The Way of the World* so well knew when she spoke of "dwindling" into a wife. Even after she had bargained with Mirabel to preserve at least some of her prerogatives in marriage, she said, "these articles subscribed, if I continue to endure you a little longer, I may by degrees dwindle into a wife." And Mirabel recognized that his status would be enhanced: "Well, have I liberty to offer conditions, that when you are dwindled into a wife I may not be beyond measure enlarged into a husband?"

the pygmalion effect

"Dwindling" into a wife takes time. It involves a redefinition of the self and an active reshaping of the personality to conform to the wishes or needs or demands of husbands. Roland G. Tharp, a psychologist, concludes from a summary of the research literature, that wives "conform more to husbands' expectations than husbands do to wives.' " This tendency of wives to shape themselves to conform to their husbands has been documented in recent research in some detail. Among freshman women who were the top 1 percent of their class at Michigan State University, for example, Dorothy Robinson Ross found that those who married lost independence and "impulse expression"; after marriage they became more submissive and conservative. Cheraskin and Ringdorf found that, in emotional state, young married women resembled other young women more than they resembled their husbands, but older wives resembled their husbands more than they resembled other unrelated women. (The authors of this study note laconically that the same kind of marital convergence results in blood-glucose concentration.) The young husbands did not resemble either their wives or the unrelated women; but the older husbands were more like the older unrelated women—as well as more like their wives—than the younger husbands were like the younger unrelated women, suggesting a kind of sexual convergence with age, quite apart from, and in addition to, convergence with marriage.

We do not have to imagine a man enforcing conformity with a whip or clenched fists or even a sculptor lovingly shaping the woman of his dreams to account for the Pygmalion effect. The conditions of marriage itself as now structured lead to this result. Women who are quite able to take care of themselves before marriage may become helpless after fifteen or twenty years of marriage. Genevieve Knupfer describes a woman who had managed a travel agency before marriage, for example, who when widowed at the age of fifty-five had to ask friends how to get a passport. No wonder the self-image of wives becomes more negative with age. No wonder Alice Rossi warns us that "the possibility must be faced . . . that women lose ground in personal development and self-esteem during the early and middle years of adulthood, whereas men gain ground in these respects during the same years." For it is the husband's role—not necessarily his own wishes, desires, or demands—that proves to be the key to the marriage and requires the wife to be more accommodating.

wives make more adjustments

This Pygmalion effect tallies with the finding generally reported that wives make more of the adjustments called for in marriage than do husbands. Understandably so. Because the wife has put so many eggs into the one basket of marriage, to the exclusion of almost every other, she has more at stake in making a go of it. If anything happens to that one basket, she loses everything; she has no fallback position. She tends, therefore, to have to make more of the concessions called for by it. Thus, when a sample of husbands and wives were asked by Burgess and Wallin three to five years after marriage who had made the greater adjustment in marriage, "the preponderance of replies . . . was that the wives had made the greater adjustment." The husband upon marriage maintains his old life routines, with no thought or expectation of changing them to suit his wife's wishes. "Often she submits without voicing a protest," Burgess and Wallin found. "In other cases the wife may put up a contest, although she generally loses." Both wives and husbands in this study agreed that the wives had made the greater adjustment. Sometimes, when the wife concedes that the husband has made more adjustments, he reports himself to be quite unaware of making any; they were probably too trivial for him even to notice.

One of the most poignant adjustments that wives have to make is in the pattern of emotional expression between themselves and their husbands. Almost invariably, they mind the letdown in emotional expression that comes when the husband's job takes more out of him, or the original warmth subsides. Lee Rainwater found in marriages between men and women in the lower-lower classes that wives tended to adopt their husbands' taciturnity and lack of demonstrativeness rather than insist on winning him over to theirs. They settled for a fairly low emotional diet. "I support you, don't I?" is a common reply to the question desperate women sometimes ask, "Do you still love me?" Not a very nutritious one for a starving person. Some women call it dehumanizing.

The psychological and emotional costs of all these

adjustments show up in the increasing unhappiness of wives with the passage of time and in their increasingly negative and passive outlook on life. One measure of these costs can be found in the increasing rate of alcoholism with time. Thus, for example, although there is no difference between married and single women in deathrates from cirrhosis of the liver when they are very young, beyond the teens up to the mid-thirties, cirrhosis of the liver is only half as common among married as among single women. Thereafter, however, the difference declines so that, by middle age, the married women have not only caught up with the single women but have even surpassed them. (See table 26.) It is not simply a matter of taking over the drinking habits of husbands, for the married women remain more like the single women than like the married men. Something or many things about marriage itself must be involved, the Pygmalion effects being perhaps only one.

female into neuter

Some of the changes brought about by marriage are extremely subtle. In sexuality, for example. Women at marriage move from the status of female to that of neuter being. In the East European shtetl this important change was recognized and marked by a rite of passage, the cutting off of a woman's hair; she must not be attractive to other men. Much of the alleged decline in sexual attractiveness of women which is attributed to age is really attributable to the prescriptions for the role of wife. Women who remain active in nonmarital roles often retain their attractiveness far into middle age and even beyond, for modern women are potentially "sexier" than women were in the past. They mature as sexual beings earlier and reach menopause later than in the past, and Kinsey and his associates noted that early sexual maturation was associated with greater sexual activity and longer duration of sexual interest.

In the 1890s, as Henry Seidel Canby remembered it, "women past their twenties, or married, suffered dumbly from an imagination that made them sexless, because they did not know what was wrong and would not have admitted the truth if it had been told to them." Married women were "cinders—agreeable, yes, admirable often, interesting often, yet cinders, . . . long emptied of fire—and like cinders they responded." Nor, according to Philip Slater, has the situation changed much since then. Stylistically, he tells us, "it is only young unmarried girls who are allowed to be entirely female. . . . As soon as they are married they are expected to mute their sexuality somewhat, and when they become mothers this neutralization is carried even further." Some women in desperation to validate their own sexuality engage in flirtation or even serious affairs to prove to themselves that they are still sexual beings.

All of these changes brought about by marriage can contribute something to the explanation that we are seeking for the sad picture of the mental health of married women. But there is still another change which may outweigh them. It has to do with the position of the housewife.

marriage and life style

We are going to have a great deal to say later about households and life styles. They are inextricably bound up with marriage. Marriage has to do with the commitment of husbands and wives to one another; life styles have to do, obviously, with the way they live. And the way in which most husbands and wives live today is alone, or with their young children, in a separate isolated household, the care of which is the wife's almost exclusive responsibility. This life style, Philippe Ariès has taught us, is not very old—a few centuries—and, if trends now incipient continue, may not have a very long future ahead of it in its present form. But for the present and at least the immediate future, the individual, separate, isolated, privatized household will be the stage on which most marriages will play themselves out. And it will be the wife's responsibility to take care of it.

occupational change in marriage

One of the basic differences in the wife's and the husband's marriages results from this life style—namely, the almost complete change in work that marriage brings in her life but not in his. Until yesterday, and for most women even today, every wife becomes a *house*wife. And this is not always a congenial role. Militant feminists have argued that this occupational change amounts to the same thing as requiring all men upon marriage to give up their jobs and become janitors, whether they like janitor work or not. Regardless of whether this analogy is fair or not, it is true that interest in and aptitude for housework are not as equally distributed among the female population as is the occupation of housework, wherefore a large number of vocational misfits is almost inevitable. For, as it happens, not all women have an interest in or aptitude for the job of housewife—just as, no doubt, there are many men who do and would prefer it to what they are doing.

Thus, for example, despite the powerful engines of socialization which almost from infancy begin to prepare girls for domesticity, only about a third of the girls among high school graduates showed interest in the domestic arts a generation ago, and even fewer—less than a fifth—among college women. The figures would doubtless be less today. These data, taken at their face value, indicate that a fairly large number of women are drawn into housework as an occupation by marriage, in spite of an absence of positive interest in the domestic arts. Coming to terms with domesticity is not the least of the housewife's trauma, however much the sheer drudgery has been alleviated. Housekeeping remains an uncongenial occupation to many women.

"The housewife is a nobody," says Philip Slater, and almost everyone agrees. Her work is menial labor. Even more status-degrading is the unpaid nature of her job. Few deny the economic as well as the sociological importance of housework and homemaking. Housework is part of the great infrastructure on which, as David Riesman has reminded us, the entire superstructure of the economy and the government rests. If women did not supply the services of taking care of the living arrangements of workers, industry would have to do so, as in the case of lumber camps, ships, and the military. But housewives are not in the labor force. They are not paid for the services that they perform.

The low status of the wife's work has ramifications all through her marriage. Since her husband's work is not only higher in status but usually competitive, as hers is not, and he has to meet certain clothing and grooming standards or lose his job, his needs have to be catered to. If there has to be a choice, his new suit is more important than hers. This, quite apart from whatever personal or institutional prestige his work confers, tends to put him in a position of status superiority to the wife.[3]

Housework is a dead-end job; there is no chance of promotion. One cannot grow in it. There is a saying that passes as wit to the effect that Washington is full of talented men and the women they married when they were young. The couple who began their marriage at the same stages of their development find themselves far apart in later years. "Persons who took the initiative in seeking divorce," Nelson Foote has noted, "in explaining their experience, and likewise observers of broken marriages, speak frequently of a mate's having outgrown the other. It is the husband who usually outgrows the wife." Not only does the wife not grow, but the nonspecialized and detailed nature of housework may actually have a deteriorating effect on her mind, as Mary

Roberts Coolidge observed long ago, rendering her incapable of prolonged concentration on any single task. No wonder that after hours of passive, often solitary, absorption in television and radio soap operas, she comes to seem dumb as well as dull.

Nelson Foote assesses to the husband some of the responsibility for the deterioration of housewives in his developmental theory of marriage. He points out that

> one's direction of growth as well as the rate of learning is powerfully affected by the responses of those particular others upon whom he inescapably depends for evaluations of his behavior. . . . Husbands are hardly prepared by cultural history [to perform the role of] the most beneficent other in the development of wives for whom the performance of household duties no longer seems to challenge their capacities. . . . The commonest picture in American marriages is that in which the husband has no concept whatever of contributing by his manner of speaking and listening to the elaboration of his wife's career, particularly when she has no ostensible professional career. While her constructive achievements with home and children may be honored, her ventures in other directions appear more often to be subject to insensitive disparagement than to insightful and competent facilitation.

Sympathetic encouragement instead of indifference or positive belittling from husbands would doubtless lessen the alienating effect of housework as an occupation on the marriage, but in and of itself could not overcome it, for the sympathy would be, in effect, patronizing.

The difference in the work of wives and husbands has other alienating effects on the relationship also. It is quite hard even for men in occupations that differ widely to maintain close friendships. They do not share the same kinds of problems. For example, imagine a case like this:

"Jim and I were great friends at college; we belonged to the same fraternity. We enjoyed one another's company and had lots of good times together. After graduation I took a management trainee job in a large establishment and he opened up a small neighborhood grocery shop. We maintained contacts for a while but we soon drifted apart. Our interests began to diverge. He couldn't appreciate the kinds of problems I had to face in a large bureaucracy and his own absorption in the piddling problems of running his little operation seemed uninteresting to me."

The same kind of alienation can occur in marriage. Change Jim's name to Jane, the grocery shop to a household, a graduation to marriage, and the story would not have to be changed very much. The occupational split that occurs at marriage can have the same kind of alienating effect on married partners as on friends of the same sex.

The occupation of the housewife has other than intellectual effects that can be damaging. As life is now organized in small, private living units, housework is isolating. "The idea of imprisoning each woman alone in a small, self-contained, and architecturally isolating dwelling is a modern invention," Philip Slater reminds us, "dependent upon an advanced technology. In Muslim societies, for example, the wife may be a prisoner, but she is at least not in solitary confinement. In our society the housewife may move about freely, but since she has nowhere in particular to go and is not a part of anything her prison needs no walls. This is in striking contrast to her premarital life, especially if she is a college graduate. In college she was typically embedded in an active group life with constant emotional and intellectual stimulation. College life is in this sense an urban life. Marriage typically eliminates much of this way of life for her, and children deliver the coup de grace. Her only significant relationships tend to be with her husband who, however, is absent most of the day. Most of her social and emotional needs must be satisfied by her children, who are hardly adequate to the task."

Isolation has negative psychological effects on people. It encourages brooding; it leads to erratic judgments, untempered by the leavening effect of contact with others. It renders one more susceptible to psychoses. Melvin Seeman has found that it also heightens one's sense of powerlessness. Anything, therefore, that increases isolation constitutes a hazard, even something as seemingly trivial as the increase in isolation contributed by which story of a building you live on. A study by D. M. Fanning of the families of servicemen in Germany, published in 1967, found, for example, that women living in apartment buildings were more susceptible to psychoneurotic disorders than women who lived in houses, and the higher the apartment the greater the susceptibility. "The incidence of psychoneurotic disorders was nearly three times as high among women living in flats as [it was among] those living in houses, and this [incidence] increased as the height of homes increased. . . . For mothers with preschool children, the confinement within flats provided an added irritant to the monotony and boredom of their lives."

the housewife syndrome

That it is being relegated to the role of housewife rather than marriage itself which contributes heavily to the poor mental and emotional health of married women can be demonstrated by comparing housewives, all of whom may be presumed to be married, with working women, three-fifths of whom are also married. Marriage per se is thus at least partially ruled out as an explanation of differences between them. The comparison shows that wives who are rescued from the isolation of the household by outside employment show up very well. They may be neurotic, but, as Sharp and Nye have shown, they are less likely than women who are exclusively housewives to be psychotic. And even the allegation of neuroticism can be challenged. For Sheila Feld tells us that "working mothers are less likely than housewives to complain of pains and ailments in different parts of their body and of not feeling healthy enough to carry out things they would like to do."[4]

But the truly spectacular evidence for the destructive effects of the occupation of housewife on the mental and emotional health of married women is provided by the relative incidence of the symptoms of psychological distress among housewives and working women. In all except one of twelve such symptoms—having felt an impending nervous breakdown—the working women were overwhelmingly better off than the housewives. Far fewer than expected of the working women and more than expected of the housewives, for example, had actually had a nervous breakdown. Fewer than expected of the working women and more than expected of the housewives suffered from nervousness, inertia, insomnia, trembling hands, nightmares, perspiring hands, fainting, headaches, dizziness, and heart palpitations. The housewife syndrome is far from a figment of anyone's imagination.

If this chapter were a musical composition, table 27 would be accompanied by a loud clash of cymbals. And a long silence would ensue to give a chance for its emotional impact to be fully experienced. For table 27 provides one of the most cogent critiques yet made of marriage as it is structured today.

Dismissing the housewife syndrome, as some unsympathetic observers do, is like telling a man dying of malnutrition that he's lucky he isn't dying of cancer. Perhaps he is. But this is no reason to dismiss malnutrition because it is slower and less dramatic. The conditions producing both are worthy of attack as epidemiological challenges. In terms of the number of people involved, the housewife syndrome might well be viewed as Public Health Problem Number One.

comment

I pause here a moment to say that I consider this chapter to be the most important one in the book. And

I have been so tediously careful to document the mental
and emotional state of health of wives and the possible
reasons for it—especially the status denigration that
marriage brings—because I believe it important to put
the evidence beyond cavil or frivolous disparagement or
ridicule. For the woman suffering from the housewife
syndrome is not likely to elicit much sympathy; she's
sitting pretty, and has no cause for complaint. She
annoys us if she even mentions any symptoms of psychological distress. They are not worth anyone's attention. Who but advertisers could take the housewife
seriously? And even to the advertisers she seems to be
only a laughable idiot.[5]

In 1970, Margaret Mead was quoted by Robert
Williams as warning women in the Women's Liberation
Movement that they might literally be driving men insane. The reverse seems more likely. It is wives who are
driven mad, not by men but by the anachronistic way
in which marriage is structured today—or, rather, the
life style which accompanies marriage today and which
demands that all wives be housewives. In truth, being
a housewife makes women sick.

If we were, in fact, epidemiologists and saw bright,
promising young people enter a certain occupation and
little by little begin to droop and finally succumb, we
would be alerted at once and bend all our research
efforts to locate the hazards and remove them. But we
are complacent when we see what happens to women in
marriage. We have, in fact, almost boxed women into
a corner. Or, to change the figure of speech, we have
primed young fillies to run fast and then put impossible
hurdles in their way. We tell young women that they are
free to embark on careers, and then make it almost impossible for them to succeed in them. We tell them they
may have access to all the privileges and prerogatives
of professionals, and then punish them if they accept
the challenge. More important still, we put an enormous
premium on their getting married, but make them pay
an unconscionable price for falling in with our expecta-

tions. We then blame them no matter what they do—refuse to run, kick over the traces, run wild, or become inert.

happiness is . . .?

If the wife's marriage is really so pathogenic, why do women marry at all? They marry for a wide variety of reasons. They want emancipation from the parental home, and marriage is one way to achieve it. They want babies, and marriage is the only sanctioned way—as yet —to get babies in our society. In addition, there is the pressure of social expectations, what some radical young women call an "idolatry" of marriage. There are, in fact, few if any better alternatives to marriage for young women in their late teens and early twenties. Most of the alternatives are—or, to date, have seemed to be—too awful. If marriage helps young women to achieve any of these goals and to avoid worse alternatives, their stampede into marriage is understandable.

The problem is not why do young women marry, but why, in the face of all the evidence, do more married than unmarried women report themselves as happy? As, in fact, they do. For it is strange to find wives, such a large proportion of whom are filled with fears and anxieties, so many of whom are depressed, reporting themselves as happy. More of the young than of the old, more of the college-educated than of the less well-educated, and among the college-educated, more of them even than of their husbands. (See tables 28 through 33.)

There are several ways to look at the seeming anomaly involved here. One is that happiness is interpreted in terms of conformity. Wives may, in effect, be judging themselves happy by definition. They are conforming to expectations and are therefore less vulnerable to the strains accompanying nonconformity. The pressures to conform are so great that few young women can resist them. Better, as the radical women put it, dead than unwed. Those who do not marry are made to feel inferior, failures. What's a nice girl like you doing unmarried? The situation may not be as bad as it was in colonial times when sanctions were actually brought against the unmarried, but the opprobrium still remains. Rozanne Brooks, a sociologist, studying the stereotypes of the unmarried, asked her students to describe unmarried women. They did, and the conventional image of a frustrated, repressed, pursed-lipped, unnatural being came through. When asked to describe some specific unmarried woman they knew well, a quite different image came through, one more conformable to the statistical picture drawn above. Escape from being "an old maid" is one definition of happiness.

Such conformity to the norm of marriage does not have to be imposed from the outside. Women have internalized the norms prescribing marriage so completely that the role of wife seems the only acceptable one. And since marriage is set up as the summum bonum of life for women, they interpret their achievement of marriage as happiness, no matter how unhappy the marriage itself may be. They have been told that their happiness depends on marriage, so, even if they are miserable, they *are* married, aren't they? They *must* therefore be happy.

Another way to explain the anomaly of depressed, phobic, and psychologically distressed women reporting themselves as happy may be that they are interpreting happiness in terms of adjustment. Even researchers have confused happiness and adjustment. In their measures of success in marriage, "happiness," "satisfaction," and "adjustment" have received different weights; in all but one, adjustment has received far greater weight than either happiness or satisfaction. If the researchers define success in marriage in terms of adjustment, it is understandable why wives do too. The married woman has adjusted to the demands of marriage; she is reconciled to them. She interprets her reconciliation as happiness, no matter how much she is paying for it in terms of psychological distress.

Orden and Bradburn offer corroboration of such a "calculus." They found that marital happiness, like individual psychological well-being, was a matter of "affect balance." There were both pluses and minuses in the marital relationship, one positive (relating to companionship and sociability) and one negative (relating to tension). The positive contribution made to wives' happiness by companionship and sociability—small as it may be—was apparently great enough to overcome the negative effect of tension. It was not, therefore, anomalous when wives reported more marital stress than husbands but at the same time more overall marital satisfaction also. It was just that they had to pay more than husbands for companionship and sociability.

the hidden deformities of women

Another way to solve the paradox of depressed wives reporting their marriages as happy is to view the socialization process as one which "deforms" them in order to fit them for marriage as now structured. We cut the motivational wings of young women or bind their intellectual feet, all the time reassuring them that it is all for their own good. Otherwise, no one would love them or marry them or take care of them. Or, if anyone did, they would be unhappy and feel caged if they had wings and could not fly, or unbound feet and could not run.

There may have been a time when this made sense. It might well be asked if it still does. But whether it makes sense or not, we are quite remarkably successful. We do not clip wings or bind feet, but we do make girls sick. For to be happy in a relationship which imposes so many impediments on her, as traditional marriage does, a woman must be slightly ill mentally. Women accustomed to expressing themselves freely could not be happy in such a relationship; it would be too confining and too punitive. We therefore "deform" the minds of girls, as traditional Chinese used to deform their feet, in order to shape them for happiness in marriage. It may therefore be that married women say they are happy because they are sick rather than sick because they are married.

There are some researchers who believe that this is indeed the case. They note that our standards of mental health for men are quite different from those for women, that if we judged women by the standards which we apply to men they would show up as far from well. A generation ago, Terman could judge women who were conformist, conservative, docile, unaggressive, lacking in decisiveness, cautious, nontolerant to be emotionally stable and well balanced. They were the women who had achieved an adjustment standard of mental health. They fitted the situation they were trained from infancy to fit. They enjoyed conformity to it. They were his "happily" married women.

But modern clinicians see them in a different light. Inge K. Broverman and her associates, for example, ask whether a constellation of traits which includes "being more submissive, less independent, less adventurous, more easily influenced, less aggressive, less competitive, more excitable in minor crises, having their feelings more easily hurt, being more emotional, more conceited about their appearance, less objective"—a constellation of traits which a set of clinicians attributed to mature adult women—isn't a strange way of "describing any mature, healthy individual." These researchers conclude that we have a double standard of mental health, one for men and one for women. We incorporate into our standards of mental health for women the defects necessary for successful adjustment in marriage.

We do our socializing of girls so well, in fact, that many wives, perhaps most, not only feel that they are fulfilled by marriage but even hotly resent anyone who raises questions about their marital happiness. They have been so completely shaped for their dependency and passivity that the very threat of changes that would force them to greater independence frightens them. They have successfully come to terms with the conditions of their lives. They do not know any other. They do not know that other patterns of living might yield greater satisfactions, or want to know. Their cage can be open. They will stay put.

solution to the paradox

"But what about love? Isn't that what marriage is all about?" the young bride cries. "None of what you say has even included the word!" True, love has been what marriage has been partially if not all about at least since the seventeenth century. Love is, in fact, so important to women that they are willing to pay an exorbitant price for it—even all the costs that marriage exacts.

Women need and want the love and companionship and the mere presence of men in some kind of close relationship. They demonstrate this need by clinging to marriage regardless of the cost. They are willing to pay dearly for it. This fact assures its future.

But the basic question is, does the satisfaction of these needs for love and companionship have to extort such excessive costs? Should young women have to pay so much for them? Should we not try to reduce the costs of marriage to them? Shouldn't it be possible to devise a structure that permits them to eat some of the cake and still have a little left over? We shall return to these questions later on, in chapters 11 and 12.

chapter four

their children

the future of reproduction

Experiments in genetic engineering and in embryology portend a host of future possibilities for reproduction, some with profound effects on marriage. Alvin Toffler supplies us with some of the possibilities. He foresees a future in which embryological transplants will be possible; he sees the possibility of parenthood postponed until later years since it will be more or less independent of biology. He sees the possibility of certain couples specialized to rear children for others, leaving the others free to pursue their own interests, for why should all parents have to rear their own children? Other seers envision mechanical gestating machines replacing the human womb. At least the first impact of these ideas —recognition of what is possible, whether probable or not—is being met. We may reel a bit, but a generation from now the new techniques may no longer seem shocking, however unpalatable. For the near future of marriage, however, we can discount these modifications in the process of reproduction and continue to think in the old-fashioned way about parenthood.

marriage into family

Having children has always been viewed as one of the major functions of marriage. For a married couple to remain deliberately childless was anathema. "To contract before that they will have no children makes it no marriage, but an adultery," preached John Donne in a sermon on May 30, 1621, and doubtless all decent people agreed with him.

Parenthood expands marriage into a family, and everything changes. And the changes are not all for the better, for although having children may do a great deal for the character of parents, schooling them in unselfishness and sacrifice, it does not always do much for their marriage.

the future of parenthood

In the future, more married couples will fall into "adultery" as defined by John Donne; that is, we may expect fewer marriages to involve children. For childlessness, which, Paul C. Glick reminds us, has been on the decline for some time, seems likely to increase. The evidence for this conclusion is as yet not statistically documentable, but rather implicit in the general tenor of the times and in the antimotherhood ambience generated by the concern about population.[1] And even those who do plan to have children will have fewer of them.[2] The effects on both the husbands' and the wives' marriages of both these trends will be profound, and all to the good.

It is possible that the time might come when fertility may have to be encouraged. Anything is possible. If that time does arrive, marriage will doubtless adjust to fit those demands. But for now that seems a remote contingency. Immediately and for the foreseeable future, marriage either without any children or with only two or three is in the cards.

the benign effects on marriage of childlessness

In the past, the concern of reformers and researchers has been with the effect of parents on their children. Increasingly, there is concern also for the effect that children have on the marriage of their parents. What we have had on this subject has been mostly an array of folk clichés: children held a marriage together, a child would win back a disaffected spouse, children forged a stronger bond between the parents, and the like. And when people are asked directly about the effect of children on their own happiness and that of their spouses, they give the predictable replies: children had added greatly to both their own and their partners' happiness.

But, the researchers ask, "can what the couples say be taken as evidence of the happiness-producing effect of a child in the early years of marriage?" and they answer "no" to their own question, or "only with reservations." For, as Burgess and Wallin have pointed out,

our society, like most, if not all, societies, glorifies the experience of parenthood. Children, especially in the period of early childhood, are culturally idealized as "bundles of joy." Parents who fail to regard them as such run the risk in many groups of being judged at best as unconventional and at worst as immoral or abnormal. Consequently persons who find the satisfactions from their offspring outweighed by the various demands and restrictions of parenthood may be reluctant to state that the net result of having a child has been a decrease rather than an increase in their happiness. This might account for the high proportion of parents who reported a strong favorable reaction to having a child.[3]

Reluctant, therefore, as parents are to state that children have decreased rather than increased their marital happiness, this is exactly what, overall, the researchers find.

It is true that divorce is more common among childless couples—though even this is less true than it was formerly—because it is psychologically and emotionally easier to get a divorce if there are no children, and the financial burden on the husband is less onerous. Children may also provide substitute personal satisfactions for unhappy marital relationships: "husband or wife," Burgess and Wallin comment, "can be made individually happier because of the pleasure derived from the child and yet not be any the more satisfied with their marriage, except in that it has given them a child." Preserving the marriage thus becomes easier. To this extent, the presence of children may be said to keep a marriage legally intact, however impaired the actual relationship may be.

But, contrary to all the clichés, childless marriages that do survive are happier than marriages with children. Mothers far more than childless wives find marriage restrictive; slightly fewer are very happy. Far more, expectably of course, report problems in the marriage; considerably fewer report satisfaction in the marital relationship; and more feel dissatisfied with themselves. (See table 34.)

The benign effect of childlessness is even more marked in the husbands' marriages than in the wives'. Thus, although there was only a small difference between childless men and fathers in the proportion expressing marital satisfaction, an impressively larger proportion of childless men than of fathers were very happy. Conversely, more fathers felt marriage to be restrictive, and more reported problems. Twice as many fathers as childless men felt dissatisfied with themselves; three times as many, inadequate. (Who, male or female, facing at least their teen-age children today *can* feel adequate or satisfied with themselves?)

The data on which these results were based were gathered in the 1950s, when motherhood was almost a mania and admitting to negative effects was not acceptable. Their significance is therefore even more impressive than it would be today, when having children is less fashionable and hence admitting negative effects more acceptable. Still, the same results were reported in a study based on data a decade later. Even when race and income were held constant, Karen Renne found that "contrary to popular belief, childless marriages are more satisfactory than others; parents, especially those currently raising children, were definitely less apt to be satisfied with their marriages." Whatever the general social ambience, then—encouraging or discouraging to motherhood—the presence of children in the marriage had an admittedly negative effect.[4]

The major concern of society with marriage has always rested on its concern for children. Where there are no children, marriage becomes a totally different relationship, one that calls for little if any public surveillance. If it weren't for babies and children, the problems associated with marriage, though never easy, would be vastly simplified. Men and women would continue to love each other and cease to love each other; they would continue to attract and cease to attract each other—but in ways quite different from those that characterize relationships in which children are involved. Already there is unofficial recognition of marriages with and without children. If there are no children, divorce is easier to get. And if, in addition, there is little property involved, marriage does, indeed, become a very private affair. To the extent that childlessness becomes common in the future, marriage will be increasingly private and personal and, for many husbands and wives, also more satisfactory.

is childlessness harmful for women?

Some people argue that having children satisfies a fundamental, even instinctive, drive, especially in women, that childlessness may therefore have an adverse effect on them by depriving them of this channel for self-expression by frustrating an intrinsic need. Conversely, others argue that some women do not want children, even reject them,[5] that the desire for children is a culturally imposed need[6] and that if such pressures on women are relaxed they will not feel the need to bear children.

An enormous literature on the maternal instinct is far from convincing as an explanation for the desire of women for children. Still, there is no denying that birth does have a powerful, even mystical, claim on our imaginations. It has overwhelming significance for peoples of all times and climes. No more can one deny that a well-fed happy infant is a pleasurable sight or that small children can be entertaining as well as enjoyable. But enjoying children is not the same as parenthood with all the responsibilities that go with it. Parents undoubtedly do love their children, but parenthood is not for everyone a fully rewarding experience. And when, in addition, there is no special praise forthcoming for having children, there will be less socially-induced sense of frustration for not having them.

The wave of the future does not, however, seem to be childlessness so much, of course, as just smaller families. And small families should be enough to satisfy whatever motives lead women to want children. These may vary widely. For some, having children is primarily a matter of wanting the experience of giving birth; they want "to use the apparatus." They want to know what it is like to have a child. Some also feel the general pressure which still makes women without children feel unfulfilled. But usually, when girls and young women say they want babies, they mean, in fact, babies—infants to hold close to their bodies and cuddle. They do not want sons and daughters who will grow up, especially when reminded that their children may be as hostile to them as they are to their own parents.

One or two children would probably prove to be enough to supply answers to these expressed wishes, and not at all impossible. For the birthrate, although not responsive to legislated incentives, seems to be remarkably amenable to public pressures.

Increased longevity and reduced fertility mean that a woman is going to be devoting a decreasing proportion of her married life to childbearing and child rearing. Women born in the 1880s, for example, spent almost a third of their married life in childbearing and practically all of it in child rearing. There was little left after that. Today, women may be married for fifty years but, with only one or two children, engaged in both childbearing and intensive child rearing for only about ten.

the small family and marriage

Although the difference between childless marriages and those with children is clear-cut and unequivocal, the same is not true with respect to differences between small and large numbers of children. Most studies report that the number of children has no effect on marriage; some report bad effects of a large number. Few, if any, corroborate the old "one big happy family" myth. The research results dealing with the negative effects of large families, especially on the wives' marriages, have been summarized by James Lieberman like this:

A recent British study found more ill health—both physical and mental—in parents of larger families, especially mothers. These differences were not attributed to disparities of income or wealth but to the increased strain imposed upon mothers who had to care for a larger number of children. Other studies have found that:

1 in discordant marriages, the chance for a successful outcome decreases as the number of children increases;
2 happiness is associated with the desire for children, whether or not couples have them at the time, and the poorest [marital] adjustment is found among those with unwanted children;
3 an inverse relationship exists between marital adjustment and family size, the more children, the less adjustment . . . ;

4 having more than one child early in marriage is correlated
  with poorer marital adjustment.

The highest marital satisfaction scores were reported
by Blood and Wolfe to be among women with three
children; the authors concluded that the point of dimin-
ishing returns came at the fourth.[7]

Actually, Frederick Campbell found, the introduction
of successive children has different effects on the relationship between husbands and wives. The first and
second child produce an increasingly heavy burden of
household tasks on the wife. By the time the fourth
child appears, these chores have become so overwhelming that husbands begin to relieve their wives of some
of them. Decision making also changes with the advent
of successive children. Husbands come to take a larger
part in decisions about the amount of money spent on
children and about the responsibilities and habits of the
children, while wives achieve greater say in such social
decisions as visiting and going out for an evening.

The general conclusion warranted from the research
is that childless marriages tend to be happier than those
with children, and that small families tend to be happier
than large ones. Both of these findings bode well for the
future of marriage, especially of the wife's, for childless
marriages and small families seem to be the wave of at
least the near future. With concern for children out of
the way, a greater flexibility will be permissible in marriage, more experimentation, more tailoring of the relationship to the personalities of those involved. With the
procreative function minimized, marriage may be permitted to perform other functions more adequately.

The stupendous research literature on parent-child
relations per se is only tangential to the present discussion. Only when parent-child relations affect husband-
wife relations are they relevant here. And, inevitably,
they often do. The mother who is overly involved with
her children, for example, may be compensating for un-
satisfactory relations with her husband; the father who

beats his son may be expressing hostility to his wife. And it is a common observation that children are often used as pawns in divorce cases. Family therapy is also based on the intrinsic connection between husband-wife and parent-child relationships. It would, however, take us too far afield to explore all these complex ramifications here. My emphasis is on the husband-wife relations, with only minimal concern for the parent-child relationships.

"the family drama"

A considerable proportion of the literature on the effect of children on the marital relationship of their parents has had a psychoanalytic slant. Oedipal and Electra complexes have been viewed as reflecting the subtle impact which the introduction of rivals into a marriage has had on its members. Fathers allegedly come to fear and resent the sexual threat of the son, and mothers, of the daughter. Situations in which the mother becomes the victim or go-between in a violent father-son battle are standard fare in theater and fiction. It is difficult to document such insights scientifically, but it cannot be denied that the presence of children does make a difference in the subtleties of the parents' marriage. One does not, however, have to invoke psychoanalytic concepts. The commonplace facts of ordinary day-by-day coping supply much of the data needed to interpret the impact that children can have on the partners in marriage.

the natural history of parenthood

Whether or not the wife's marriage is worse than the husband's, it is usually conceded that motherhood is more rewarding than fatherhood. And Burgess and Wallin found that wives more than husbands did tend to report that children have added to their happiness. In fact, despite the curse of Eden, it is alleged that giving birth is one female prerogative that men envy and covet for themselves. The custom of the couvade, common throughout the preliterate world, according to which the father goes to bed at the birth of a child to receive congratulations, is said to reflect his desire to participate in this creative event. And even today, Veroff and Feld note, "motherhood still remains a role in which [even] an educated woman can find the personal gratification she needs to justify her existence."

Actually, the effect of children on marriage varies widely according to the age of the children; but it also varies according to the education and motivations of the parents. The first child's entrance into the marriage is especially crucial; but so is the exit of the last one. School-age children (six to fourteen) have a different effect from that of teen-age children. And the effect of children on the wife's marriage may differ from the effect on the husband's.

It had long been known that marriage success, as measured by all the instruments, tended to decline with time, reaching a low point when the partners were in their forties. The process was called one of "disenchantment." But not until recently have the researchers tied these trends up with the presence or absence of children. The new researches corroborate and refine the findings of the older studies and, in addition, contribute new insights.

Before examining any of the trees in this forest of research, let us take an aerial view to show the general contour and lay of the land. Encapsulated in graphic form, the story told in figure 2 says that children whoosh through their parents' marriage, leaving it sometimes in shambles, and then whoosh out again, making it possible for the marriages to bounce back to the pre-child condition. Most middle-class urban marriages are apparently resilient enough to survive this "trashing."

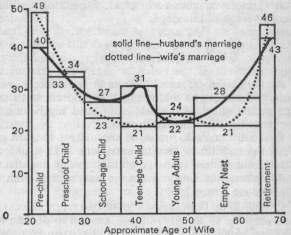

Figure 2.

the effect of children on the marriage of parents

SOURCE: Boyd C. Rollins and Harold Feldman, "Marital Satisfaction over the Family Life Cycle," *Journal of Marriage and the Family* 32 (February 1970):20–28. The age of the youngest child is represented.

*general marital satisfaction; positive companionship; satisfaction with present stage in the life cycle; and absence of negative feeling

the pre-child stage

When people are asked what they remember as the happiest time of their lives, almost all of them, H. Meltzer found, include the first years of marriage. We know from Harold Feldman's work that marital communication is at a high point in these early years; perhaps, Wesley Burr's work suggests, even egalitarianism. We know that companionship is higher than at any other time in the marriage and satisfaction with that stage of the marriage is also very high. There is the joy of hav-

ing found each other, the enhancement of self by interaction with the other; the glow of mutual appreciation.
Disenchantment has not yet reached great depths, and
the novelty of the new relationship casts a halo over
everything. It is all to the good, therefore, that there is
a trend, not yet completely clear, for a lengthening of
this first stage of marriage.

the first child

As long as there are children in a marriage at all,
there will always be a first child. So the research findings on the effect of the first child have a good deal of
relevance for the future of marriage.

The effect may be traumatizing. There is a drop in
all of the indexes of marital satisfaction. Diverging interests—the wife's in her maternal and household responsibilities, the husband's in his professional career—
can produce a drop in daily companionship. The marital
interaction pattern seems to be muted.

In marriages of lower-class or lower-middle-class
women, husbands and wives tend to live relatively segregated lives, and among them, Helena Lopata found,
children add a new dimension to the relationship, bringing them closer together. But among college-educated
women the effect is more equivocal. In reply to the
question, "How is the relation between husband and
wife changed by the presence of children?" wives emphasize the decrease in companionship with their husbands and hence the greater social distance between
them. "Before we had children we did more things together. You give your husband more attention. You
can't go out as much, and probably were more carefree.
You can't always get babysitters and, if you go out
every night, I feel you're neglecting your children," is
the way one suburban mother answered Helena Lopata's
question. Thus, although "the early modification [in
the marriage] brought about by the birth of children

worries middle-class women, if it is seen as a separation of interest worlds," Helena Lopata continues, "an increased social distance, and a decreased opportunity for companionship, it pleases the lower-class woman, if she finds it creating a bridge across sex-segregated social worlds."

The advent of the first child may not be a crisis, as some researchers call it, but it does represent a profound transition, even discontinuity, in the lives of the parents, especially for the mother, inside and outside of the marriage—even an "identity crisis." It can have both negative and positive effects not only on the mother and father as individuals but also on both as part of the marital relationship itself.

A great deal is made of the lack of preparation for the first child—indeed, of the impossibility of preparing for this monumental event—and certainly among marriages in which the first child is born less than a year after marriage. The parents have scarcely had an opportunity to work out their marital roles, let alone prepare for parental ones. This is especially true for the youngest husbands and wives, for the least well-educated, as well as for those with the lowest incomes.

It is not necessary to invoke esoteric psychiatric mechanisms to interpret the strains introduced by a first child at any age. The sheer fatigue factor, including sleeplessness, would be enough to account for much of it. Young mothers "develop a transient but recurring state called the 'tired mother syndrome,'" Beverly Jones notes. "In its severe form it is, or resembles, a psychosis. . . . They complain of being utterly exhausted, irritable, unable to concentrate. They may wander about somewhat aimlessly, they may have physical pains. They are depressed, anxious, sometimes paranoid, and they cry a lot."

There are reverberations in the marital relationship: "The greater burden of parental responsibilities is," Burgess and Wallin found, "borne by the mother. Mothers who report that they find their duties too much for them may be expressing indirectly dissatisfaction with the extent to which their husbands are assuming their share of responsibility. Even if this dissatisfaction is not present, the irritability of harassed mothers with their children may manifest itself in their marital relationships. Strong marriages can assimilate such pressures and perhaps be the stronger for them, but weak marriages may be weakened by them."

The husband's marriage may suffer also. The sex relationship may be interfered with, as Burgess and Wallin noted, social activities curtailed, customary routines of postwork relaxation upset, and his "monopoly on his wife's attentions and ministrations . . . inevitably shattered with the advent of a child." In fact, Daniel Hobbs reported the stress of the first child to be greater for the husband's than for the wife's marriage. But for both, the sheer weight of coping with problems would be enough to weigh heavily on any relationship.

Burgess and Wallin concluded that "in the majority of cases a child may intensify the attachment of husband and wife and deepen their mutual regard and affection only if their preparental relationship is characterized by love and accord. If the latter situation does not obtain, the net impact of parenthood is likely to be negative. . . . Given a satisfactory marital relationship, the potential stresses of parenthood can be assimilated and can even serve to strengthen the union of the couple."

Nor is it only the original transition to parenthood that reverberates widely throughout all aspects of the marital relationship. The impact of the presence of children is different not only for successive children but also in different stages of the child's development.

low points in the natural history of parenthood

School-age children, from six to fourteen, seem to have an especially distressing effect on marriage. This period in the life cycle is the nadir of general marital satisfaction in the marriages of both husband and wife. This stage seems to be especially hard on wives. Everything seems to go wrong. Positive companionship is reported at its lowest level, as is also satisfaction with children. Understandably, therefore, negative feelings are at their highest. The wife is usually in her thirties, probably swamped by the demands being made on her from all sides; and her husband is probably devoting most of his energies to his profession. No wonder relations between husband and wife suffer.

Some wives are, further, going through a developmental stage of their own. At about the age of thirty-five, some are just beginning to achieve autonomy, overcoming their earlier feelings of inadequacy. The restrictions on achievement imposed by children now begin to loom up. It becomes clear, moreover, that children are not going to become suitable sources of companionship, as some had hoped.

The situation improves little when the children become teenagers. General marital satisfaction remains low for both husbands and wives; again, the wife's marriage suffers, and she does not find that stage of her marriage very satisfying. Being the father of teen-agers is especially difficult. The variable "satisfaction with children" at this stage of life is at its lowest ebb. Fathers and teen-age sons are in almost perpetual hassles, sons disobeying, fathers struggling to maintain status.

Teen-agers are hard on the marriages of both husbands and wives. General marital satisfaction is low, as is companionship. Parent-child difficulties exacerbate any irritations in the husband-wife relationship. It is at the teen-age stage that children are more likely to become delinquents, to have troubles in school, to have their first brushes with the law; for the first time, the product of the parental input has public exposure, revealing parents' own shortcomings or failures—or at least the shortcomings that the public attributes to them. Each parent may blame the other. It couldn't be my fault; it has to be yours. You have been too easy on the boy. You have been too harsh with the girl. I told you not to let him go on that trip. You never let him go anywhere. You have babied him. You always expected too much from him. And so on.

Child rearing is one of the major issues in husband-wife relations, and any failure of a child can become a very sore spot indeed. The teen-age stage is the time when such failures—or seeming failures—begin to show.

late teen-age and early twenties

Young unmarried sons and daughters over eighteen can be devastating to a marriage. For both husbands and wives, this is the time when fewest say that the present stage of the marriage is very satisfying. The difficulties that arise when two adult generations try to live amicably together in a modern household are accentuated by their effect on the parental marriage at this so-called launching stage.

Fortunately for the marriages of the parents, there has been a marked tendency—documented in greater detail in chapter 8—for young people to leave the parental roof when they reach the age of about eighteen. Fewer and fewer now remain at home. This trend, measurable since 1940, is projected into the future as well. The extrusion of these young adults from the family may perform a benign function for the marriages of their parents—as well, of course, as for the young people themselves.

exit of the last child

A large proportion of the young people who leave the parental household do so now, as in the past, to marry and establish their own homes. In the past, however, a woman was likely to have been widowed before her last child was married. Nowadays, she has ten to fifteen years of marriage left. To women for whom the wife role has remained salient, taking precedence over the maternal role, this segment of her marriage can be the best of all. They revel in having the nest empty.

This postparental stage of marriage is a brand-new phenomenon in human history. People did not live long enough in the past to reach it. One spouse or the other had died long before the youngest child had left home or was married. After the first year or two of marriage, there was never a time when husbands and wives had each other to themselves without the distraction of children around them. We are only now beginning to recognize the importance of this wholly new form of marriage; its potentials for happiness have hardly been explored. It will constitute an increasing proportion of all marriages in the future. And they can be very good. We are bound to hear more and more about them.

However, for women who have invested themselves completely in the maternal role or who have at least given it priority, the empty nest may be traumatic. Those who have found a sense of achievement in motherhood may find themselves frustrated; those who have hoped for companionship from their children may find themselves deprived; and for those who have derived satisfaction from the exercise of power over their children, the changes that come with the empty nest may be on the red side of the ledger. All these points have been self-evident for a long time in the time-hallowed mother-in-law joke. Still, despite these hazards of too great investment in motherhood for both mothers and their grown children, at least up to now women have tended to favor motherhood over wifehood.

wife or mother?

There is just enough specialization in the reproductive function to maximize human difficulties. If there had been a third sex whose function it was simply to produce offspring for the whole society, like, for example, the queen bee of a hive, that would have freed men and women for other activities, erotic, supportive, companionable, and recreative, among others. But a host of incompatible functions were dumped on the gestating sex, much to the confusion of all of them.

In our country today, motherhood takes precedence over wifehood. In her study of homemakers, Helena Lopata found that the largest number (38 percent) gave motherhood as a source of satisfaction; only 8 percent specified wifehood. Suburban women gave somewhat more recognition to the role of wife than urban women. Another report on six hundred suburban housewives in their thirties with family incomes of $6,000 to $10,000, found that about two-thirds viewed men as breadwinners first, as fathers second, and as husbands third.

Although the effect of children on a marriage may not be benign, still, children may supply surrogate personal, if not marital, satisfaction. Eleanor Luckey found, for example, that among those in unsuccessful marriages, children were the primary source of satisfaction as compared with those in successful marriages, for whom companionship was the major source of satisfaction.

The conclusion of Veroff and Feld on the wife-versus-mother issue is not at all reassuring:

What all this suggests is that in more educated groups the marital relationship, despite its presumed intimacy, does not offer women many personal gratifications. [But] motherhood still remains a role in which an educated woman can find the personal gratification she needs to justify her existence. A highly educated American woman's investment in her children seems more deeply personalized, more richly rewarding and, perhaps as a result, more intensely frustrating than are her commitments to her husband. This may occur because these women can easily learn to be indifferent to their marriages. Even if they find their interpersonal marital gratifications wanting, they usually feel well provided for and can adopt an air of indifference to their mates. But they will generally find it impossible to maintain an indifferent attitude to their children. No matter how much they may want to escape, the responsibilities of parenthood are too demanding. . . . Highly educated women may desperately need to be married, but motherhood rather than marriage seems to be the role that engages their deepest personal core.

The data on which the above analyses were made were gathered during an era when motherhood was the stamp validating femininity. By the time the authors were preparing their material for publication, a decade later, they recognized that there may have been a shift since 1957. Lopata's data on the salience of motherhood over wifehood among housewives were gathered in the midsixties, about one decade later, and the situation had not changed. But almost certainly the situation will not remain the same two decades later. Among the oncoming generation there seems to be no such overwhelming preference for the maternal over the wifely role.

At least, the conditions that led to so much emphasis on the motherhood role are being challenged. Helena Lopata has summarized the forces that have led to such concentration on the role of mother: young mothers spend most of their waking hours with children; there has been a strong child orientation in our society; it takes a lot of concentration on motherhood to learn how to carry out prescribed child-rearing practices; society places almost complete responsibility for child rearing on the mother's shoulders; modern medicine and modern social science have given women the idea that health—both physical and mental—depends on their doing a good job. But young women are coming increasingly to challenge these conditions. They want to be relieved of some of the care and responsibility for child rearing; and they are shaking their fists at Dr. Spock who for so many years—however unwittingly—filled them with guilt if they did not devote their whole lives to child care.

In addition, the results of recent research indicate

that too great a concentration on the maternal role is connected with the depression of middle age. Pauline Bart found among middle-aged hospitalized women that those who had put their maternal role before all others were most likely to have succumbed to depression when they had to relinquish that role. Once their children were gone, they felt worthless and useless. They had been overcommitted to motherhood and were suffering the consequences when deprived of that function.

Finally, the zero-growth population goal will also mute the motherhood role. The importance of the husband to the wife will increase as the importance of children subsides. Marriage will have an additional weight to bear when motherhood is no longer a full-time escape from wifehood. Hopefully, marriage will have improved enough to bear it.

the work of mothers: refuge from, or salvation of, marriage?

When a childless wife takes a job, the only accommodation which must be made is to the effect it has on the husband-wife relationship. The accommodation is by no means trivial, to be sure, but it is limited. The job usually calls for a reallocation of household responsibilities and a new balance of power between the partners. But when a mother of young children takes a job, the readjustment in both of the marriages has to take account of third persons also. And neither marriage as it has been structured up to now is easily bent to meet this new contingency.

There is no unequivocal evidence that outside employment of mothers affects children favorably or unfavorably. So many other factors enter into the picture —social class, full-time versus part-time employment, age and sex of the child, and the mother's attitude toward the employment—that the impact of employment per se is lost in the shuffle. In view of the complexities involved, Lois Hoffman, after a careful evaluation of the research, concludes that the concept of maternal employment is too broad to make possible valid generalizations. Our concern here is not, however, with the effect of maternal employment on children but rather with its effect on the marriages of husbands and wives.

F. Ivan Nye reported that, by and large, there was more quarreling in marriages of employed than of unemployed mothers, and that more employed than nonemployed mothers had thought of divorce at some time. Still, there were no significant differences in the happiness or satisfaction of the two sets of mothers. It is possible that some of the mothers who might once have sought a divorce now found enough fulfillment in their work to keep the marriage viable. Alternatively, the working mothers may have found compensatory satisfaction in their work—for working mothers did seem to derive sufficient satisfaction from their work to compensate for their lower marital adjustment scores. As usual, we are confronted with the chicken-and-egg dilemma: Were the working mothers in the labor force as a refuge from an unsatisfying marriage, or was the marriage bad because the mother was working? A hint comes from Nye's study of remarriages. When mothers who were in a first marriage were compared with those in a second marriage, the working mothers, in the remarriages did not show marital satisfaction lower than the nonworking mothers. This finding suggests that in some first marriages the lowered marital adjustment of employed mothers is the cause rather than the result of the job.

The age of the children affects the marital happiness of the working mother. When there are preschool children, both husband and wife are happier if the wife stays home, but when there are grade school children, all the comparisons favor work for the wife. When the children are of high school age, there is no difference between working and nonworking wives.

Viewed over a long period of time rather than i
cross section, the work of mothers seems to have
benign effect on marriage. Jan Dizard, reporting on
study inaugurated by Burgess and Wallin a generatio
ago (and therefore unique in research on marriage i
that it followed four hundred out of a thousand couple
through some fifteen to twenty years of marriage)
found that marriages in which the wife had restricte
herself to her domestic roles were more likely to be
come "empty shells" than marriages in which the wive
had had more expanded roles. And Arnold Rose i
another study of the mothers of college students foun
that those who were dissatisfied in their middle year
were less likely to have assumed a paying job.

the future of marriage: shared roles

Accommodating the marriages of both husbands an
wives to the demands of working mothers is going to b
one of the first priorities of the future. We shall have a
good deal more to say about this in chapter 11, but i
is so important that we anticipate that discussion here
So far, practically all of the adjustments proposed fo
accommodating marriage to the needs of the working
mother deal with the wife's marriage. Part-time jobs o
day-care centers or cooperative nursery schools o
what-have-you are advocated on the assumption that o
course child care is exclusively a woman's job. Increasingly, however, the idea is gaining currency that th
husband has a share also. The idea of having both husband and wife share not only the provider but also the
child-care role is gaining currency. In 1968, the Swedish
government even made such sharing of roles a goal o
official policy. In a report to the United Nations, it said:
"the division of functions as between the sexes must be
changed in such a way that both the man and the
woman in a family are afforded the same practical
opportunities of participating in both active parenthood

and gainful employment." And an observer of the Swedish scene reports that "men in increasing numbers are taking their home responsibilities more seriously and are more fully participating in the raising of children. No better illustration of *man's* emancipation could be offered." This kind of sharing of both child-rearing and provider roles may be down the road quite a piece, but it is undoubtedly the wave of the future. Motherhood will then no longer completely overshadow wifehood.

This, then, is the present scene. This is the starting point of the future. These are the marriages whose future we are going to be talking about, the husband's and the wife's. His, not bad, and getting better; hers, not good, and badly in need of change.

2

the past and the present future of marriage

chapter five

marriage's past and its present future

does marriage have a past?

To be able to predict from the past, there must *be* a past. Does marriage have one? In a certain sense, no, it does not. For there is something timeless running through the accounts of specific husbands and wives from the past and from the present, a thread of human continuity which runs through all the institutional diversity. Despite the enormous differences between Homer's world and ours, for example, we all recognize at once the relation between Hector and Andromache. The baby is frightened by his father's helmet, so Hector laughingly removes it from his head before he takes the infant in his arms. We all understand Andromache's plea: "What can possess you? Your own might will destroy you, nor have you any pity on your infant son or hapless me, who soon shall be your widow. For soon will the Achaeans all set upon you and slay you. When I am bereft of you, it would be better for me to pass beneath the earth. There will be no more warm comfort for me when you have met your doom, but only grief." And Hector's reply: "I, too, take thought of these things, dear wife. But I feel great shame before the Trojans and their long-robed wives if like a coward I skulk from war. Nor does my own heart permit it; for I have learned to be valiant always and to fight among the foremost Trojans, striving greatly for my father's glory and my own."

Or the little vignette of Elkanah and Hannah, Samuel's parents. The season has come to go to Shiloh to make the yearly sacrifice. "And the man Elkanah, and all his house, went up to offer unto the Lord the yearly sacrifice, and his vow. But Hannah went not up; for she said to her husband, 'I will not go up until the child be weaned, and then I will bring him, that he may appear before the Lord, and there abide for ever.' And Elkanah her husband said unto her, 'Do what seemeth thee good; tarry until thou have weaned him: only the Lord establish his word.' So the woman abode, and gave her son suck until she weaned him." They could be our neighbors.

For whatever may be the institutional or structured relationships between husbands and wives—and they have been enormously variegated—still there is this human substratum that we recognize as familiar. There is an inner dynamic that does not change. Socrates and Xanthippe are as archetypical as Maggie and Jiggs. And we have little reason to expect that they will be all that different in the future. There have been loving, gentle, tender relationships and hostile, harsh, and brutal ones. In this sense, then, there is neither past nor future for marriage. There is a past or a present or a future only in the sense that some kinds of relationships are more common at one time, some at another.

A pageant of past institutional forms spreads itself out before our eyes; but behind all the diversity, there are husbands and wives interacting in fairly stable ways. This is how one sociologist, W. G. Sumner, put it early in the century:

The definition of marriage consists in stating what, at any time and place, the mores have imposed as regulations on the [timeless] relations of a man and woman who are cooperatively carrying on the struggle for existence and the reproduction of the species. . . . It has no structure. . . . Marriage has always been an elastic and variable usage, as it now is. Each pair, or other marital combination, has always chosen its own "ways" of living within the limits set by the mores. In fact the use of language reflects the vagueness of marriage, for we use the word "marriage" for wedding, nuptials, or matrimony (wedlock). . . . Wedlock is . . . as variable as circumstances, interests, and character make it within the conditions. No rules or laws can control it. They only affect the condition against which the individuals react. No laws can do more than specify ways of entering into wedlock, and the rights and duties which the society will enforce. These, however, are but indifferent externals. All the intimate daily play of interests, emotions, character, taste, etc., are beyond the reach of the bystanders, and that play is what makes wedlock what it is for every pair. Nevertheless the relations of the parties are always deeply controlled by the current opinions of the society, the prevalent ethical standards, the approval or condemnation passed by the bystanders on cases between husbands and wives, and by the precepts and traditions.

If marriage as an interpersonal relationship has neither past nor future, the same cannot be said of marriage as an institutionalized relationship, of "the prevalent ethical standards" and "the precepts and traditions" Sumner talks about. In this institutional sense, marriage has many pasts and, no doubt, many futures.

marriage as commitment

No matter how or where one looks for the future of marriage, or what one looks for, one fundamental fact underlies the conception of marriage itself. Some kind of commitment must be involved. Without such commitment a marriage may hardly be said to exist at all, even in the most avant-garde patterns.

The form of the commitment is less important than the emotional contents it underlines. It may be a written contract or simply vows and promises made before

witnesses or even simply an "understanding" or consensual arrangement. Merely fly-by-night, touch-and-go
relationships do not qualify.

the function of commitments

It has never been supposed by anyone over twenty-
five that the world operates according to its prescribed
rules. It is not expected that spouses will never violate
any of their marital vows. A certain amount of violation
of all kinds of norms is taken for granted—even provided for in sub-rosa or unofficial ways. Only the very
young label this hypocrisy. No one argues seriously that,
because vows may be violated, they should therefore be
abolished, or that they serve no useful function.

The function performed by the marital commitment
resembles that performed by our Constitution. It protects the relationship from the vagaries of everyday
living. When we poll the man in the street, we often
find that in the heat of passion he sometimes regrets,
even rejects, the Bill of Rights; but he does not really
want the Constitution repealed. Similarly, we want a
commitment to the vows which constitute the "constitution" of our marriage. To be sure, there will be times
when we will want to throw the book at it, wish we had
never ratified it. But in our hearts we want the decision
we made in thoughtful, perhaps in some cases even
prayerful, contemplation to be the one we accept, not
the momentary decision we may come to in the heat of
passion. The restrictions imposed by the commitment
are even recognized, however reluctantly at times, as
beneficial, no matter how much they may interfere with
our freedom.

Emile Durkheim, as we noted in chapter 2, showed
that men needed the restraints of marriage to prevent
them from dashing themselves to pieces. The desires
of men, he reminded us, had no limits; they had to be
restrained. The commitments of marriage provided such

restraints. The Catholic church for centuries justified the all-but-adamant Bible-based position on divorce on precisely this line of argument. If men knew that such restraints were impregnable, they would come to terms with them, learn to live with them, and thus be preserved from the destructiveness inherent in normlessness. The commitment not only protects against such destructiveness for one partner, but in addition it also safeguards the security of the other partner as well.

For—and it can hardly be said too often—there is an intrinsic and inescapable conflict in marriage. Human beings want incompatible things. They want to eat their cake and have it too. They want excitement and adventure. They also want safety and security. These desiderata are difficult to combine in one relationship. Without a commitment, one has freedom but not security; with a commitment, one has security but little freedom.

In the past, the desire for security, though present in both marital partners, has tended to be stronger among women than among men, and the desire for outside—especially sexual—adventure greater among men than among women. There is no assurance that this difference will survive the decline in the importance of motherhood in the future, or the increase in labor-force participation by women, or the lengthened years of sexual attractiveness in women. My own observation of young people convinces me that in the future the emphasis among both men and women may well be on freedom rather than on security, at least to a far greater extent than today. Conceivably to a too great extent.

public and private commitment

From the point of view of public policy there has always been strong pressure to regularize and thus control the form of the commitment, to make it firm, public, official, documented, provable, clear-cut, unequiv-

ocal. Church and state have bent their efforts to
achieve such a goal. The existence of a document verify-
ing marital status is a useful bureaucratic prop. A great
many prerogatives are made to depend on it, including
inheritance rights, pension rights, and parental rights.
So there is always support for any measure that will
eliminate any other form of commitment.

But despite these efforts at control, in one form or
another, unofficial, undocumented, unprovable kinds of
commitment have taken place, and some kind of recognition has been accorded to them in the form of the
so-called common-law or consensual marriage. Their
current status is moot. One court denies benefits to a
widowed woman because she cannot prove her marriage, and urges Congress to abolish consensual marriages: "the conditions which . . . gave rise to judicial
recognition of such informal and unrecorded marital
agreements can hardly justify modern-day perpetuation.
. . . Few people really understand that such marriage
requires more than mere cohabitation coupled with the
adoption of the husband's surname. Certainly most of
those who live together in such a relationship lack any
understanding of all the ingredients and permanency
of such marriages. . . . Indeed, one might question
whether any valid reason exists to encourage and sanction future circumvention of the established system for
getting married." But another government agency re-
forms its administrative policies to accommodate such
marriages. The National Capital Housing Authority, for
example, had initially refused to accept the application
of a family because the parents of the seven children
were not legally married though their union had lasted
thirteen years. The parents brought suit, and even before the case was settled in court the policy was changed
and they were accepted. The Post Office Department,
in another case, was rebuked by a federal judge for
firing a mailman living with a woman without benefit of
clergy. The firing, the judge said, violated the man's
right to privacy guaranteed by the Ninth Amendment.

At least some legal scholars believe that it might be wise to retain the common-law form of commitment.

The legal recognition of consensual marriages may have unexpected consequences. Young couples who wish to live together outside of marriage may find themselves, willy-nilly, viewed as officially bound to each other. One lawyer in the District of Columbia thus advised the young people that they would do well to make a formal, public statement to the effect that they were *not* committed to each other. Otherwise, they might have to go through divorce proceedings in order to separate.

The problem of offbeat, unconventional forms of commitment has most often surfaced in lower socio-economic unions. But such forms are by no means limited to them. They occur, Cuber and Harroff tell us, among other classes also, some of them assuming the stability of ordinary marriages. In the past, they may have had a "back-street" quality, but, apparently, now they do so less and less frequently. In fact, such unions are becoming common enough to find their way into the etiquette books. A woman asks Elizabeth L. Post, for example, how to introduce the lovely woman her father-in-law is living with. Another woman asks Ann Landers whether she should return to the man's son his father's personal belongings, such as his Phi Beta Kappa key, now that the father has died, after a six-year relationship with her. A French etiquette book informs us that couples living openly together may be invited together to a dinner party but that they should be sent separate invitations. These unions, in brief, have increasing social as well as legal sanction.

Penelope Orth, studying the "mistress role"—defined as that of a "single" woman who is having an affair with a married man she loves, who may support her but today more frequently subsidizes her or merely improves her standard of living—finds that although the custom of having mistresses is not increasing in its traditional form, it still does persist. "Most mistresses," Orth tells us, "work now, often for their lovers, they are rarely completely supported and sometimes they live with their men." This researcher attributes the decline in the number of mistresses to relaxed divorce laws which make it more feasible to regularize the relationship, better employment opportunities for women who therefore do not have to settle for less than a formal commitment, and an environment in which sexual relations are available without any commitment at all. "But mistresses continue to exist, and the fact that they do in an environment where men can 'get it free' indicates or even exaggerates the fact that an emotional relationship exists which is desirable and satisfies needs not being met elsewhere," certainly not in the formal commitment.

Among young people of college age, the form of the commitment is usually implicit. One sociologist, Robert Whitehurst, has found most of the partners in such relationships to be serious in their search for meaning and not, as adults sometimes fantasy them, primarily concerned with the hedonic, sexual aspects.

Parenthood, as we noted in chapter 4, changes everything. And ordinarily, at least in the higher socioeconomic classes, and among relationships based on offbeat kinds of commitments, it is assumed that there will be no children, for the fate of the child of any union depends on there being a commitment between his parents. But in recent years even this has changed among the extreme avant-garde. Thus a spate of young women, including popular stars, have borne children in such unconventional unions. And one young actress asks, "What difference does a piece of paper make?" The piece of paper makes no difference, of course; but the commitment which it represents does.

It seems safe to predict, at least for the near future, that these informal, unsanctioned forms of commitment will increase. But the elimination of the binding, formal commitment is by no means in the stars. The formal, even religious, commitment will remain the preferred model for most people for a long time to come.

the contents of the commitment

What each prospective husband or wife commits himself or herself to is usually spelled out precisely and in detail. The commitment may range from the most solemn spiritual vows to the most mundane property arrangements, and sometimes both may have equal weight. In a patriarchal system in which convenance and property are important considerations, the emphasis will be on material goods; in a system that emphasizes the conjugal relationship, it will be on loyalty.

The ketuba, or Hebrew marriage document, illustrates the patriarchal orientation. It was a one-sided commitment "made for the daughters of Israel in accordance with the institutions of our sages" that only the husband was obliged to make; it was intended to protect the wife. The future husband "said to this virgin, . . . 'Be thou my wife according to the law of Moses and Israel, and I will work for thee, honor, support, and maintain thee in accordance with the custom of Jewish husbands who work for their wives, honor, support, and maintain them in truth.'" He set aside 200 zuz "in lieu of . . . [her] virginity." And thereafter he promised he would live with her in "conjugal relations according to universal custom." Then the virgin consented and became his wife. The amount of her dowry was specified, and he promised to increase it. He took upon himself and all his heirs "the responsibility of this marriage contract, of the dowry, and of the additional sum, so that all this shall be paid from the best part of my property, real and personal, that I now possess or may hereafter acquire. All my property, even the mantle on my shoulders, shall be mortgaged for the security of this contract and of the dowry and of the addition made thereto." This contract was not just a piece of paper. It was "not to be regarded as an illusory obligation or as a mere form of document." The participants had "followed the legal formality of symbolical delivery between . . . the bridegroom, and . . . this virgin and . . . employed an instrument legally fit for the purpose to strengthen all that is stated above, and everything is valid and established." This ironclad document was signed by the bridegroom and two witnesses. The agreement was formidable, valid, and established. All the wife had to do was consent to live with the groom in conjugal relations "according to universal custom." The significance, implications, and ramifications of this one-sided set of commitments invite ambiguous interpretations. The woman, with the status of a minor, made no commitment; all she did was consent. It is interesting that no mention was made of love on the part of either partner. What was important was the security of the wife. She could, apparently, not threaten his security; so no provision was required to safeguard it. But he could threaten hers; so provision was required to safeguard it.

In a modern French antenuptial contract, the parties may commit themselves to anything they please provided it is not contrary to good behavior and does not interfere with public order. It is forbidden that any such contracts derogate marital rights vis-à-vis wife, children, or husband; change the law of succession; or stipulate that their relationship will be governed by any custom, law, or local statute forbidden by the civil code. The antenuptial contract is thus left with a rather short tether; in practice, it deals primarily with property and can be enforced like any other contract.

At the other end of the gamut from these solemn, no-nonsense provisions of the commitment are those airily set forth in Congreve's *Way of the World*. Mirabel and Mistress Millamant each specify what they want commitments on. Her specifications: he must continue to solicit her favors; let her stay in bed as long as she pleases; permit her to pay and receive visits from whomever she pleases; write and receive letters without question or expressions of displeasure from him; wear what she wants; be under no obligation to be pleasant with his dull relatives; have complete privacy; and the like. If he promises to subscribe to her demands, she may,

s we saw in chapter 3, "by degrees dwindle into a
ife." Mirabel, for his part, specifies that she must have
o conspiratorial women friends, use only limited
mounts of cosmetics, indulge in no tight lacing (espe-
ially in pregnancy), and serve only non-alcoholic
everages at her tea table. If she accepts, then he may
e "enlarged into a husband."

Wide as the variety of forms of marriage commit-
nent may be, the contents usually consist of some com-
ination or permutation of two fundamental dimensions
f the marital relationship: exclusivity and permanence.
 marriage may combine them, as conventional mariage in the Judeo-Christian tradition now does. Or it
nay call for permanence but not exclusivity, as in
olygamy or the concubinate. Alternatively, it may de-
nand exclusivity but not permanence, as in "serial
olygamy," as the marry-divorce-remarry pattern has
een called, or as in the unofficial liaisons of young
eople today. If it calls for neither permanence nor ex-
lusivity it can hardly be called a marriage at all but
nly a more or less casual affair.

The Christian, as contrasted with the patriarchal,
onception of marriage added to the commitment an
mphasis on love. Thus the Book of Common Prayer
pecifies for the groom an affirmative answer to the
uestion: "Wilt thou love her, comfort her, honor her,
herish her, and keep her; forsaking all others, cleave
nee only unto her, so long as ye both shall live?" And
ne bride answers affirmatively to this question: "Wilt
hou love him, honor him, inspire him, cherish him, and
eep him; and forsaking all others, cleave thee only
nto him, so long as ye both shall live?" The several
enominations play variations on the same themes. But
y and large, the commitment, whether religious or
ivil, specifies these promises. Only yesterday did the
vife's promise to obey her husband, reflecting the patri-
rchal conception of marriage, disappear from the wife's
romises. (As recently as 1938, only three-fifths of the

women polled by the *Ladies' Home Journal* objecte
to the word *obey* in the marriage ceremony.)

some nineteenth-century
anti-establishment commitments

As early as the first third of the nineteenth centur
there were already beginning to appear repudiations
the traditional commitments of marriage. Robert Da
Owen, for example, drew up a document to which Ma
Jane Robinson concurred. In this form, it was mal
oriented, much as the ketuba was. He was the one wh
entered into the "matrimonial engagement," and th
first person singular was prominent throughout. Still, f
the date, 1832, it was radical and, for that matte
still is.

This afternoon I enter into a matrimonial engagement wi
Mary Jane Robinson, a young person whose opinions on a
important subjects, whose mode of thinking and feeling coinci
more intimately with my own than do those of any other i
dividual with whom I am acquainted. . . . We have selected th
simplest ceremony which the laws of this State recognize. .
This ceremony involves not the necessity of making promis
regarding that over which we have no control, the state
human affections in the distant future, nor of repeating form
which we deem offensive, inasmuch as they outrage the pri
ciples of human liberty and equality, by conferring rights ar
imposing duties unequally on the sexes. The ceremony consis
of a simply written contract in which we agree to take eac
other as husband and wife according to the laws of the Sta
of New York, our signatures being attested by those frien
who are present.
    Of the unjust rights which in virtue of this ceremony a
iniquitous law tacitly gives me over the person and property
another, I can not legally, but I can morally divest myself. Ar
I hereby distinctly and emphatically declare that I consid
myself, and earnestly desire to be considered by others,
utterly divested, now and during the rest of my life, of ar
such rights, the barbarous relics of a feudal, despotic syster
soon destined, in the onward course of improvement, to l

wholly swept away; and the existence of which is a tacit insult to the good sense and good feeling of this comparatively civilized age.

Henry B. Blackwell and Lucy Stone in 1855 made their commitment in the form of a protest. Throughout, it is the first person plural that speaks, and the protest is against almost everything the establishment commitment called for—except permanence. These two partners believed that "marriage should be an equal and permanent" relationship.

While acknowledging our mutual affection by publicly assuming the relationship of husband and wife, yet in justice to ourselves and a great principle, we deem it a duty to declare that this act on our part implies no sanction of, nor promise of voluntary obedience to such of the present laws of marriage, as refuse to recognize the wife as an independent, rational being, while they confer upon the husband an injurious and unnatural superiority, investing him with legal powers which no honorable man would exercise, and which no man should possess. We protest especially against the laws which give to the husband:

1. The custody of the wife's person.

2. The exclusive control and guardianship of their children.

3. The sole ownership of her personal property, and use of her real estate, unless previously settled upon her, or placed in the hands of trustees, as in the case of minors, lunatics, and idiots.

4. The absolute right to the product of her industry.

5. Also against laws which give to the widower so much larger and more permanent an interest in the property of his deceased wife, than they give to the widow in that of the deceased husband.

6. Finally, against the whole system by which "the legal existence of the wife is suspended during marriage," so that in most States, she neither has a legal part in the choice of her residence, nor can she make a will, nor sue or be sued in her own name, nor inherit property.

We believe that personal independence and equal human rights can never be forfeited, except for crime; that marriage should be an equal and permanent partnership, and so recognized by law; that until it is so recognized, married partners should provide against the radical injustice of present laws, by every means in their power.

We believe that where domestic difficulties arise, no appea should be made to legal tribunals under existing laws, but tha all difficulties should be submitted to the equitable adjustmen of arbitrators mutually chosen.

Thus reverencing law, we enter our protest against rules an customs which are unworthy of the name, since they violat justice, the essence of law.

There could hardly be a greater repudiation of th traditional concept of marriage than these nineteenth century commitments. In the ketuba everything wa done to make it "valid and established"; the partner were to follow "universal custom." And the same sub mission to custom and established ways characterize formal marriage commitments for millennia.

Now they were being rejected out of hand, not out c irresponsibility but on principle. Robert Dale Owen an Henry B. Blackwell and Lucy Stone were committin themselves in ways that were not only different from those required by the establishment but in ways tha were diametrically opposed to them.

some current commitments

Even after most of what the early protesters had ob jected to had been meliorated, rejection of the tradi tional model of marriage continued. However, in recen examples of protesting commitments, the emphasis i on the subtler aspects of the relationship. Here is on example of the kind of commitment now the subject c experiment:

Both of us commit ourselves to: (1) continue to grow, eac in his or her unique way; (2) retain future choices about ou relationship, recognizing that the risks of growth include th risks of growing apart; (3) give room for the process of grow ing, being patient with no-growth plateaus, being "there" whe it's painful, giving space for the bursts of joy; (4) provide climate that stimulates and invites growing—confronting with out judging, sensing when the most help is no help; (5) tak risks of self-exposure, confrontation, pain, shame, also risks c joy, fun, play; (6) respect differences of belief or viewpoint, without requiring agreement but expecting a curiosity to understand, or acceptance.

This may be, for the kinds of personality which modern life produces, the equivalent of loving, comforting, honoring, and cherishing called for by the conventional commitment. It differs drastically, mainly in its rejection of the insistence on permanence, recognizing "that the risks of growth include the risks of growing apart," and in its complete ignoring of the idea of sexual exclusivity. Having extramarital relations would not, presumably, violate any of the commitments. Aside from these differences, it is hard to see how anyone could take exception to this difficult and idealistic commitment. It, or some variation of the same themes, will doubtless become the model for many marriages of the future. In the hands of responsible adults, almost any commitment is acceptable.

A different emphasis is reported in the press in the commitment of a younger couple's marriage. In the presence of their families and friends, this is what they said:

The Bride: This ceremony marks the beginning of a time in which we will try to create as best we can, a true and honest marriage. We might fail. We hope not. We feel that certain things in the world as it is will impede our efforts. We first reject the legal vestiges of the definition of marriage that treats two people as one, and that one being the husband, such as laws that require a woman to maintain her legal residence at the place of her husband's. We also reject the traditional definition of marriage that divides human activity into two parts—one for men and one for women. Work done by men at the expense of their identity as part of a home and as a parent diminishes their humanity. Homemaking and child raising done by women at the expense of their need to establish their self-sufficiency cannot but injure, restrict, and confine not only women but also their husbands and the children in their care.

We would like to share with you a few decisions that we have made regarding our marriage. I will keep my maiden name.

The Groom: I will keep my name. Neither of us will, in the event of separation or divorce, ask for or accept alimony, but we both recognize our responsibility for child support.

The Bride: We recognize that neither of us to the exclusion of the other is solely responsible for the support of the other or of any children.

The Groom: I don't think men should view the liberation of women as a threat. Too often the man is trapped in the role of the breadwinner, in effect, the hero; and the consequences, if related only in terms of ulcers, are not always pleasant.

Like its nineteenth-century forerunner, this defiance of "legal vestiges" and "traditional definition of marriage" is a far cry from the ketuba's insistence on conformity with "the law of Moses and Israel," "the custom of Jewish husbands," and the "institutions of our sages." Or from the restrictions on French antenuptial contracts forbidding violation of "any custom, law, or local statute." These young people are shaking their fists at such establishmentarian restrictions—but substituting equally difficult ones.

The promise that they will try "to create, as best we can, a true and honest marriage" is, again, a restatement of the traditional commitment. Only their definition of what constitutes a true and honest marriage does not include the bride's taking her husband's name; it does not include the customary division of labor within the household; it does not include sole responsibility by the husband for family support nor by the wife of child raising. (Neither, to be sure, does the traditional vow.) They want to share both provider and child-rearing roles. The major change in these new commitments as compared to the old is the omission of a promise of permanence or of sexual exclusiveness.

To friends who were "turned off" by the cold self-centeredness of this commitment, the young couple replied with a talmudic verse:

> If I am not for myself, who will be for me?
> If I am for myself only, what am I?
> If not now—when?

A great many people do tailor their marriage commitments to make the adjustments called for in this ceremony, but, one respondent asks, do they have to put it in the ceremony? "It's getting a bit tiresome," she notes, "to be a wedding guest these days, when people have their Our Relationship talks in front of everyone."

Unique and unprecedented was the commitment of one couple, reported by a San Francisco minister, "to work for the liberation of all people, for frustrated, lonely people, . . . to love, embrace, to commit ourselves to do battle through the journey which is the celebration of life." Such a commitment may have been implicit in the marriage of missionaries in the past. Its analogue is implicit in some of the unions among "collectives" of revolutionary young people today. Still, "the liberation of all people" does constitute a new function for marriage.

Since the contents of the commitment made at marriage have varied over time, there is no reason to suppose that they will not continue to change in the future. A fairly safe prediction is that more and more young people will design their own commitments, and that a substantial proportion will decide to include—in one kind of terminology or another, whether in King James sonorities and rhythms or Women's Liberation jargon—love, honor, comfort, cherish . . . but not necessarily till death does them part.

In the long haul demanded by permanence, low-keyed emotion has more staying power, but for some of the modern relationships, intensity is more prized. At the present time, there is even a cult of intensity. Emotion at a high pitch for however long the relationship lasts is valued more than more equable emotion over a lifetime.

Both the form and the content of commitments, then, are in process of change. And both of the traditional commitments—permanence and exclusivity—are being reconsidered. It seems to me not at all unthinkable that we may one day arrive at the idea not of an all-or nothing marital status, an either-or one, but one of degrees of being married. "How committed are you?" we may ask rather than merely "What is your marital status?" One may be 100-percent committed to a spouse, permanently and exclusively, or only contingently committed, both the duration and the exclusiveness being contingent on a host of other—specified—factors such, for example, as how well do I love my partner, how dependent am I on the relationship, how much more is my work (or whatever) worth to me than my relationship, and so on. We may even come to have symbols telling the world the degree of our commitment, from one indicating only, let us say, ten degrees of commitment to one indicating a hundred degrees. It hardly seems more fanciful than the old-fashioned symbolism of fraternity pin, engagement ring, and wedding ring.

interpreting commitments

No commitment, however detailed it may be, is self-interpreting. What constitutes a violation—infidelity, for example—even in conventional marriages is not always self-evident. And the interpretation varies from time to time as concepts of marriage change. What is cruelty today was not cruelty in the past; grounds for divorce acceptable today were not acceptable in the nineteenth century. And even the subtler dimensions of the promises change and demand interpretation. The interpretations of one pair of commentators, Easton and Robbins, have been summarized this way:

love . . . means that one will treat the spouse affectionately. Comfort means that one will impart strength, cheer, encourage, gladden, as opposed to dispiriting, distressing, discouraging, saddening, or nagging. And the promise or vow to forsake all others includes more than other men or women as objects of attraction. It may include loving one's mother more than one's spouse, or children more than husband. It includes even imaginary clinging to old flames. Just thinking "If I had only married so-and-so instead of you" constitutes a breach of this promise. And the fantasy of other sex partners does also.

On the basis of this interpretation, it could be argued that if a man remains in a marriage, cleaving to his wife, he has not forsaken her even if he has relations with another woman. Especially in the context of "swinging," to be discussed in chapter 9.

Divorce grounds usually specify exactly what constitues violation of the marital commitment: adultery, almost universally; cruelty, physical or mental; non-support by the husband or abandonment or desertion by either. The trend nowadays is no longer to think in terms of violation of a commitment but in terms of incompatibility, a state of affairs rather than a violation of a promise. No one can be blamed for it.

If even in conventional unions it is not always easy to interpret a commitment, it is even more difficult to do so in unconventional ones. In the commitment of the mature couple described above to "continue to grow" or to "provide a climate that stimulates and invites growing," how would one know when or if it was being violated? What standards should one apply? The young couple's commitments are more matter-of-fact and easily interpreted; but even they would require some interpretation. Both recognize responsibility for child support; but which responsibilities are whose? And, of course, enforcement of an interpretation is by no means automatic. In the last analysis, in these commitments, as in any other, the ultimate sanction comes from the individuals themselves. If they cannot or will not honor their commitments, there is no recourse, with or without the sanction of the law.

duration of the commitment

No matter what else the Christian commitment of marriage has or has not included in the past, it has always tended to include permanence; permanence nailed down the security function of marriage. A commitment that was less than permanent was hardly a guarantee of security at all. For centuries, therefore, stability was considered almost the only component of the commitment that absolutely had to be insisted upon. Till death do us part was the indisputable rule.

Still, some provision for divorce has usually been made available for marriages that were utterly destructive. John Milton, in *The Doctrine and Discipline of Divorce* (1643), was among the first to teach that incompatibility—that is, "indisposition, unfitness or contrariety of mind arising in nature and unchangeably hindering and ever likely to hinder the main benefits of conjugal society, which are happiness and peace"— should be sufficient grounds for divorce.

The very fact that Milton was even thinking of divorce reflects an important change then going on in the conception of marriage, especially among the English divines. When the family was, in effect, an economic or productive enterprise, especially among the propertied classes, marriage was a businesslike arrangement. Estate, income, family connections were important considerations; the nature of the relationship between the spouses was secondary. Certainly, convenance was more important than mere love. Even in humbler establishments, the nature of the relationship was as much economic, or property-related, as personal. It was always considered desirable if the partners also found one another congenial; but, in any event, they had to learn to come to terms with each other no matter what happened. The institution was far more important than the individuals themselves.

In the sixteenth and seventeenth centuries, however, the English divines began to reexamine the nature of the relationship between spouses, and for a long time two different conceptions, one which emphasized the institutional aspect and one which emphasized the personal, fought it out. The importance of love in marriage became increasingly emphasized, with implications only now becoming wholly clear.

The emerging emphasis on companionship, now included as one of the purposes of marriage, and on love in marriage, tended to enhance its value, making it a positive good as well as merely a negative bulwark against sin. At the same time, it tended to weaken the patriarchal or institutional structure. The two conceptions of marriage were finally reconciled by the rule that the institution was not to absorb the individuals; but neither were the individuals to defy the institution.

The emphasis on love by the Romantics of the late eighteenth and early nineteenth centuries was only a logical extension of the thinking which the seventeenth-century divines had arrived at: they "prepared the way," Richard Bulger Schlatter tells us, "for the middle-class ideal which became dominant in the nineteenth century: the ideal of the monogamous family founded on mutual love; and . . . for a still more modern idea of marriage: a relation justified solely by the mutual affection of the partners, and the necessity of divorce when this justification no longer exists. Even the condonation of adultery where legal or economic restrictions make divorce or marriage impossible, is a logical result of this exaltation of mutual love."

This was a dangerous course to pursue. As extended by young moderns, it has come to be read like this: the seventeenth-century divines "prepared the way for a very modern idea, namely of sexual relations justified solely by the mutual affection of the partners, and the necessity of a break-up when this justification no longer exists." We shall examine this in more detail later on.

One modern trend seems to be in the direction of marriage commitments which last for only a limited period. The idea is not to wait until Milton's grounds—indisposition, unfitness, and contrariety of mind—have proved to be unchangeably hindering happiness and peace, but to head them off before they get that far by making the commitment at marriage for only a limited period of time, albeit renewable if both still want it to continue.

In the United States, the commitment to permanence has been greatly attenuated in fact if not in theory in the last century. Increasingly, the procedural requirements for divorce, if not necessarily the grounds, have been eased, making possible the abrogation of the original commitment to permanence. However, the current trend seems to be in the direction of commitment for only as long as the relationship between the partners is a good one. The thinking of the so-called no-fault divorce follows this line. When the partners, one or both, feel that the relationship has irretrievably broken down, they may ask a court to recognize this fact officially.

There are some who argue for open admission of this abrogation of the permanency principle by accepting, or even requiring, commitments of only limited duration. "Renewable marriages" they have been called. A five-year commitment, or a ten-year commitment, or a three-year commitment would be made. The partners would promise to maintain the marriage at least for this limited period of time. If at the end of that period they felt that the relationship was not a good one, they could renege. Alternatively, if they felt that it was a good one, they could recommit themselves to it. The realization of this conception is not very far away; in Maryland in 1971 a bill was introduced in the legislature to institutionalize such limited-commitment marriages.

The argument given in favor of the nonpermanent commitment is that it puts both partners on their mettle and prevents either from sinking into a taken-for-granted status of neglect. This is how a twenty-eight-year-old woman lawyer in a renewable marriage to a thirty-five-year-old divorced man, put it: "We are the sexiest, grooviest one person that I know. We work together, we live together, it's a beautiful one life. The agreement helps. Nobody feels tied down. When we meet someone who's attractive and good looking, we don't say to ourselves, 'Oh, I'm tied down.' We can relax. Only a fool would sign a contract for life. . . . It sounds queer I know, but it helps sustain the loving type of thing we had before our marriage." One couple, in order to maintain such "universal, permanent availability" as Bernard Farber calls it, even dissolved their marriage—ostentatiously, with a ceremony amidst friends—while retaining the relationship. Being married or "churched" had ruined it. In another instance, the man had been traumatized by an earlier marriage to an extravagant woman who had run up unconscionable bills and made exorbitant alimony demands on him; provision was therefore made in a remarriage that if or when he and his new wife did decide on a divorce, property would be divided equally and there would·be no demand for alimony.

There are advantages to women as well as to men in renewable marriages, the argument runs, for "there are men who take their wives so much for granted that they turn them into servant-functionaries because their fathers treated their mothers that way, because that's their idea of masculinity, because it's easier. The threat of nonrenewal may make the men pay more attention." Under the threat of nonrenewal, the argument continues, the partners can "delight and love each other with an enduring, fresh enthusiasm because they treat each other as man and woman, as lovers first, and as occupants of social roles only in a secondary sense." Couples who depend on the law or on other outside institutional props to support their marriage, advocates of renewable marriage go on to say, are likely to let the conscious, voluntary props decay. In fact, "often men and women who've lived happily together for years in unwedded bliss get married and are divorced in a year or two. . . . They cease to seek security in a person and find it in an institution." Without the coercion of the formal institutional structure, however, "each day the unmarried man and woman living together are more likely than married people to reaffirm their decision to be a couple and do what's needed to make the relationship stronger and happier. What they do, they do in relation to each other, not because once, long ago, they made a promise to live together the rest of their natural born lives, not because of money or social pressure."

The logic of this line of thought is incontrovertible. It has long been noted that job security has a deadening effect on many workers. The tenured professor can, and sometimes does, rest on his oars. Without the threat of being fired, the worker can relax. This principle operates, too, the proponents of renewable marriage point out, in marriage. Once sealed into a permanent, secure relationship, the partners can let down. The other side of the coin, however, is that the worker who is too insecure and anxiety-ridden cannot perform at his best. It is a nice question, how to balance the costs and benefits of security and freedom in any aspect of life. They are both desirable; they are both costly. Whichever we choose, we will always look longingly toward the other. Such intrinsic conflicts are in the nature of things. Incompatible desires constitute the fabric of life. They are built into the human condition, in marriage no less than anywhere else.

One final word about permanence. In the past, marriages did not last as long as they do today because life itself was shorter. A vow to remain together until death parted them was not so hard for brides and grooms to take when death was not so far off. Childbirth, for instance, exacted an enormous toll among women. The story revealed by New England tombstones shows that in colonial days a man might go through several wives in his lifetime. In those days, the serial polygamy we now speak of in connection with divorce was the result of death rather than divorce. Nowadays, people have a much longer time in which to discover how unhappy their marriages are.

Proponents of the limited-duration commitment recognize that they remain parents even when they cease to be spouses, and, at least in the commitment quoted above, "both recognize our responsibility for child support" upon termination of the marriage, although the specific provisions for such support are not spelled out. They would probably have to be worked out individually in each case. At least this amount of security is recognized, for the children, if not for the spouses.

There should, however, be no illusion that breaking up a marriage is any easier because its possibility was anticipated. There is always heartache in the breakdown of a human relationship as intense as that of marriage. Neither a change in the law nor brave-new-world resolutions can change that fact. Divorce or nonrenewal, call it what you like, will be as painful in the future under one name as under any other.

pyrrhic victory

If emphasis on permanence shored up the need for security, the commitment to sexual exclusivity in marriage hedged the human desire for excitement and new experience. The Christian conception of sex in marriage included, in addition to permanence and monogamy, the limitation of sexual intercourse to marriage. Although the promises made at marriage could refer only to the future, the Christian conception of marriage implied pre- as well as post-marital sexual restrictions to the marital partner.

It is difficult for young people today to realize why virginity or sexual exclusiveness seemed so all-important in the past, why religion for centuries seemed organized primarily to ensure virginity before marriage and sexual exclusivity after marriage. Why was it so urgent? Why did virginity make so much difference? Why did people care so much? Why did virginity have such great value in the marriage market?

There were, of course, many reasons, though not necessarily the same reasons everywhere. Sexual imperatives and taboos are not likely to be merely whimsical or random or accidental. Virginity and chastity are important wherever paternity is important, for whatever reason, either to protect property or to avoid incest. Paternity is important wherever "blood" makes a difference, as in connection with mating. And the limitation and confining of sexual relations to marriage protect women when their status is one of dependency. Without such confinement of sexual relations to marriage, women would, as Richard Baxter warned, be cast out when men were through with them sexually. Whatever the reasons—in addition to the magical and mystical taboos almost universally associated with sex—they were basic to the Christian concept of marriage. Indeed, one of the major functions of marriage was precisely to supply the sexual controls that were felt to be needed.

In recent times, however, a curious inversion, or perhaps extension, of the Christian emphasis on love has occurred. If the Christian model, with its emphasis on love, had struck a powerful blow against the patriarchal conception, with its emphasis on institutional stability, one might say whimsically that the patriarchal model was revenged. For the demise of the patriarchal conception also struck a blow at the Christian model, as the generation gap today illustrates. Thus, whereas the divines had insisted that marriage was justified solely by the mutual affection of the partners, today young people are saying that not only marriage, but all sexual relations—outside as well as inside of marriage—are justified by the mutual affection of the partners. We noted earlier that what the seventeenth-century divines were doing—preparing the way for the ideal of the monogamous family founded on mutual love—was dangerous, for, as extended by young people today, they were also preparing the way for sexual relations justified solely by the mutual affection of the partners.

Research comparing adults and students illustrates the gap between generations with respect to premarital sexual relations. Ira L. Reiss, for example, compared them with respect to attitudes toward petting, sexual relations between engaged couples, sexual relations between couples in love, sexual relations when there is strong affection, and sexual relations even if there is no particularly affectionate relationship present. The disparity between the generations showed that the movement of change is in the direction of greater acceptance, for both males and females, of premarital sexual relations. Far more interesting, though, is the fact that the disparity between the generations tended to diminish as one moved to the "cold" position—that is, nonaffectionate sexual relations. The students differed less from the adults with respect to such "cold," or nonaffectionate, relations than with respect to "warm" or affectionate ones. And even with respect to "cold" relations, only about a fifth of the students accepted them for men and even fewer—a tenth—for women.

Even more relevant for the future of marriage, however, is the changing conception of extramarital relations. Under the Christian model, extramarital sexual relations were sinful. When wives were chattels, such relations constituted also a form of theft. Not all theologians, to be sure, were adamant on the subject. Martin Luther could find it in his heart, A. C. Calhoun tells us, to condone it under certain circumstances. "If," for example, "a healthy woman is joined in wedlock to an impotent man and could not, nor would not for her honor's sake openly choose another, she should speak to her husband thus: 'See, my dear husband, thou hast deceived me and my young body and endangered by honor and salvation; before God there is no honor between us. Suffer that I maintain secret marriage with thy brother or closest friend while thou remainest my husband in name. That thy property may not fall heir to strangers, willingly be deceived by me as you have unwillingly deceived me." What was sauce for the goose was also sauce for the gander. "I confess," Luther also said, "for my part that if a man wishes to marry two or more wives, I cannot forbid him, nor is his conduct repugnant to the Holy Scriptures."

Not, however, until the twentieth century was the subject of extramarital relations seriously discussed. In 1929, Bertrand Russell was beginning to point out that if a marriage was solid and substantial, based on love and affection, it had nothing to lose if it permitted outside sexual relations. Kinsey and his associates found that sometimes extramarital relations improved sexual relations within a marriage; harm resulted only when they became known to an unwilling spouse. M. R. Sapirstein, a psychiatrist, reported that some of his patients were willing to accept extramarital relations on the part of their spouses if that would help them. John Cuber, Morton Hunt, and Gerhard Neubeck, among others, have already defused some of the opposition.

We seem, in fact, to be moving in the direction of at least tacit, if not as yet formal, acceptance of extramarital relations. There are several straws in the wind to give us hints. Researchers are beginning to point out the positive contribution that such relations may make to marriage. Counselors are beginning to specify what is "extra" in such relations; one even specifies the standards for "healthy adulterous behavior." Theologians and church leaders are beginning to accept them, individually if not officially. Joseph Fletcher, for example, notes that "there is nothing against extramarital sex as such . . . and in *some* cases it is good." A Presbyterian study group produced a document that states that "there may be exceptional circumstances where extramarital sexual activity may not be contrary to the interests and a faithful concern for the well-being of the marriage partner"; for marital fidelity did not imply that coital exclusivity was synonymous with faithfullness in marriage. And a document produced for, but not accepted by, a Lutheran assembly held that sexual relations outside of legal marriage could be permissible.

Even more telling is the generational trend in attitudes toward extramarital relations. Data gathered by Daniel Yankelovich comparing parents and youth on attitudes toward pre- and extramarital sexual relations show an incipient trend, presently a cloud on the horizon no larger than a man's fist, but apparently edging its way into our thinking. For although young people, in college and outside, agree that extramarital sexual relations are morally wrong, fewer of them than of their parents hold this position. The direction is clearly toward a more permissive position.

Of at least equal significance is the simple fact that such a question could even be asked in a national survey. For, as I pointed out long ago, "when an attitude has become subject to statistical study, when we are privileged to have an opinion on a subject, it is no longer, strictly speaking, within the category of the mores. For mores are not subject to controversy or argument or differences of opinion. . . . It is only when the mores become the subject of controversy that we study people's attitudes toward them. But by the time we become critically conscious of the mores they are already beginning to lose control over us."

As a subject of moral debate extramarital sexual relations now seems to be in the same position as premarital sexual relations about, let us say, fifty years ago. Then as now, controversy and debate were catching up with behavior. A considerable literature on the subject is already in being and more, no doubt, is in process. Popular motion pictures take it for granted that extramarital relations are de rigueur.

Traditionally and historically, extramarital relations have been tolerated more in men than in women, and tolerance of infidelity was more common in women than in men. It was, in fact, alleged that male jealousy precluded acceptance of extramarital relations for women. Male jealousy was the major prop of monogamy. Darwin, for example, was of the opinion that female chastity was buttressed and supported by human jealousy. "Looking far enough back in the stream of time, and judging from the social habits of man as he now exists, the most probable view is that he originally lived in small communities, each with a single wife, or if powerful, with several, whom he jealously guarded against all other men." And Westermarck, after surveying the anthropological literature on male jealousy, concluded that it "has not only been a powerful obstacle to promiscuity, but that its peculiar violence may possibly serve the very purpose of preventing it." If male jealousy were, in fact, so innate and so powerful, the future of extramarital relations for women would be negative, but Kingsley Davis, a sociologist, reverses the Darwin-Westermarck thesis: monogamy gives rise to jealousy rather than the other way round.

Whatever may have been the relation between monogamy and male jealousy in the past, it seems to be different today. What seems to be new is not so much a tacit tolerance of extramarital relations for men—which is fairly old, however unpalatable—as tolerance of such relations for women. There is as yet only a modicum of authentic research on wife swapping or swinging, but there are shreds of evidence that it is more appealing to husbands than to wives: it is, in the first place, called "wife swapping" rather than "husband swapping" or even "spouse swapping." We do not yet know in what proportion of cases the idea is proposed by wives, but what we do know suggests that it is proposed by husbands more often than by wives. (See chapter 9 for evidence.)

We also know that the desire for extramarital intercourse is reported to be far more characteristic of husbands than of wives. In Terman's study, roughly three-fourths of the women but only one-quarter of the men said that they had never experienced the desire. And 43 percent of the men, as compared with 12 percent of the women, stated they had felt the desire sometimes or more frequently. Kinsey and his associates noted what all men throughout the ages had known, "that extramarital relations are generally desired." There has been corroborative evidence in a long series of studies. For the men and women of the first half of the twentieth century there is no reason to doubt it.

If extramarital relations do become acceptable, it may mean either of two things about a marriage: it may men it is so strong, so secure, so unthreatened that it can tolerate such relations without strain; or it may mean that the marital relationship is so brittle and so insignificant that the partners do not care if there are extramarital relations. If there is a difference between the spouses, the chances are that the wife will have to make the adjustment.

confusion worse confounded

It is by no means easy to enter a new world, especially when one is carrying a considerable load of hang-ups from the old. There are booby traps all along the way. Some of them have been mapped for us by Kafka, Ryder, and Olson in the approximately 1 percent of a sample of young marriages that were nonconventional in intention if not wholly in fact.

In this particular sample, the wife's position was not improved. There were still conflicts between role expectations and performance. The wife, for example, "may feel herself to be a 'sucker' in supporting a husband thought to be indolent, or the husband may deeply resent his wife's prowess at earning money. Cases have been seen where the termination of the marriage was at least threatened by concerns relating to this issue." It sounds distressingly familiar.

The inferior position of the wife showed up also in the fact that although she was often the provider, her interpretation of the new life style was not accepted as authentic. The husband was the expert or professional on the new life style; he was expected to be "the theoretician who is well informed about various aspects of appropriate ways to live. . . . The wife was seen as less expert at the couple's way of life, and might even be thought of as an empty-headed amateur who is tolerated and perhaps protected by her husband." Doubtless she is an amateur. She probably entered into the nonconventional pattern on the basis of his, not her own, wishes. Unprepared, "some wives manifest dependence of a high order, and seem unable to make independent evaluations of themselves or their talents. The wives may be extremely distressed at the slightest sign of abandonment or at trivial separations." The wives, at least, had achieved the worst of both worlds.

Nor does the husband escape his old hang-ups. He is the "verbal champion of modernity and the relatively clear theoretician of [sexual] permissiveness." So the wife, being only an amateur in the new life style, takes him seriously. Since she has been led to believe that sexual possessiveness and monogamous obligations are passé in the new life style, she may "think it all right to engage in sexual activity outside the marriage." The husband is shocked; he had expected the double standard to be too deeply ingrained in her for that. She soon learns that to him "sexual activity outside the marriage is either never all right in actual practice or permissible only under circumstances defined by him." Is *this*, one wonders, what all the shouting is about?

Hopefully, not all of it, but the nonconventional marriages sketched here do remind us how male-oriented most of the thinking about the future of marriage has been.

the male bias

Practically all of the thinking about the commitment which marriage represents has, until recently, been by and, for the most part, for men.[1] It is, in fact, quite astonishing how little women themselves have been invited to participate in the discussion, or even listened to when they have participated. Considering how involved women are in marriage and how bad marriage has been for them, their lack of contribution to the pool of ideas on the future of marriage is remarkable. Only recently have we begun to hear from them. This is a good thing, too, for, obviously, the future of the husband's marriage is going to depend on the future of the wife's.

The women who are now entering the lists of designers of the future are less preoccupied with the ancient dimensions of permanence and exclusivity than they are with new ways for wives and husbands to relate to each other. Whereas men, as we shall see in chapter 9, are thinking of new-style commitments about sexual relationships, women are thinking of new-style commitments about all marital roles (chapter 10).

This brief overview of the trends in marital commitments suggests that as between freedom and security the trend has been increasingly in the direction of freedom. The commitments of the past made as little room for freedom as possible. The ketuba tried to nail down every possible contingency that would permit an inch of freedom. The French antenuptial agreement specifies in great detail what such contracts may not provide for. The great goal in the past was fixity, stability. The marital relationship was not to be tampered with. Young people today are moving toward the other extreme. Security, stability, fixity is the last thing they want; it is freedom, not security, that has to be built into the commitment. Some people believe that the pendulum has swung too far.

costs and benefits to women of the new-style commitments

"You really don't have to sign this! He can't make you do it!" This warning cry came from older women when the young bride whose commitment was quoted above told them of its contents. It was an echo of thousands of years of female wisdom painfully garnered.

The young woman was—voluntarily, even flauntingly—throwing away all the protections built into marriage by men themselves who knew what their own weaknesses were and those of other men and that women had to be protected against them. They were minor corrections of the enormous balance against women. True, these laws remained; the young woman could not abrogate them even if she wanted to, and they were still available to her if she ever needed to use them. The husband still had a legal obligation to support her however cavalierly she might insist that he did not have exclusive responsibility for her support. Without the protections built into marriage by the law, women would be at the mercy of inconstant man.

In the eyes of traditional women, therefore, the bride was giving up much more than she was receiving in the new-style commitments. She was promising in advance to share the provider role, accept no alimony in case of divorce, and share responsibility for child support. In exchange, all she got was the right to keep her own name, have a separate domicile, and get out of some of the housework and child care. The old right to lifelong support was being given up. The whole arrangement was a poor bargain in their eyes.

The new-style commitments looked dangerously prejudicial to traditional women. And if you have in mind the kind of woman our society has been creating in the past, they are. The new-style commitment would be fatal for the passive, dependent, phobic, and psychologically distressed woman we met in chapter 3. Women trained for dependencies or molded into them by marriage are at a great disadvantage in their relationships with the world. The kind of women we have been rearing until recently have been dependent, and therefore they have needed a great deal of protection. They were vulnerable, easily exploitable, both inside and outside of marriage.

Any thinking, however, about the future of marriage that continues to assume dependent, docile, manageable, domestically inclined, "feminine" young women will be off beam—but so, too, will thinking about it which takes for granted the right of women to be supported their entire life, regardless.

The new-style commitment is a challenge. The very deprivation of assured support as long as they live may be one of the best things that could happen to women. It would demand that even in their early years they think in terms of lifelong work histories; it would demand the achievement of autonomy. They would have to learn that marriage was not the be-all and end-all of their existence. It would not free them from the necessity of knowing how to take care of themselves. It would save them from the pitfalls of too much security. All this would actually be a blessing in not very impenetrable disguise, for if it is good for men to be saved from normlessness by hemming them in, it is good for women to be forced out of their security. It costs too much.

Such a drastic change in life style would require that opportunities for women be made as available to them as to men. If marriage is to be merely a sometime thing for a wife, she has to be prepared for its termination. If she is not to have lifelong support guaranteed to her, she must be freed from the handicaps of discrimination in the outside world.

A final and not really incidental comment: one of the great nightmares which haunts traditional women is the fear of loss of sexual attractiveness—and such a loss was, as we saw in chapter 3, practically guaranteed by traditional marriage. Jane Austen assured us that no woman beyond twenty-three could hope to stir romantic impulses in a man's breast; Balzac extended the deadline to thirty. In the 1960s, a woman of fifty was permitted a love affair in a woman's magazine story. If commitments are to be limited, women will have to learn to remain attractive. Indeed, they can do so, well on into their fifties and even, folk clichés to the contrary notwithstanding, beyond.

The caveat offered above bears repeating. No change in either the form or the contents of the commitments which people make to one another mollifies the pain and suffering of a broken relationship. It hurts. It hurts if both welcome the break. It hurts even more if only one does. The measure of the joy which the partners brought to each other when they made the commitment is a measure of the grief which they bring to each other when it ends. The future promises no abrogation of that sociological "law."

chapter six

can any number play?

marriage as privilege and prerogative

There was a time when marriage was not for everyone. The Romans conceived it as a privilege for the well-born, a status mainly for patrician families, forbidden to slaves, though not forbidden to the lower classes. The Church had other ideas; as early as the twelfth century it was challenging legal restrictions on the marriage even of slaves, and finally succeeded in removing them from the civil law as well as from canon law.

It was not until the end of the nineteenth century, however, that marriage really became available for everyone, for even without legal restrictions, practical and social ones continued. Class lines remained strong. The way in which these restrictions operated has been documented by historical demographers who have pored over parish records in England and France. They reveal the existence of large segments of the population deprived of the privilege of marriage, living continent and moral lives nevertheless.

the european marriage pattern

The so-called European marriage pattern was unique, found nowhere else in the world, as contrary to "human nature" as we conceive it today as can be imagined. As much as slavery, it is entitled to the characterization of "peculiar institution." It was more a nonmarriage than a marriage pattern, for it had the effect of excluding a very considerable proportion of the population from the status of marriage. Thus, for example, at any one time, John T. Noonan tells us, as many as 60 to 65 percent of all adult women, including those who would later marry as well as those who never would, might be living outside of marriage. (In the United States in 1960, only 19 percent of women fourteen years of age and over were single; in 1970, 22 percent.) Marriage, in other words, was a minority status.

That is hard to imagine, especially since out-of-wedlock births were, according to Peter Laslett, no more common then than now and, in some countries, notably France, probably lower. (Illegitimacy, Laslett tells us, was higher in the late sixteenth and middle eighteenth centuries; higher, in general, in times of prosperity than in times of depression.) Even when marriages were delayed, there was little profligacy or moral obliquity. In fact, as E. A. Wrigley notes, the illegitimacy rate and late marriage were inversely related; if a community had an early age at marriage, it tended also to have a higher illegitimacy rate; if it opposed early marriage, the illegitimacy ratio was low also. Pauline morality was adhered to by Protestants, Catholics, Anglicans, Separatists, town dwellers, rural dwellers, commoners, and gentry alike. True, as Laslett reminds us, many brides came to their weddings pregnant—as, indeed they still do—but not to their espousals or betrothals, and such troth plighting or contract agreement did not take place until the marriage was assured.

In view of current assumptions about the nature of human sexuality, it seems incredible that such a seemingly anti-human-nature form of marriage as this European marriage pattern could ever prevail for any length of time. Still, the evidence is convincing that generations of men and women passed through their teens and twenties—the very heyday of sexual prowess—continently; and, in some times and places, almost half of them lived celibate lives until they died. People learned to live with the fact that marriage was not for everyone —for older brothers and sisters, perhaps, but not for them, especially if they were servants.

Marriage was, in brief, a kind of privilege, a prerogative, a gift bestowed by the community. One had to wait until there was a house or a cottage available, or until permission was granted to build a house or cottage on the commons. A place had to be vacant, land for the luckier ones, or a bakery, a joinery, a loom, or some other productive property. The European marriage pattern, in effect if not in intent, imposed a means test for marriage. It implied that only substantial citizens were entitled to that status. In the sixteenth century, the acquisition of these requisites might take years. When times were prosperous or after an especially heavy mortality toll, more people could get married and they did not have to wait so long. But when times were hard they might have to wait a long time—in many cases, forever. If someone had told them the time would come when everyone could get married while still young, many, looking around the village with not a single cottage or piece of land available or even in prospect, would probably have shaken their heads at this dream.

Noonan sees this late- or non-marriage pattern as a reflection of Christian, especially Catholic, ideology. Since there was a clearcut tendency for marriage rates in the short run to vary inversely with the price of bread—as in the United States they have tended to vary with depression and prosperity—Wrigley sees the pattern as a response to economic circumstances, as a way of limiting fertility to available resources. Joseph J. Spengler sees it as a form of saving or nonconsumption which made possible the accumulation of capital for investment and expansion, a kind of demographic "thrift."

Whatever the circumstances causing this European

pattern, they passed away by the nineteenth century, except in Ireland, where late marriage and nonmarriage still tend to obtain today. The old obstacles were no longer operative; life in cities made marriage possible for more and more people and at an earlier age. This, according to Etienne Van De Walle, is how it was in Holland:

Marriage had previously depended on the possession of a house and the means of livelihood. Among rural populations, the eldest son would often be the only one who could afford to marry, and then only when his father had died or was too old to take care of the farm. Younger brothers and unmarried sisters would live on the farm as dependents with ancillary status. During the "proletarian transition period," the old institutions started breaking down as a result of industrialization and urbanization. The ties became looser between employers and servants—or unlanded members of the family, the two often being synonymous. People married earlier and in larger proportions; they went to towns where they were able to earn a living in ways other than agriculture. The number of holdings ceased, therefore, to limit the number of households to the extent that it had during the earlier agrarian period. The birth rate grew, and many of the old values based on tradition were abandoned.

the american marriage pattern

The original colonists of the seventeenth and eighteenth centuries brought with them to America the generally prevailing conceptions of marriage that they shared with those in the mother country. But the same constraints on marriage were not operating on them. In fact, precisely opposite forces were at work. There was no limitation on the number of holdings. Anyone could find land and build himself a cottage or a house. One did not have to queue up for permission to marry. As population was needed, strong pressure was exerted on young people to marry. The status of bachelor and "ancient" maid was penalized. Arthur W. Calhoun quotes a law in New Haven, for example, which, in order to "suppress inconvenience, and disorders inconsistent with the mind of God in the fifth commandment, [forbade] single persons, not in service or dwelling with their relatives . . . to diet or lodge alone; but they are required to live in 'licensed' families; and the governors of such families are ordered to 'observe the course, carriage, and behavior of every such single person, whether he or she walk diligently in a constant lawful employment, attending both family duties and the public worship of God, and keeping good order day and night or otherwise.' "

The age at marriage was young in colonial times. One girl of fifteen begged to be excused from marriage until she was ready. Even so, the status of marriage did demand a certain competence and skills, and accumulating them still took some time. For men born about 1834, the average age at marriage was 25.58 and for women, 21.34; a generation later, in 1866, 27.32 and 24.08 respectively.

the democratization of marriage

For most European countries, the old marriage pattern showed remarkable resistance to change. As late as 1870, according to Wrigley, about two-fifths of the women in Lucerne, Switzerland, had not been married by the age of fifty. In fact, the real democratization of marriage in Europe, making marriage possible for almost everyone, including young people, has come only as recently as the second half of the twentieth century.

Van De Walle's study of the proportion of men and women never married by the age of fifty in eleven countries found contradictory trends among both sexes in the nineteenth century—up in some countries, down in others, constant in still others. But with the exception of French men, the proportion of both men and women who never married was down among those born in the twentieth century, precipitously in some cases.

Marriage in the twentieth century was no longer dependent on a competence, on property, nor even on maturity. One did not have to wait until one could set up an establishment or manage a large household. Marriage was no longer a class privilege. And the trend in the United States since 1890 has been, until the late 1950s, for marriage at an ever earlier age and for a larger proportion of persons. In fact, the most important characteristic of the American pattern has been the freedom to marry which it encompassed.

The test that the young journeyman and cottagers had had to pass before they could marry had been based on their ability to manage a productive enterprise in the form of a household, the basic industrial unit. Even when production moved outside the household, the ability to earn enough in wages to maintain a household remained as a prerequisite for marriage. One had had to prove himself a good provider. By the middle of the twentieth century, even the term *good provider* was losing its significance. What did providing have to do with marriage?

The idea of the household as intrinsic to marriage lingered on long after its central importance had disappeared. Until well into the twentieth century, the girl's hope chest remained a vestigial, even minuscule, descendant of the household goods a girl brought to marriage, and the custom of the kitchen shower for the bride continues to this day. It was not until well into the twentieth century that a generation came to maturity without feeling that they had to establish a household when they married. Not until the advent of a child does the household today become important, especially to the wife.

The democratization of marriage has had the effect of attenuating the difference between single and married status. Single today, married tomorrow; and all that has changed may be the woman's address, if that, or the man's. The transition may not be marked by much more than the ordering of a duplicate key.

The idea that even undergraduates could get married without a cent to their name, with no immediate prospects for setting up a proper household, would have been unentertainable in the nineteenth century. All one needs to marry now, though, is love, baby. Rose K. Goldsen reports the attitudes of college students in the 1950s:

> Gone is the caution of the young man who felt that he had to make a mark in business or the professions before he dared assume the responsibility of taking a wife. Today, more likely, many young men consider a wife an economic asset rather than a liability; if the student marries while preparing for a profession, his wife can work while he completes his studies.... Career does not determine when the student expects to marry.

Young people do not formally "demand" the right to marry without the old perquisites. They assume it. More to the point, many students do not even view it as necessary. In fact, they even demand the right not to have to marry. Since they do not plan to have babies, they feel they can forgo marriage. Since they are not interested in avoiding the sin of fornication either, that doesn't bother them. And since companionship does not depend on marriage, they may settle for it outside of marriage.

When a conventional household is no longer intrinsically related to marriage, the impact of marriage as a status change becomes mollified also. The dividing line between being married and not being married grows very blurred. The "what-difference-does-a-piece-of-paper-make?" point of view makes sense. If you can just move in together, sharing the rent, without having to worry about setting up in serious housekeeping, married or not, why bother to marry? Marriage, one might say with a good deal of truth, has for some been democratized almost out of existence.

But marriage has not, however, become completely democratized for those who want it. Quite apart from the age and health requirements for the license, marriage rates are higher for some segments of the population than for others. Black men in general do not have as good a chance to marry as white men. The road-blocks to marriage in the case of black men are similar, though, of course, far from identical, to those in English villages in the seventeenth century. Marriage rates are lower also for the unschooled and, in general, for those of lowly status. It is not that there is an articulated policy to deny the privilege of marriage to servants and apprentices as there was in seventeenth-century England, or as there was in the Old South to deny it to slaves. But the de facto situations are analogous. Black men and those in low status are less likely than white men and those in higher status to have the resources, either in hand or in prospect, to support conventional households in circles where such establishments are still expected.

mate selection, past and future

Marriage has become democratized not only in the sense that everyone now has a chance to marry sooner or later, but also in the sense that marriageable young people are now permitted to select their own mates. Because so much rides on marriage—the heredity of the children, the disposition of property, the happiness of the partners themselves—mate selection, no matter who does it, has always been a matter of supreme importance, especially to middle- and upper-class families. It was not something one could safely leave to young people.

It was important also to the man in the street. Thus, an enormous folk and homiletic literature from time immemorial has discussed not only what the process of selection was actually like but also what it ought to be like. The conventional wisdom taught that opposites attract, but also that birds of a feather flocked together. It taught that love was blind, that one married in haste but repented at leisure, that a man chased a woman until she caught him.

father knows best

In the fairly distant past, unless parents selected mates for their children long before they were ready for marriage, it is hard to see how parental mate selection could have been effective for any but the oldest children in the family. If a man married at, let us say, around twenty-five and died not much beyond his fiftieth birthday, as seems to have been likely, and if so many young people reached marriageable age without parents, how many marriages could have been arranged by parents? Only when parents lived long enough could they have a say in mate selection for all the children.

When parents did have their say about mate selection, a great many factors were taken into consideration. The "good wife" was industrious, sober, and devoted. The good woman of Proverbs was a prodigy of competence, as was the shtetl wife. When Plutarch wanted to compliment his wife, he spoke of her "economy in dress and thrifty way of living" and of the simplicity—dowdiness?—of her appearance in public. In keeping with the European marriage pattern, estate or status was important too. In fact, Samuel Pepys believed that a poor gentlemen was a better match than a rich merchant. Of course, it was always hoped that the young people would get along well with each other, for without love, as Richard Baxter had noted, the duties and suffering of marriage would be unendurable. It should, however, be rational love, not blind sexual passion.

Although a system of arranged marriages is theoretically more efficient in making sure that everyone gets married than is a system of personal choice, still the time did come in the process of democratizing marriage when young people were allowed to make up their own minds. Even so, the present, almost exclusive reliance

on love as the major support of commitments, which is
so characteristic of marriage, and especially of the new
forms of relationship with which young people are now
experimenting, was a long time evolving. And the
change in the nature of marriage implied by permitting
young people to choose their own mates, John T.
Noonan tells us, was of major significance in European
history:

Gratian's teaching that a girl could not be compelled to marry
against her will marked a distinct development in European
history. Very gradually, in a society where arranged matches
were still the model furnished by the upper classes, the principle
of freedom was applied by church courts. A milestone was
reached when the Council of Trent (1545–1563) affirmed explicitly that the consent of parents was not necessary for the
validity of a marriage; such marriages could still be illicit, but
the great sanction of invalidity was definitively removed.

This action did not mean that parental control of marriage did not continue, but only that it was no longer
absolute or definitive.

Two conceptions of marriage, one based on love and
the other on convenance, were finally reconciled by the
rule that although parents should not force children to
marry anyone they did not wish to marry, still children
should not marry without parental consent. The emphasis on love by the Romantics of the late eighteenth and
early nineteenth centuries was only a logical extension
of the thinking which the seventeenth-century divines
had arrived at. By the twentieth century, mate selection
had, at least in the United States, if not everywhere,
become a completely do-it-yourself process.

do-it-yourself mate selection

When young people themselves choose their mates,
they tend to apply criteria somewhat different from
those which parents used to apply, and the process

becomes increasingly complex as populations become increasingly differentiated. If everyone is just about like everyone else, or almost so, the choice of a specific mate is less crucial than if there is a wide variety to choose from. It is certainly not true, as George Bernard Shaw once said, that love is simply the exaggeration of small differences or that one could marry almost anyone and end up with the same marriage. Still, it is more nearly true when people are more alike. The trend today, despite the mass media and despite charges of homogenization, is in the direction of differentiation. Modern life makes possible a wide diversity of interests, life styles, and general orientation. Matching, as Bertrand Russell pointed out, thus becomes more difficult and mistakes more probable. If all the young people in a community are Catholic or Jewish or Methodist, then there is no chance of a marriage failing because of religious differences. If all have had eight years of schooling, then differences in education are not a problem. If all are white, then race differences are ciphered out. But if the choices open include a wide variety, then mate selection becomes much more complicated and compatibility harder to determine. In addition, there is more room for regret if an unfortunate choice is made. If only I had married Tom instead of John! This regret would not be so likely to occur if Tom and John are not much different, one from the other. As life becomes more complex and people less rooted, the problems of finding even suitable candidates for marriage become more and more difficult.

When young people are asked what they look for in mates, the portrait of a model but usually conventional young person emerges. They differ among themselves in the priority they assign to the several virtues, but, by and large, most young people look for a rather idealized partner. When one looks at the mates they finally end up with, however, it is difficult to reconcile the ideal and the real.

In general, physical attractiveness or sex appeal looms

larger when young people make the decision; "prospects" and stability, when parents have some say. Still, the assumption is made that young people know what they want and that what they want is best for them, an assumption which, psychiatrists tell us, is quite unfounded; for some people, they assure us, select mates for unhappiness rather than for happiness. "Men and women are infinitely ingenious," Lawrence Kubie, a psychiatrist, laconically comments, "in their ability to find new ways of being unhappy together." Or, as Edmund Bergler notes, "two neurotics look for each other with uncanny regularity." Still, it is perhaps just as well to achieve such a state of misery democratically as to have it imposed on one by parental authority.

needs as mate selectors

The adage that opposites attract was modified by the psychiatrists and social psychologists to a theory of complementarity: people were attracted to one another because each complemented the other. By itself, the concept of complementarity did not associate specific needs with each sex. Theoretically, one sex as well as the other might need to be dominant or submissive, the supporting or the supported one, the pain-inflicting or the pain-receiving one. But, in line with the old conception of the nature of marriage, there was, implicitly if not always explicitly, a tendency to find one of the pairs of complementary needs to be feminine and one masculine. Indeed, the Victorian model of complementarity was one of the clinging vine and the sturdy oak; husbands were strong, independent protectors; wives were gentle, dependent supporters and encouragers. Any other pattern was "unnatural" or "deviant." And a great deal of the research did find women more submissive, supportive, and masochistic; men more dominant and sadistic. Actually, though, the theory did not require, nor in fact, even specify such sexual specialization.

A wide variety of such complementary forms have been reported. The psychoanalysts had their construct of the sadistic-masochistic pair, each supplying the needs of the other, or the pair composed of the girl who needed a father and the man who needed a subservient acolyte; or, again, the young man who needed a mother and the woman who needed a subject.

Bela Mittelmann found five patterns: one partner aggressive, sadistic, out to humiliate and hurt the mate, the other partner dependent, submissive, enduring; one self-sufficient and emotionally detached, the other with intense, open demand to love; both wanting to dominate or both wanting to be dependent; one pleading helplessness, the other attempting to be considerate; and one alternating between periods of helpfulness and suffering and periods of intense self-assertion, and the other with periods of shouldering responsibility and disappointed desire for love and support. Sometimes both want to dominate or both want to be dependent. Sometimes one pleads helplessness while the other tries to be considerate. Obviously, not all these patterns represent complementarity; some look like recipes for frustration.

Robert Winch found a fourfold classification of matings: an Ibsenite mating, in which the husband is dominant and nurturant, the wife the opposite; a Thurberian mating, in which the husband is submissive and nurturant rather than the wife; a Master-Servant Girl mating, in which the husband is dominant and the wife receptive; and a Mother-Son mating, in which the husband is submissive and receptive. Robert Ryder reports twenty-one different mating patterns. Working out complementary patterns is a game anyone can play. But ingenuity and cleverness are no substitute for convincing evidence. It is not surprising, therefore, that Roland G. Tharp, on the basis of a résumé of the very considerable literature on mate selection beginning with the work of Karl Pearson in the 1890s, concludes that "the complementary-need hypothesis as now stated is not tenable."

Specific marital patterns, the researchers found, did

not necessarily coincide with happiness; complementarity, even when it did exist, did not guarantee it. The problem was deeper than that; it lay in a fundamental conflict between conscious and unconscious goals and needs. "Until we can [teach human beings] to distinguish between their conscious and attainable goals and needs . . . and their unconscious and unattainable goals," Lawrence Kubie warns us, "the problem of human happiness, whether in marriage or otherwise, will remain unsolved." It is a somewhat lugubrious prediction for the future of marriage, as well as for the future of mankind.

If we are, indeed, helpless in the hands of unconscious needs, so also may we be in the hands of our environment, for many of our needs are imposed on us from the outside. During World War II, for example, researchers on hunger found that healthy but hungry young men fantasied roast beef rather than pretty pin-up girls. Once well fed again, they reverted to fantasies of the pretty girls. The symbolism is far from profound.

The disparagement here of the theories of complementary needs or neurotic compulsions in mate selection does not mean that matching in marriage is not viewed as important. My own study of remarriage shows that it is, in fact, extremely important. A man and woman who fail in marriage with each other may both succeed with other mates. But one does not have to spin out fine theories of complementarity to interpret such a finding.

birds of a feather

Researchers who were willing to settle for less than a dredging up of unconscious needs found that most people tend to marry within their own cultural, class, religious, educational, and racial groupings; and, more to the point, that when they did not, their marriages ran up against more hazards than when they did. Here and there, a miner's daughter might "catch" the millionaire's son or the young-man-on-the-make, the boss's daughter. But that was not the general pattern. Mating was far from completely democratized.

Romantic literature has familiarized us with a long-standing, perhaps insoluble conflict. Love or money, workhorse or highstepping filly, unit of production or object of consumption—in one form or another some such option presents itself to people selecting mates. The general rule has been that rich people could afford the love, the high-stepping filly, the object of consumption. Poor people could not. Rich men could afford seraglios, or wives who performed, in Veblen's quaint terminology, vicarious leisure and conspicuous consumption for them. By and large, beauty and sex appeal were luxuries in a wife; members of the working classes had to settle for the less ornamental virtues. Though the young man on the make might prefer the boss's daughter, he settled for the clever stock girl, and though the rich heiress might indulge her fancy and marry the chauffeur, the poor girl had to settle for the good provider rather than the romantic stranger.

The question may be raised as to whether we really have any choice when we select our mates ourselves. According to the psychoanalytic and psychosocial view of the matter, our unconscious needs are the dominant factors; according to students of social structure, our class and cultural environment. We may not, in fact, the implication is, have done so well in substituting one set of masters for another.

computers to the rescue

It was inevitable that someone would come up sooner or later with a technological solution to the problems of efficient mate selection—the computer.

There was a time when the idea of using computers in mate selection aroused fear and revulsion, and it still does to many people. Actually, the computer is only a more effective way of doing what young people were trying to do for themselves with singles parties, bachelor cruises, introduction agencies, even advertisement of one kind or another.[1]

The computer is simply a way of performing an important function not adequately provided for now in our society. The problem is, though, what does one program the computer for? Obviously, the qualifications some seekers specify—such, for example, as those listed in one advertisement: "divorced (not angrily), very bright (and literate, though hardly an intellectual), tall and slim, sensitive, decidedly male, ebullient and tidy as hell, indulges in comfortable living and spontaneity, thinks simplicity is a virtue, enjoys wide range of music (some Bach to most rock), plays bridge, hearts, chess, scrabble or what-have-you at a moment's notice"—cannot all be accommodated on an IBM card. Some can, though, and there are agencies which promise precisely that.

But that is not the way the scientists go about it. They do not begin with what the prospective partners say they are looking for. They begin, rather, with the experience of past marriages. They try to find out what kinds of combinations of partners have succeeded or failed in the past. And it is quite amazing how much researchers can do with quite simple objective data such, for example, as: date of first marriage; when and how first marriages ended if they are not intact; date of birth; race; education of self and any other spouses; occupation; income; employment; and so on. Out of such data, the computer tells us that such and such combinations "worked," but such and such did not.

Now, the prospective bride or groom can profit by the experience of the past. The man, for example, locates his composite prototype and finds out what kinds of wives he did well with and what kinds of wives he did not. He may find that the prognosis for marriage with the kind of girl he is attracted to is not all that good; or that he is attracted to girls who, according to the past experience of men like him, are not suitable partners for him. No one can force him to select either one or the other, but he makes the choice with his eyes at least partially open. There is no guarantee that the help of the computer in mate selection would be any more welcome than similar advice proffered by friends and relatives has been from time immemorial. Love seems to remain blind, regardless, but there is certainly no harm in trying to help.

Paul Glick, one of the most perceptive and imaginative of the family demographers, is one researcher who finds room for computers in the future:

One of the first steps in an ideal system for getting the right kinds of people together in marriage . . . would be to acquaint them with a number of the potentially "best" marital partners for persons like them, well ahead of the time when they decide that they should marry. This matching process usually just happens informally through chance meeting at school or at work, or at club, recreational, or church functions. Those who are moderately aggressive generally succeed in finding a tolerable-or-better partner and proceed to become married. This group is evidently large, inasmuch as projections indicate that all but 2 to 4 percent of the young adults today will eventually marry. The problem, therefore, is much less one of helping to keep young adults from being lifelong bachelors or spinsters than it is one of helping them to select an "appropriate" person as a partner to marry during the optimal age range for them to marry.

So far, with only the grossest kinds of data to work with, all the computer can tell us about marriage is about factors related to stability. Even so, that is worth something. "Research on permanence of marriage should prove quite useful in facilitating the process of judicious mate selection," Glick notes. "The findings should be especially useful to those who lack the perspective and insight to make the most of their own potentialities for entering and continuing in a permanent marriage with a partner who comes reasonably close to being an ideal husband or wife for 'persons like them.' Even those who have a good understanding of their own strengths and weaknesses may not necessarily possess reliable intuitive knowledge about what types of persons of the opposite sex most often have permanent marriages with 'persons like them.' "

With the current fears about the potentially sinister uses of data banks, we may hesitate long and seriously about encouraging mate selection by computers. Still, it does have a future.[2] It should be especially useful for women. It permits a woman to take the initiative in a protected setting. She is supplied with candidates to judge and evaluate in the privacy of her own room, and spared the agony of face-to-face rejection or the humiliation of wallflower status. A considerable amount of the weeding-out process has already taken place by the time she meets the man. She knows that he is interested in paleobiology, does not care that she is size sixteen, does not mind stringy hair, enjoys square dancing. . . . In time we may be able to zero in on the subtler—even psychological—components of compatibility. Computer mate selection may not completely democratize the process, but it will help.

Still, use of a computer cannot eliminate the traits which make one a loser to begin with. A young man may know that the young woman weighs 175 pounds and yet not be prepared when he meets her for the ungainly shape the pounds take. She may know he is six feet tall and yet not be prepared for the gaunt, stoop-figured man when he shows up. Each may know that the other is a college graduate; neither is prepared for the utter dullness of the other. The computer cannot change the world. It can only help to make it more manageable.

Democratization does not mean that success of marriage is guaranteed. Even with computers, it is inevitable that, despite objective, rational, and deliberate efforts to bring "the right kinds of people together," there will still be failures. The goal would not be the elimination but only the minimization of marital breakdown. As such it is worth a try.

Even more cogent as a criticism is the fact that good matching at the time of marriage does not guarantee continued good matching over time. Nelson Foote introduces the concept of marriage as a pair of careers in the sense of processes of orderly development and hence not as static. "A marriage is not likely to stand still or continue unchanged for very long. Arrest in development of either partner makes it vulnerable to breakdown." If one develops and the other does not, as we noted in chapter 3, the original matching may no longer survive. A good match at twenty, Jan Dizard found, does not guarantee a good match at forty.

Granted, then, that marriage has been democratized in terms of who may marry and who selects one's mate, but has it also been democratized in terms of the relationship between the partners themselves? Or is it, in any event, at least in process of becoming democratized in this sense? There is a common assumption that the answer to these questions is, why, yes, of course marriage is becoming increasingly democratized. Actually, however, the answer is not nearly all that unequivocal.

chapter seven

are some more equal
than others?

a new conception

If there were something intrinsic, natural, divinely sanctioned about the almost universal allocation of authority to husbands, and if wives were incapable of exercising power, there would be no foolish talk about the democratization of marriage. Or if nature were as decisive about everything as about who bears the children, there would be no talk of whose prerogative any function was. Nature would conform to the institutional pattern, and all would go well. But the long history of male complaints about the difficulty of keeping women in their place belies the undemocratic assumptions about the position of wives. It isn't all that easy to keep women in their place, especially since a new egalitarian conception of marriage has arisen.

A generation ago, Ernest Mowrer, a student of the American urban family, distinguished four kinds of families: the paternal, the maternal, the filiocentric, and the egalitarian. There were two kinds of egalitarian marriages: that of conventional middle-class and professional people, and that of "emancipated" persons—the current.term would be "liberated." In these egalitarian marriages there were no children, relations were free from conventions, both partners were employed, relations with neighbors were casual, touch-and-go, contacts with others were on the basis of common interests rather than geography, interests and activities were outside rather than inside of the home, and the interests of one were not allowed to interfere with those of the other.

The egalitarian marriage was based on companionship, and reflected a new conception of the relationship between husbands and wives. In 1945, a widely used textbook on the family by Burgess and Locke had as a subtitle, "From institution to companionship."

The companionship concept of marriage (with its emphasis upon affection, comradeship, democracy, and happiness of members of the family) is replacing the old-time notion of marriage as a relation stressing respect, obedience, authority, and duty. This new concept has arisen as the result of many factors, including the loss of economic and other functions by the family, the growth of the urban way of life, the rising status of women, the continued decline in parental control of children's marriage, and the application of democracy in marital and familial relations.[1]

The key words in this description of the companionate are: comradeship, democracy, obedience, authority, rising status of women. These bland words, referring to ideas which were taken for granted, were almost clichés. Of course, the companionate was replacing the old-time notions of marriage. But the idea of the companionate proved unexpectedly elusive when the research tests came.

The idea of the relationship between husband and wife as one including, if not characterized by, companionship was by no means new. It had begun to emerge as early as the seventeenth century; indeed, the Book of Common Prayer began at that time to include companionship as one of the purposes of marriage even if, as we know from contemporaneous discussion of the nature of marriage, it was not viewed as an egalitarian relationship, as it is today.

Goodwill, love, and affection are possible between unequals—older and younger, master and servant, patron and protégée, employer and worker, teacher and pupil—and that was undoubtedly the kind of relationship the seventeenth-century writers were advocating in marriage. Genuine companionship, however, is a relationship among equals or approximate equals. It depends on the absence of both status and power barriers. As contrasted with the "old-time notion of marriage as a relation stressing" such status and power barriers as "obedience, authority, and duty," the new egalitarian notion is democratic, minimizing them. And no one (except an avant-garde radical) was seriously advocating such a model of marriage until about a generation ago. Since then, though, we have been talking about marital egalitarianism as if it could be taken for granted —and even believing what we were saying.

the egalitarian fallacy

Talking a good egalitarian game does not, however, prove that we are playing it. True, there has been a trend toward equalizing the legal obligations and rights of husbands and wives;[2] and the promise to obey no longer necessarily appears in the marriage vows of the bride. But so far as the actual relations between husbands and wives are concerned, there is no research proof that egalitarianism has been increasing.[3] Considering how hard it is to measure power or influence or control, or whatever is taken as the evidence of egalitarian relations,[4] we could expect some fuzziness in the conclusions the researchers have arrived at. However, if there had been a genuine increase in the relative number of egalitarian marriages, it should have been discernible through research. Yet if there was any trend at all—which I do not believe there has been—it seems to have been in a direction contrary to expectations, marriages in which the husband had greater power increasing and those in which the wife did, decreasing.[5]

This lack of a clear-cut trend documentable by research is the more remarkable because we know that when wives enter the labor force their "power" in the marital relationship tends to increase, and more and more wives have been entering the labor force. Thus, despite the revamping of the legal framework of marriage, the dropping of the wifely promise to obey, and the increase in at least some of the conditions making for egalitarianism, there is no clear-cut, unequivocal evidence that egalitarianism itself has kept pace.

In chapter 5 we asked if marriage had a past, and answered that although marital institutions—laws, customs, mores—had a very long and varied past, husband-wife relationships were timeless. Here, too, it is the same. No matter what the institutional structure prescribes with respect to power, authority, dominance, or control, the actual exercise of this prerogative will be by the partner best suited for it. But before attempt is made to illustrate this point, a brief parenthetical comment is interjected on the concept of equality itself.

a parenthetical aside on equality

Equality is a mathematical term. The only things that are or can be equal are the interchangeable units of measurement like inches or pounds or degrees of temperature. Science tries valiantly to reduce qualities to such interchangeable measurement units in order to compare the incomparable. We cannot compare apples and oranges unless we reduce them to some such common unit as calories or measures of sweetness. Then we can say that one is just as nutritious in terms of calories or as sweet as the other.

When we say that the average man is taller than the average woman, all we are saying is that his body has more units of height than hers. Not the bodies but the number of inches in each is compared. And since so many of the measures used to compare human beings with one another are not true measures in the sense of consisting of interchangeable units, the comparisons are always slightly spurious. The pitfalls are even greater when what is being compared is something not even reducible to units at all, such as something as amorphous and poorly conceived as power or dominance or influence.[6]

female-male, feminine-masculine

Regrettable as it may be, no discussion of egalitarianism in marriage can avoid at least paying its respects to the timeworn paradox of sex differences.

Femaleness and maleness are biological facts. Femininity and masculinity are cultural facts. It is easy to confuse the two sets of facts, because we do our best to identify femininity with femaleness and masculinity with maleness. But we know very well that the identification is spurious. The anthropologists have reminded us again and again that although what is female in one society is female in another, what is feminine in one society may be masculine in another, and vice versa.

Even in the case of biological traits, there is some overlapping. Some women are taller than the average man, and some men are weaker than the average woman. Still, the average superiority of males in size, running speed, and muscular strength has given them an enormous advantage, for in the last analysis they can exert physical force and overpower a female. They have therefore been able to define the nature of femininity and masculinity, and they have done so in terms of a polarity: weakness on the part of one and strength on the part of the other. Thus "feminine" women are delicate, dainty, yielding, passive, nurturant, emotional; in fact, by definition to be feminine is to be weak. Although women as such are not weak, feminine women are. And since femininity is the norm to which females are supposed to conform, they do their best. They are punished by rejection if they do not. Women, in brief, are rewarded for being weak, punished for being strong. An egalitarian relationship is hard to achieve under this design.

The polarity gives a sense of balance, of complementarity. By making femininity and masculinity as complementary as femaleness and maleness, it results in a fundamental distortion in our thinking. We feel that if all men are not dominant, then all women must be; if all women are not subservient, then all men must be. When thinking of change, therefore, we tend to think in terms of role reversal rather than in terms of roles assigned on the basis of individual temperament and talents, whatever they may be. Thinking in terms of sexual polarities makes it difficult to think of human beings rather than of stereotypes.

Women who are frankly and unintimidatedly female, unglossed with femininity, can be not only powerful but also fascinating and exciting and even fun. Men who have acquired a taste for them find them delightful and feminine women dull, useful as servants and assistants and underlings but not as companions or even sex partners. Relatively few women, though, make it to frank femaleness. Most gloss it with femininity.

the hidden agenda of marriage

At all kinds of meetings there are at least two sets of interactions going on, one the formal, the manifest, and the other undercover. So, analogously, in marriage. No matter what the formal, institutional structure of the marital-bond may be, there is always an informal, personal one which may not only not conform to the formal, but may actually subvert it.

Husbands enter marriage with an initial advantage in the institutional prescription of superiority to them. A generation ago, A. H. Maslow reported that men showed up as more "dominant" than women as measured in personality tests then available, and Eleanor Maccoby's summary of recent studies tends to corroborate this finding. Men are, further, more likely to be equipped by training and motivation for the exercise of power; I am even willing to concede a biological basis for it in average size, aggressiveness, and hormonal activation.

All right, then. Take a young woman who has been trained for feminine dependencies, who wants to "look up" to the man she marries. Put her at a disadvantage in the labor market. Then marry her to a man who has a slight initial advantage over her in age, income, and education, shored up by an ideology with a male bias and an institutional framework tilted in his favor. Denigrate her status further at marriage by lowering her occupation still more. (The directions for doing this were specified in chapter 3.) Then expect an egalitarian relationship?

Yet, in spite of everything we can do to disqualify this young woman, it does sometimes happen that, because of the subversiveness of nature which does not distribute human characteristics in nonoverlapping curves, like Lady Macbeth she does have the talent and temperament to run the show.

When marriages are arranged, perceptive and insightful matchmakers take into account such personality differences and try to arrange a good fit between spouses. Compliant young women are matched with dominant young men, and if a young woman seems temperamentally insubordinate, a mate who is older or who has other compensating assets is sought to tame her. This is a situation, it might be added, not uncommon in folk tales and in literature, including Shake-speare's version of the taming of the shrew. Where mate selection is permitted to the young people themselves, we are told that they tend also to select mates who complement one another. In some cases, the result co-incides with the structural imperatives; the husband is dominant and the wife dependent. In some cases the husband is only overtly dominant; covertly he is de-pendent, and the wife, who has traditional views on the position of women, exercises her power covertly. In still other cases, however, the wife is dominant and the hus-band passive and nonaggressive; such a pattern, how-ever congenial it may be to the partners themselves, goes against the prescribed pattern.

Still, it is hard to imagine a strong, competent wife allowing an incompetent or passive husband to make deleterious decisions or to pursue harmful goals. By wiles or by sheer determination she would almost cer-tainly assume control—perhaps even to his relief, pro-vided it was made unmistakably clear that he was boss. And, as a matter of fact, the nearer we get to specific, concrete husbands and wives and the farther away from the prescribed rules, the less powerful many of the flesh-and-blood husbands look. And the more powerful the wives, as so many biblical or shtetl women were, for example, or African or Alorese women are today. (Have you, for example, ever even heard of Lapidoth, Deborah's husband?)

The almost passionate insistence on the subservience of wives in the past rested on a conception of the nature of women which such flesh-and-blood women belie. There is no way of knowing whether or to what extent there has been a change in the hidden agenda of mar-riage over the centuries. But it is hard to imagine women like Deborah, the biblical general, docilely ac-cepting anything but pro forma domination by their husbands. In the day-by-day business of coping, power has, we repeat, always undoubtedly rested in the hands of those able to use it. And that, as Benjamin Franklin wisely noted, is as it should be.

so what difference does it make?

If it is true that women can prevail in marriage as well as men can, does it make any difference, really that wherever the power has actually rested, the assumption has always been made that it rested with the husband?

Yes, it does, for dominance has one effect if exercised by the husband and quite a different one if exercised by the wife. The wife who is dominant is a misfit in the relationship as prescribed by the marital structure; the husband who is, is not. There is probably enough plasticity in the heredity of human beings that most can be successfully socialized into the models demanded by their culture, but it will be more costly for some than for others, for the Katherines than for the Biancas.

Among men, power and prestige go together. And prestige can more than compensate for lack of power. Not so among women. Women have to pretend that they do not have power and to convince the world that they do not. In the case of men, failures to conform to the institutional imperatives can be masked more easily than in the case of women, for wives try to save their husbands' faces. They tend to act out their part in a way that reassures husbands. They try to build them up, support them, give them at least the illusion that they conform to the prescribed pattern. Wives are less likely to have this support. They are less likely to be protected by husbands trying to give them the illusion of conformity.

Even worse. Because of the male bias which has shaped our mentality for so many years, not only do women who exercise power receive no reward for it in the form of prestige or deference, but they are actually punished. They are "henpecking" their husbands. They are "castrating bitches," or worse. They are unwomanly, unnatural, deviant, and hence execrable. Unless, that is —and this is the heart of the matter—they are clever enough, as they usually are, to hide their light under a bushel, and to convince everyone, including their husbands, how brightly the masculine light shines.

There is some evidence that under the impact of the egalitarian ideal things are changing, though, and that modern women are less and less inclined to play charades. This is a change with, apparently, disturbing effects on husbands.

how successful are egalitarian marriages?

If, as we saw above, it is practically impossible to answer even the simple question, What proportion of all marriages are egalitarian? it is even harder to answer the more difficult question, How successful are they? What test of success should we apply? What criteria of egalitarianism? How should we measure either success or egalitarianism? And how shall we make provision to discount the tendency of both partners to overestimate the egalitarian nature of their marriages, or the tendency for wives to underplay their own power in the marriage? Despite all these difficulties, I venture a very general answer to the question: egalitarian marriages show up well when we apply the criteria of adjustment and happiness.

Among marriages that are not egalitarian, the less they deviate from this mold the better. Thus, although a general slant in favor of mild husband-dominance or wife-dominance makes for good marriage, extremes in the direction of dominance by either partner, but especially by wives, show unfavorable results.

However, the most interesting conclusion to be drawn from a generation of research is that the results vary over time. Studies made in the 1930s and 1940s, for example, reported results more favorable for the egalitarian marriage than do those made in the 1950s and 1960s. Whereas more of the egalitarian than of the nonegalitarian marriages were found to be happy in one of the early studies, in the 1960s, egalitarian marriages

were said to be "confused, irresponsible, and characterized by an inability to resolve problems and by a low
level of sex differentiation, which creates difficulties in
identity and ego development"—quite a bill of particulars against egalitarianism.

Especially intriguing was the finding in the early
studies that among nonegalitarian marriages, the wife-
dominant ones showed up better than husband-domi-
nant ones, for both husbands and wives. These husbands
seemed not to mind it when their wives were dominant;
but wives did mind it when their husbands were. And
so, unexpectedly, did the men themselves. Husband-
dominated marriages scored low, wife-dominant marriages intermediate, and egalitarian marriages, intermediate to high.[7]

Later studies did not report such successful accommodation of men to the egalitarian ideal. The father-led
—but not father-dominant—family was the one which
now won the accolade. It was, in fact, the only type,
allegedly, producing predominantly healthy children.[8]

Something seemed to have happened either to the
researchers or to marriages between the early and the
later studies. I believe it had to do with marital style.

the lady macbeth syndrome

Traditional wives were content with the covert exercise of power in the marriage; they did not mind having
to dissemble. Dissembling was so much a part of the
wife's personality that she did not even notice she was
dissembling, or if she did, she enjoyed it. This was
especially typical of wives in blue-collar marriages. In
fact, Veroff and Feld tell us, the covert power was
gratifying because it *was* covert. On the current scene,
older women and less educated women are the ones
most likely to conform to this traditional pattern. But
it is not the wave of the future. Even in the 1950s,
younger women were beginning to show evidence of

frustration in the traditional marital pattern, and even some of the older high school educated wives were also beginning to chafe.

But the real impact was occurring among the less traditional, more egalitarian marriages of the college educated. Women with strong power motivation, Veroff and Feld tell us, found egalitarian relationships congenial; they "felt unrestricted, happy, and free of problems." Egalitarian relationships made it possible for them to assert themselves, and they liked that. They reported fewer marital problems and more marital happiness than women with less power drive. The egalitarian model suited them just fine.

Not so, however, their husbands. Egalitarianism created difficulties for the power-oriented college-educated man. It challenged his position of power and threatened to reveal his weakness. We begin to catch a glimpse of the reasons back of the differences in reported success of egalitarian marriages in the early and in the later studies. "Even for men who presumably accept the egalitarian marital role," Veroff and Feld report, "this role poses a threat to the masculine self-image of men with strong power motivations; they felt restricted and had marital problems. For them there is a lack of congruence between their motivation and the role demands." The egalitarian ideal shakes a finger at their desire to exert power and evokes "fear of weakness."

These results applied to men and women interested in power. Whether in the future more women will, like some avant-garde women, become power-oriented or, like the idealists among the Women's Liberation Movement, decry the very concept of power, is a matter of conjecture only. My own preference lies in the direction of the downgrading of power in either sex.

Whatever the trend of the future may be, there are some men who fear that the pendulum may have swung too far in the direction of the wife already. "It does appear that the myth of the aggressive, dominating husband and the shy submissive wife may be laid to rest," Harold Feldman tells us. He saw wives "as more out-going, aggressive, verbal persons with a wider range of emotionality both felt and expressed. . . . Men, on the other hand, seem to be constricted in their emotional makeup, less forceful, more calm, and less demanding of marriage. These marriages may reflect the conse-quences of the trend toward the companionate egal-itarian marriage with the possibility of the pendulum's having swung past the midpoint."

Men, in brief, despite lip service to the egalitarian model, were finding it difficult actually to accept it in practice. It was as true in the 1960s as it was a genera-tion ago, as Terman said, that "the new mores empha-sizing equality of the sexes in marriage have not as yet entirely displaced the old attitude that the husband should be dominant."

What has really changed, I am convinced, was not power but style. In the egalitarian model the wife was no longer dissembling. She was rejecting the idea of a misfit between the institutional or theoretical pattern and the actual pattern. This rejection was not neces-sarily of the "real" power structure, but reflected wives' increasing reluctance to go along with the institutional conception of marriage which put them down and re-duced them to manipulative operators. They no longer wanted to have to be devious, to simulate, to be patron-ized. They wanted to be themselves, whatever those selves—dominant or subservient—happened to be. They did not, like Veroff and Feld's blue-collar wives, enjoy covert power because it was covert.

Another change was also occurring in the area of achievement as well as of power. Achievement for women has tended to be derivative, vicarious. For ex-ample, when the public is asked who are the women they admire most, the resulting list consists largely of the wives of men who have achieved rather than women who have achieved in their own right. Women are socialized into believing that although they cannot in their own right become great "doctors, lawyers, merchants, or chiefs," they can do so through their husbands. The old cliché that behind every successful man there is a woman on whom the success depended is accepted. And in the 1950s William Whyte told them that the corporation wife was an integral part of the system, performing an essental service for it. (Strangely enough, no one seemed to think it odd that if her services were so important, the corporation did not pay her for them.) At least wives could feel they were contributing to their husbands' success in the traditional manner and thus enjoy a sense of achievement, however farfetched.

It is not surprising, therefore, to find how salient women have judged ambition in a man to be. Roland Tharp reports on a national survey of high school girls that found that almost all of them put ambition at or near the top of the list of qualities preferred in a husband, following only honesty and physical attractiveness. Nor is it surprising to find that a considerable proportion of all traits desired in a mate by college women were achievement-related, such as getting ahead, being ambitious, enjoying working, being energetic, and having a high-status profession. Women have had a great stake in their husbands' achievement, having put their eggs in the basket of the husband's achievement rather than in their own.

Modern women are now learning, according to Lois Wyse, that a man's business success does not depend on a wife, the popular myth to the contrary notwithstanding. Further, the world in which surrogate success could be taken for granted has vanished, or is in process of vanishing, for a sizable segment of the population. Young men, especially among the avant-garde college-educated segment—bellwether of the future—are less and less willing to invest themselves in the (to them) mindless competition required for business or professional success. They are not as highly motivated to climb to the top as were earlier generations. They are willing to settle for less, for a slower pace, for a lower level of achievement. The psychologist's "achievement motivation"—once the very hallmark of maleness—has become attenuated in them. If they are married to women in whom achievement orientation is also muted, there is no problem. But for women who still expect to satisfy a desire for achievement by way of their husbands, this new trend may be frustrating. Even men who do have a strong desire for achievement do not always succeed. Despite their emphasis on achievement in future husbands, not all women marry men who rate high on this quality. Even derivative achievement by way of their husbands is denied to them.

Women are beginning to chafe at their power-behind-the-throne status; many want to play the game themselves rather than vicariously through someone else. Marriage comes to seem restrictive to them; they feel frustrated. But even if they pursue careers on their own, their achievement must be muted, for, Margaret Poloma has found, if a wife contributes to the family income her power in the family is increased. In fact, sometimes in traditional marriage her contribution is not even recognized; she is presumed to be just having fun. There seems to be a nice gradation between acceptance of the wife's contribution to the family income and the power accorded to her.

Poloma's study of professional wives found four patterns of relationship in their marriages: (1) traditional or patriarchal, in which the wife's career was viewed primarily as just a hobby, while the husband's was the source of income and status; (2) neotraditional, in which the wife's profession was taken more seriously, but she was still responsible for the children and the household; (3) egalitarian, in which the women deliberately kept their incomes down in order not to surpass their husbands (strange kind of egalitarianism); and (4) matriarchal, in which the wife's income was larger and in which there were many problems.

This is the way one successfully achieving woman laid it out, off the record, to a—rejecting—group of young listeners:

The success of the career woman lies in not expecting your husband to see you in the career role at home. Don't expect him to be in the position of a fan, worshipping you or kow-towing to you. He may be proud of your success if his is greater but if you insist that he treat you as a successful professional it may bore him. If you're an adoring wife rather than a patronizing star maybe he can take your success in stride. He must also be protected from people who *have* to see you as a successful professional. Beware of them. They can come between you. I found as I climbed the ladder of my profession I got used to being treated with formal respect and deference. OK. But it's a mistake to expect your man to do the same. You're still a wife, entitled to his love but certainly not to deference. And don't throw your weight around at home. Being a boss on the job doesn't entitle you to be boss at home.

Ugh! shuddered one of the young women in her audience, who happened to be supporting a young man in an unconventional relationship. Still she had to admit that egalitarian relationships did take a bit of female maneuvering.

Hewing our way through the jungle of inadequate conceptualization, poor measurement, and conflicting findings, we conclude—without backup from research —that from time immemorial, despite the institutional pattern conferring authority on husbands, whichever spouse had the talent for running the show did so. If the wife was the power in the marriage she exerted her power in a way that did not show; she did not flaunt it; she was satisfied with the "power-behind-the-throne" position. Since companionship was not expected from marriage, egalitarianism was not an issue. It is only now that we are beginning to face the issues involved in egalitarian relationships and especially one—the possibility of a conflict between companionship and sexuality in marriage.

companionship and sex: an unexpected obstacle

Difficult as it was proving to be to bridge the institutionalized authority gap between husbands and wives, it was proving even more difficult to bridge the companionship gap. All the studies of middle-class marriages show that companionship, the hallmark of the egalitarian marriage, is one of the most important ingredients for a successful marriage, especially for the wife, no matter what criterion or index is used to measure success. In the Blood and Wolfe sample, almost half of the wives felt that companionship was the most valuable aspect of their marriages, far ahead even of love, understanding, standard of living, and children. These findings, the researchers concluded, "show that when modern Americans think of marriage, they think of companionship more than anything else." An understandable, but, unfortunately, not easily realized dream, for companionship is one of the hardest of all marital goals to achieve.

The difficulty of achieving companionship in egalitarian marriages was unexpected. That it was difficult in the old patriarchal model was taken for granted; but the modern pattern would change all that. In the past, Blood and Wolfe remind us, "If female companionship was desired, it could hardly be obtained from one's wife since she dwelled in a different world—uneducated in the ways of men, and too submissive to achieve the equality which companionship requires. . . . Fortunately, the same economic developments which made leisure available to men also made education available to women. And the shift from patriarchate to equality in decision making broke down the barriers of reserve and respect between men and women, enabling them to enjoy each other as persons." If only it were that simple!

Alas, it was not so. It wasn't working out that way. The English divines of the sixteenth and seventeenth centuries had noted that companionship tended to enhance the value of marriage, making it a positive good as well as merely a negative bulwark against sin, read sex. But it was now beginning to look as though companionship in marriage was proving too successful as a bulwark against sex, especially in the more educated classes. By the middle of the twentieth century, in fact, Veroff and Feld were beginning to raise disturbing questions about the way an ideology oriented toward egalitarian companionship might affect the sexual component of marriage. They were wondering out loud whether companionship might "cost" too much in terms of sexual relations, whether a companionate relationship in marriage was even compatible with a good sexual relationship. On the basis of their data, gathered in the 1950s, at the height of the era dominated by the feminine mystique, they were speculating that the conception of the "traditional marital relationship [as] a friendship may play havoc with the potential that the marital role has to permit sexual and interpersonal activity." In other words, can you mix companionship and sex? The future of marriage rides on the answer.

The dilemma is particularly painful because sexual satisfaction and companionship have been found to be about equally related to marital happiness and general satisfaction. If they are, indeed, incompatible, the companionate marriage has tall hurdles to overcome. Companionship might have to be achieved at the expense of sexuality.

Apparently appalled by the direction in which data had led them, Veroff and Feld remind us that the possible incompatibility between companionship and sexuality is only hypothetical, merely speculative. Still, they do take it seriously enough to lay out possible alternative ways to accommodate the conflict, just in case.

alternatives: sex versus companionship

Companionship in marriage, they hypothesize, calls for similarities between the partners. This assumption is implicit in a great deal of discussion of mate selection in which common interests and backgrounds are assumed to be desirable. Sexuality, on the other hand, depends on differentiation between the sexes. If you prefer companionship, you will try to make the sexes as like each other as feasible, you will underplay the differences; if you prefer sexuality, you will favor anything that makes the sexes different; *"vive la différence!"* will be your motto.

A third alternative proposed not by Veroff and Feld but by others is to change the nature of marriage itself, reserving sex for marriage and seeking companionship elsewhere. A fourth alternative, suggested by a psychiatrist, Robert Seidenberg, is to evolve a sexual style that accommodates companionship in what he calls "afterplay."

By and large, men have preferred the alternative that emphasizes sexuality over companionship, especially the kind of sexuality involved in the chase and conquest. They complain that life would become intolerably dull without a "battle of the sexes" based on sex differences.

In another place I have distinguished relations between the sexes from sexual relations, the first dealing with any kind of relationship between men and women —employer and employee, buyer and seller, mother and son, father and daughter, teacher and pupil—and the second to only one very special kind, which has to do with excitement, thrills, romance, fun and games, the sort of thing that advertisements, romantic movies, and much popular culture deals with. It is a kind of relationship that probably accounts for three-fourths of the fantasy life of most people. There is great concern that any change in the direction of emphasizing the similarities rather than the differences between the sexes would jeopardize such relations, especially the difference which highlights sexual aggression on the part of men and resistance but inevitable submission on the part of women.

Veroff and Feld suggest that husbands and wives may maintain their differences and individuality in another way, by emphasizing their separate roles, the men turning to their work and women to motherhood. The data on which this outmoded suggestion was based were gathered, we remind ourselves, in the 1950s. Since that time there has been such a reversal of trends that the proposal sounds almost ludicrous. Women are no longer turning so exclusively to maternity, and men are beginning to reexamine the whole philosophy back of their own work mystique. That road does not look promising.

Another prescription by those who favor emphasis on sex differences is to encourage any kind of specialization just so it's sexual. Says Charles Winick, "Almost any male-female role structure is viable, so long as there is clear [sexual] division of labor and responsibilities." He concludes sadly that the kind of sex-role ambiguity that we tolerate in our open society "might ultimately prove to be almost as hazardous as the rigidities of authoritarianism." Equality, in other words, is subversive.

Women and other minority groups tend to be suspicious of emphasis on differences, for all too often it undergirds some version of the separate-but-equal form of discrimination. The "you-are-just-as-good-as-we-are-only-different" point of view is certainly valid. But it is almost always interpreted by patronizing men in their favor.

Parenthetically, it is interesting to observe that the men who are most vocal about sexual polarity in almost every other area show an anomalous inconsistency in one sector: that of grievances. When women raise any particular grievance, these men are the first to cry, "Men, too!" If women need liberation, so do men. If housework is dull, so is the work of most men. If marriage is disillusioning to women, so is it to men. They want it both ways—unisex in grievances, polarity in sexual relations. It is, of course, quite true that men, too, have grievances. There has certainly been no lack of recognition of them, since men have been complaining of their lot from time immemorial, and, a good deal of the time, not only blaming it on women but also convincing women of their culpability. It is only recently that at least some men have stopped their complaints long enough to hear those of women. And it will take a long time to show that many of their grievances can be ameliorated with the women's. A great many of the things men complain about in wives result precisely from the polarization they have favored. Why can't a woman be more like a man? whines Henry Higgins. Because so many men have insisted on the polarization that makes her different—and segregated her, cutting her out of almost all except sexual contacts. Companionship with husbands could help cultivate the male virtues, the lack of which Henry Higgins so plaintively deplored; and, in return, the female virtues in men, be it noted, so lacking in him.

The second of the Veroff-Feld alternatives—playing up similarities between the sexes—is the current trend among young people today. There is a minimization of sexual polarities, a blurring of sex differences, a movement in the direction of unisex or monosex rather than toward more polarization. Charles Winick, a sociologist, lists some of the evidence, namely—the names given to children that do not indicate sex; the haircuts of children; dolls for boys; reading materials; courses in school; dating behavior involving sexual aggressiveness in girls; clothing and appearance; cosmetics use; recreation and leisure activities; employment; tasks about the home; the "feminization" of alcoholic beverages; the feminization of decor, architecture; the predominance of women in the performing arts. These, by emphasizing similarities, lean in the direction of encouraging the companionate aspect of marriage.

Neither of these two alternatives is compelling, and it would be depressing if one really believed that good sexual relations in marriage depended on either one. There is little likelihood that sexual polarity will be purposely increased in the future or that women will soon return to a concentration on the maternal role.

Nor will the future alter the basic biological differences between the sexes. The advocates of sexual polarization need have no fear on that score. The future may reduce the artificially exaggerated differences, but if sex differences are truly immutable—as I believe they are—they will survive all the forms of unisex specified above.

In the case of race, anthropologists tell us that there is value in cross-mating. By analogy, I would argue that mixing of "maleness" and "femaleness" has value, that such "mixed" products are superior to either "pure" maleness or "pure" femaleness. The stereotypical "he-man," the male with a large dose of "maleness," is far from an appealing character as either companion or sex partner. (I refrain from invoking the reported research findings that men with an extra male chromosome show more than the expected number of defects, including low intelligence and high aggressiveness.) Similarly, the corresponding "she-woman," the female with an over-dose of "femaleness," is so passive, so sacrificial, so static, and so colorless as to be an all-around nullity as either companion or sex partner. "What is needed is not sexlessness," says Edgar Z. Friedenberg, "but decent people and institutional arrangements that acknowledge the force [of sex] in human affairs while minimizing its potential for insult and injury."

I do not see the cultivation of tenderness and gentleness in men or aggressiveness in women as something to be bemoaned. A combination of the characterizing traits of men and women results in the most attractive human types of either gender as both companions and sex partners. And attempts to exaggerate the characterizing traits of either one is retrograde. Let men who have a flair for homemaking do just that and women who have nondomestic interests pursue them. There is little danger that permitting roles to be filled by those individually most qualified for them, regardless of sex, will have the calamitous effect on marriage that some men fear. The result, as a matter of fact, might not be all that different from what advocates of sexual polarity seek. We'll never know until we try.

The third alternative for reconciling the alleged incompatibility between sexuality and companionship recommends sex to be left to the marriage but does not demand that companionship also be provided by it. Margaret Mead has suggested that we might play tennis with one man or woman, go to the theater with another, ride horseback with another, and still remain married to a fourth. This is a kind of specialization with which the Greeks were familiar. A well-born Athenian had a female slave for hard work, a concubine for valet service, a mistress for sexual pleasure, a wife for bearing legitimate children, and hetaerae for companionship. Clifford Kirkpatrick has commented on the difficulty for modern women of combining all these functions in one person.

Sometimes this alternative has taken the form of companionship in the marriage and sexuality outside of it, the prostitute supplying the sexual component and the wife the companionship, or at least the conventional façade of companionship. This may have been acceptable in the nineteenth century, but it would have low priority for modern women, or men.

The fourth alternative leans heavily on an old insight. *To converse* originally signified "to have sexual relations." And this verbal aspect of sexual relations remains to this day an important component of sexual pleasure. Robert Seidenberg has incorporated this important insight in his emphasis on what he calls after-play.

We have paid so much attention to foreplay and the orgasm that an area of sexuality that I would term "afterplay" is virtually unexplored. By this I mean those events which follow "conventional" intercourse between people—events that may be crucial to the enjoyment of the relationship. . . . For those who have not succumbed to boredom and indifference, afterplay is apt to consist of a great deal of talk and inquiry. . . . Prostitutes report that the bottlenecks of production in their work are the men who want to linger and talk. For many people it is far easier to find someone to have sex with than someone who will hear them out. The sexual act is far easier to master than that of conversation. For women who have been kept out of public life and have little voice in the world, this opportunity to talk to a man, especially if he is intelligent and worldly, becomes the most fulfilling part of the coital experience.

Seidenberg is not unaware of the pitfalls of such after-play—women can use it for blackmail, for example—but the possibility for misuse does not detract from its potential for providing companionship along with sexuality in marriage. In a poor relationship there is either no afterplay at all or exploitative afterplay. But in a good relationship it takes the form of intimate conversation, close sharing, and warm appreciation. Seidenberg is not implying, of course, that such intimacy has to be restricted to afterplay. In any event, there is no incontrovertible evidence that good sexual relations in marriage have to be paid for by loss of companionship, or vice versa.

The four alternatives imply the validity of the thesis that the companionship of the egalitarian marriage, by threatening men's power impairs their sexuality. If companionship is a relationship between equals, as Burgess and Locke say it is, the implication of the Veroff-Feld findings is that sexual relations, by way of contrast, are relations between unequals, between a man whose feelings of power and hence of sexual adequacy are threatened by egalitarian conceptions and a woman who must, therefore, settle for inferior status and power.

sex and status

Status in sexual relations is bafflingly subtle. Since men have appropriated the area of sex, practically all we know on the subject is what they have written about it. Men have generally had more sexual experience; they have therefore been the teachers, the experts. Because they were more knowledgeable, they had higher status in the relationship (just as Mrs. Robinson in *The Graduate* did in her teacher role). They therefore felt they were entitled to take charge.

That there may be some difficulty in moving from the egalitarian status of companionship, in which neither is presumably superior to the other, to the sexual act, in which, until recently, the man was superior, is understandable. An intuitive sociologist, Willard Waller, described two faculty members faced with the uncertainties involved in such a status transition: "when a woman has been talking [as an equal] about philology in the tone of mature scholarship, one cannot just begin making passes at her." The transition from the language of words in the companionship relation to the language of seductive action in the sexual relation changes the status relationship. He takes over and she is no longer his equal.

Subtler still is the status degradation implied by the panicky young girl who asks anxiously if he will still respect her if she engages in sexual relations with him, or by the young women who feel they will "lower themselves" by consenting to them, or the wife whose frigidity evens up—or even reverses—the status differential. Or the wife who is fearful that if she takes the initiative —a prerogative that constitutes one of the indexes of status superiority—her husband will consider her unfeminine, not satisfied with her properly inferior sexual status. For in any social relationship—nonsexual as well as sexual—the higher-status person is the one who has the privilege of taking the initiative.

A survey by Gordon and Shankweiler of eighteen best-selling marriage manuals of the past two decades shows how right these girls and women are. For "women in this century have been granted the right to experience sexual desire and have this desire satisfied, but always with the man calling the tune. This . . . is a manifestation of the minority group status of women."

Men, we are told—by a man, Philip E. Slater—have

maintained these myths about women in order to enhance their own superior status: "one of the oldest gambits . . . has been to maintain that dominance is sex-linked (as indeed it is, in some species). Thus if a woman assumes any other than a submissive pose she is accused of being 'unfeminine.' This is an ingenious device for maintaining superior status and has been quite successful."

There is, however, a fallacy imbedded in our words that can mislead us here. We have stereotyped the sexual patterns "passive" and "aggressive" so that they imply status inferiority and superiority, subordination and superordination. Actually, there are many styles of being passive, ranging all the way from demeaning, servile, hostile, resentful, resigned, to cordial. To illustrate, there is the story of a young woman, brilliant, talented, beautiful, and determined to be as superlative in bed as in the classroom and laboratory. She prepared for her first sexual rendezvous with a fellow student by studying up, as she would have prepared for a critical examination. Only after several years did she confess that she had just learned "the pleasures of passivity." But it was not the passivity of subordination implied by the stereotype. In her words: "it was fun to receive his caresses, like a queen accepting homage, and it was pleasant to let him do all the work." In this definition of the situation, passivity was far from servile or demeaning and aggressiveness from dominating. Her partner was also entitled to passivity—as, in fact, the geisha girl knew, and as to this day many prostitutes do, too. Sometimes, that is, men want their sex partners "to do all the work." Status differences? Perhaps, but not intrinsically along sex lines.

There is, of course, much more to the matter. Status is a sociological, not a biological, phenomenon. In the nineteenth century there was reported a kind of status-based aberration in men, this time not an incompatibility between companionship and sex but between love and sex. There were some men whose sexuality depended on contempt for their partners. Thus, although they could function well with prostitutes who were their status inferiors, they could not function at all with women of their own class who, they had been taught, were their moral superiors. They could not degrade such women by sexual relations. We know that there was nothing biologically intrinsic involved here. If the incompatibility between love and sex was not intrinsic, should we accept as intrinsic an incompatibility between companionship and sex?

Not only does companionship suffer if we accept such an incompatibility but so also does sexuality itself. Slater reminds us that men lose as well as gain by hobbling their wives' personalities, concluding that "women who have been taught too well that aggressiveness is 'unladylike' often seem a bit asexual." And in quite a different context, Dr. Malcolm Brown, a psychological therapist, in rejecting the therapeutic value of sexual relations between therapist and patient because that relationship is one of dependency, concludes that "really satisfying sex has to be egalitarian."

So far as status goes, I think we have only a generation gap to contend with in achieving companionate or egalitarian marriages. But the power angle is more difficult. Status is purely a social phenomenon, but power involves biological inequality and that complicates the situation.

sex and power

Veroff and Feld had traced the difficulties they found in companionate marriages to the fact that the egalitarianism of such marriages threatened men's feelings of power and, since in the male mystique sexuality and power are closely identified with one another, their sexual adequacy as well.

Is this identification of sexuality with physical power intrinsic, or is it, like so many other aspects of masculinity, a cultural artifact, perhaps once functional but long since become anachronistic? Do we have here a more-or-less minor sex difference which culture in the form of the male mystique has elaborated all out of proportion? A difference primarily in incidence rather than in kind? Granted—and I grant it only for the sake of argument—that male power may once have served some purpose—for capturing a wife, for example, or for overcoming the built-in chastity belt that protected access to a woman's body—have not the conditions that once may have justified it long since disappeared?

To answer these questions a distinction has to be made between the physical power of men and the male mystique which identifies it with sexuality. It is true that on the average men are larger and muscularly stronger than women. In the archetypical sexual encounter, therefore, the male has greater physical power. (This has nothing to do with coital position or the possibility of greater strength of libidinal interest or frequency of erotic desire or orgasmic capacity, in all of which women may excel men.) The ancient cliché remains: although women may be able to "castrate," they cannot rape men. But men can rape them. Husbands can, and legally may, force wives to have sexual relations with them. Although men can be socialized into concern for their sexual partners they can, if they please, also ignore their partners' feelings and get away with it. The male mystique not only permits such use of power, it may even demand it. The fallacy of the mystique lies in identifying physical and sexual prowess. The fact that a man *can* overpower a woman does not demonstrate his sexual prowess, but only his physical strength.

If we defined masculinity as the ability to chin oneself twenty times or to do twenty push-ups every morning, the men who could not achieve this level would feel emasculated. For whatever is identified with masculinity is imposed, willy-nilly, on all males, and failure to conform to the criteria is "castrating." So with power. If power is measured as the ability to conquer a woman and if masculinity is defined as such power, the subjugation of women is demanded for potency. And, in fact, such a definition of masculinity has characterized the male mystique for centuries. The criteria for dominance in studies of personality parallel point for point the criteria for masculinity.

From time immemorial, therefore, sex has meant power to men. The thrill of victory in the chase, conquest, subjugation has enhanced if not actually surpassed the thrill of the sexual act itself. The man boasting of his conquests at the tavern gets no points for sexual relations with his wife even if his achievement is prodigious; no conquest there, no proof of power. He scores only when he has succeeded in overpowering a—however pro forma—reluctant woman. Among young men, "making" a hard-to-get coed counts more in the bull session than "making" a less popular young woman or a more approachable one. In fact, young women in a talk session with Robert E. Gould pointed out that when they comply too readily with the proposals of young men, the men find themselves unable to perform. Their sexual potency does, apparently, depend on their ability to overcome resistance—an example, one might say, of "castration by female compliance."

The very term *impotence* betrays the power component in the male mystique. Sexual athleticism among males is identified with power, and power with sex. In the therapy developed by Masters and Johnson, the women partners of men undergoing treatment for impotence are instructed not to make demands on the men because such demands are threatening. (A functional explanation for the need to give priority to the male is invoked in the dependence of reproduction on the male's sexual performance rather than on his partner's. For nonprocreative relations, however, the increasing acceptance of manual and oral sexuality may mitigate the pressure on males for 100 percent penile readiness.)

It is not the ultimate power of the penile thrust that is under discussion here; there is no way or, for that matter, wish to challenge that by either men or women. There is this much truth in the anatomy-is-destiny dictum. But this is not the same as the identification of physical power with sexuality.

There is no proof that physical power is identical to sexual power, that rapists, for example, are more sexually potent than normal men. Great "masculine" he-men like athletes, further, are not necessarily any more sexually powerful than sedentary men. "There is," Kinsey has told us, "no invariable correlation [between sexual and physical activity]. The list of top athletes includes persons with both low and high rates of sexual outlet." And surprise is sometimes expressed when an extremely "masculine"-looking man turns out to be a homosexual.

Men make a good case for the identification of power with masculinity, and most believe it. Their case is almost convincing, but not quite, for the identification of masculinity with power is not total, any more than is the identification of femininity with passivity. The male mystique fits all men no better than the feminine mystique fits all women. We know that there are some men who enjoy sexual passivity; they seek the ministrations of the geisha-girl type, coital or noncoital. Some men, as we noted earlier, want women "to do all the work." In exaggerated form, this preference may be masochistic, even pathological, as when men even require whipping by women for sexual stimulation. In a journal addressed to swingers, there are advertisements by women offering their dominating skills, such, for example, as a "dominatrix" who specializes in training docile men with the leather equipment to make them obey, or as another dominant mistress who is looking for men for strict training, or as still another woman seeking docile males who want to be commanded.

My own reading of the situation is that the conflict between companionship and sexuality based on an identification of masculinity with power is not biologically intrinsic but a result of the imposition of the male mystique on men. What reduces men to impotence is not the deprivation of power in egalitarian relations but the male mystique that defines masculinity in terms of power. I do not have any illusions that overcoming this impediment to companionate marriages is going to be easy, but I do not think it will be as difficult as Robert Seidenberg does when he asks, "Is sex without sexism possible?" and answers, for the present, no, because of the way in which we have socialized both men and women. Here is his perceptive analysis of the power obstacle to egalitarian relationships between the sexes at the present time.

We must accept the premise that at this point in history both sexes have operated under the rule of sexism, i.e., the male asserting his superiority and dominance, the female accepting her place of inferiority and servility. In this dominance-submission dyad, the sexual act by and large has been highly satisfactory for most men and to most, but by no means all women. The dissatisfaction experienced by women has many origins—one of which must be a resentment of the role of subjection. But it is also true that many "subjugated" women experience great sexual satisfaction. Women say: "I feel best when I am dominated." "I want a strong male to overwhelm me." Hearing such statements probably prompted Freud to state that masochism must be normal for the female. Yet this phenomenon parallels the political one—the majority in most nations very often lead happy lives under benign tyrants without much protest or dissent. It is the minority that is conscious of oppression—the majority seem to take oppression as a protective cloak. Freedom truly becomes a curse. And so with women; so very many have accepted the myth of their own inferiority and demand to take a servile role in coitus as in the other areas of their existence. . . . Women, having been taught in a thousand ways that they are inferior, may ironically demand that the sexual act confirm their demeaned status. Only rarely do men and women come together on a basis of equality. No one can say as yet whether sex between equals of the opposite sex will be satisfactory or enjoyable. There is, sadly, evidence that marriage and other unions dissolve quickly when the dominance-submission model is threatened. If unions between equals are to succeed, a massive reorientation must occur, hardly a likelihood in a generation or two.

We have said nothing here about women in the male mystique. In its extreme form, women as human beings are not implicated at all; they are merely means to an end, objects needed in counting coups; they are trophies, validators of masculinity, or, as Sheldon Messinger put it, commenting on a stag movie he had seen, masturbatory devices. Now to the female point of view of power in sexual relationship.

"massive reorientation": new battle of the sexes

Seidenberg's gloomy prognosis for the future of egalitarian mariage is, I believe, premature. It is not likely that the domination-subjugation pattern can long persist once it has been exposed for what it is and enough women become sufficiently brave to puncture the myth of the woman glorying in her sexual subjugation, and at least to stop acting out that myth to please her partner.

For millions of women have played the male scenario so well that they have convinced men of their masochism. All the while, that woman underneath him, writhing in the pleasure he was conferring on her, was in many cases actually revolted by the whole scene. A woman's "wild enjoyment of sex," says Dana Densmore, "is supposed to make her just adore every nauseating bit of the role playing. . . . If it's demeaning, you should love it that way because it makes for better sex. . . . Revel in your subservience, they tell us. What they are saying is, be masochistic."

So far from wanting strong males to overpower them, demanding a servile role in coitus, or seeing freedom as a curse, untold millions of women have resented the submission to power, surrender, giving in. Much of the revulsion against sexual relations on their part rested on the humiliation of defeat; they felt "used." The more hostile have fought the inequality by fighting sex itself.

We anticipate here the discussion in chapter 10 on the disappointment that women have experienced in modern sexual freedom by stating their power-inequality argument against sex. Roxanne Dunbar, one of the most militant of the early leaders in the Women's Liberation Movement, put it this way: "For most women, right now, sex means brutalization, rape, submission, someone having power over them. . . . The man has to feel a kind of dizzying, sick sense of power. . . . The woman feels, quite accurately, defiled and humiliated. . . . Sex still means power. . . . Sexual relations in this society are not 'degraded' because it [sic] is a commodity, or because technology has 'dehumanized' such relations. Traditional as well as contemporary sexual relations are based on power of male over female. Pleasure is derived from that power." Her observations are especially cogent because they span a lower-class childhood and a radical campus background; they are thus less class-bound than most.

And, again, from Roxanne Dunbar: "Sexual relations [for women, even] in the world today (and perhaps in all past ages) are oppressive. . . . Sex for a man is the only or best way to prove or express his virility, both by the demonstration of sexual potency and by the imposing of his will on her. . . . As women have frequently observed, sex can be a fast way to ruin a good relationship. Either because the man just can't treat her as an equal . . . or because he doesn't know how to treat a woman equally in a sexual relationship, or because he was secretly or subconsciously after the conquest all along."

The kernel of truth in the theory of female masochism is, according to Dana Densmore, to be found in the woman's desire to share the man's power. "There is no question that sexual love among women contains as a strong component the desire to become powerful by merging with the powerful. She sees herself as impotent and ineffectual, him as masterful and competent. She longs for that sense of competence and the confidence that comes to him from knowing it's 'his world.' In the intimacy and ecstasy of sex she seeks to lose herself, become one with him."

Seidenberg offers an interesting solution to the problem of the pitfalls between companionship and sexual relations arrived at by a talented young woman who decided that the only way to achieve companionship was to get the sexual hurdle over with right away. She therefore made advances, engaged in relations, and then, having that out of the way, went on to see if companionship was now possible. If sexual relations were all the man wanted, she had now weeded him out of her companionship possibilities. She dropped him. But if, once having that settled, the man was still interested, companionship became possible. She thus controverted the old pattern. In that pattern, the attempt was made to achieve companionship before engaging in sexual relations. The idea was to get to know one another on a friendly basis before proceeding on to sexual relations. The difficult was that too often the urgency of the sexual challenge was too strong. The couple engaged in sexual relations, much easier to achieve than companionship, before they had really gotten to know each other as friends. But, in the strategy of this young woman, once the challenge had been met, it was possible to explore to see if there was anything but sex left.

Before leaving the topic of the male mystique, it is only fair to note that there is a more benign, romantic version, called by Dorothy Lee Jackson the rescue or service version. It has to do with the fantasy of the strong, powerful male using his superior strength not to subjugate but to rescue or protect the less powerful woman. This fantasy has as long a history as the harsher one; it was embodied in the medieval romances of chivalry. It is preserved today in the great-he-man and helpless-little-woman charade played out by countless dating couples every day. The difficulty of both the harsh and the tender versions of the male mystique is their unsuitability for life in the real world. Men become bored with having to protect the weaker vessel, and women become resentful at having to submit to the stronger male.

If the companionship model of marriage implied a reversal of power relationships, there would be serious reasons for rejecting it. It would be no more palatable to most women than the present relationship. Such power reversals, in fact, are, as Roxanne Dunbar points out, characteristic of pornography, which "rests on the accurate assumption that sexual 'pleasure' is equal to power and dominance among men. It expresses a masculine ideology of male power over females. . . . Often in pornography females are shown in the role of dominator. This is the other side of the ideology. Dominance is still the rule. Either the male dominates, or the female dominates. Both concepts are part of the masculine ideology of power." Egalitarian companionship means that neither exerts domination over the other.

The current battle being waged by women against the male mystique will undoubtedly contribute to the massive reorientation that Seidenberg sees to be necessary. But there are other forces working toward the achievement of this goal, also, for example, the new sexual morality, referred to in chapter 5, which justifies sexual relations only on the basis of an affectionate relationship between the partners. To the extent that this morality comes to prevail, it will demythologize the masculine mystique and put a brake on the male power advantage inside as well as outside of marriage. "The Greeks were right," Isaac Asimov tells us, "it *is* much better to love an equal." And, he then asks, "if that be so, why not hasten the time when we . . . can have love at its best?" Why not, indeed?

We said above that the future of marriage rode on

the reply to the question, Can you mix companionship and sex? My own answer is, Yes, you can.

I still hold, however, that outside of the bedroom, the same "law" will continue to prevail in the future as in the past, namely, that whichever partner has greater talent for management and decision making will tend to take over these functions.

chapter eight

"other things being equal"
but *are* they?

the present as the future of the past

In 1927, John Watson, the psychologist, by projecting current trends, concluded that by 1977 marriage would no longer exist. Here it is, almost 1977, and marriage is still very much with us. In the 1930s, Lewis M. Terman, also a psychologist, projected his statistical curves dealing with the premarital sexual behavior of women, and concluded that no girl born after 1940 would enter marriage a virgin. The women born in the 1940s are now in their thirties. A majority of them did enter marriage as virgins.[1] In 1937, Pitirim Sorokin, a sociologist, predicted that divorce and separation would increase to such an extent that there would no longer be any real difference between sanctioned marriage and illicit sexual relations, and that the home would be merely an overnight parking place. With no specific date set for the arrival of this outcome, we cannot judge its correctness. In 1947, C. C. Zimmerman, another sociologist, projected historical trends, and concluded that the family was doomed unless we returned to more traditional forms.

The search for the future by way of the projection of past and current statistical trends presupposes that the future will be like the past in the sense that the same forces will continue to operate in the same way. Projections of statistical trends look like the safest way to search for cues to the future. Despite the history of error in such projections, therefore, and despite Nisbet's cautionary reminder that they are subject to unpredictable change by madmen, geniuses, prophets, and random events, our need for some kind of guidance in thinking about the future is so great that we continue to demand them. As we noted in the Introduction, industry has to know how many consumers of different kinds of goods and services—houses, household furnishings, appliances—to plan for; communities have to know how many schoolchildren to be prepared for. A veritable information industry has grown up to supply this need to know about trends. Thus, every day, miles of printouts issue from the computers of government agencies alone, and over a year many hundreds of thousands, perhaps millions, of tables, charts, graphs, and diagrams result to help us look for cues to the future. It is hard to find one's way around this statistical jungle, but if one looks long enough he finds the people behind the tables and charts—people courting, marrying, having children, divorcing, separating, remarrying. With the help of perceptive demographers, we begin to be able to focus on the confusing picture and make some sense out of it.

some projections

Two such perceptive demographers, Paul C. Glick and Robert Parke, Jr., have given us some of the most relevant projections about marriage. Among them are the following:

1 Persons now in their late twenties and their thirties are

more likely to marry at some time in their life than any other group on record.

2 The rate of teen-age marriage, which is now on the decline, will continue to go down for a while, then level off.

3 The relative oversupply of young women will tend to produce a further rise (over the short term) in the age at which women will marry for the first time.

4 Over and above any general decline in mortality, the decline in the differences between the ages of the husband and wife will reduce the frequency of widowhood and increase the proportion of couples who survive jointly to retirement age.

5 Declines in the relative frequency of divorce and separation should result to the extent that there are reductions in poverty and general improvements in the socioeconomic status of the population. (There seems to be a real likelihood that desertions will diminish, assuming that the education and economic levels of the population improve over time.)

6 Nearly all married couples now maintain their own households. Within the next twenty years, four out of every five aged individuals not in institutions will keep house on their own, as will half the adult individuals of other ages.

The authors of these projections make the usual disclaimers, noting that "the future patterns could actually veer off in new directions not anticipated in the projections." True or false, however, there are *people* lurking in the background of all the curves and projections, snapping their fingers at some, happily conforming to others, utterly ignoring the rest, and all shaping the future.

a thriving prospect, but marriage for *anyone*?

The democratization of marriage described in chapter 6 is reflected in the first projection. The proportion of men and women who were married increased for a long time, especially after 1940. Practically everyone marries sometime or other nowadays—97 percent of the women and 96 percent of the men, it was estimated of the generation in their late twenties and early thirties in the 1960s. The never-married were three times more common a generation ago than in the sixties. It was no longer a question whether or not young people would ever marry but the age at which they would marry. "Bachelors" and "old maids" were on the way out, certainly as defined in those pejorative terms, but also as defined as simply unmarried individuals.

Since, as we saw in chapter 2, marriage is good for mature men and hence, as the social indicator suggests, good for our total society also, this was a seemingly benign trend. Still, although we may grant that marriage is good for men, can we also say that all men are good for marriage? Is it really a good sign when *every* man is married? The poor marital bets as well as the good?

There are no precise and accurate figures on the actual number of alcoholics in this country, and estimates vary. A current estimate is about nine million. Many of them are married and making their spouses—especially wives, since there are more male than female alcoholics —miserable. In addition, there is an indeterminate number of sociopaths who are making life insufferable for an indeterminate number of spouses. There are millions of mentally or emotionally crippled men and women rendering normal married life impossible for their mates. There are many men and women who are marginal in mental health: mean, hostile, aggressive, punitive, suspicious, pugnacious, irresponsible, dependent, not always enough to warrant a diagnosis as abnormal or pathological or sick—the legally insane are forbidden to marry—but enough to make those about them suffer. Some are weeded out of marriage by the selective forces referred to earlier, but some may look to marriage for relief.

In addition to these sick and near-sick people, there is an indeterminate number who, with no diagnosable defect or deficiency, are just not suited for the discipline that living with another person in an intimate relationship under any circumstances calls for. Lewis M. Terman called the lack of this quality a lack of marital aptitude. People who lack this aptitude are quite normal, indeed sometimes superior, in many ways. There is nothing intrinsically wrong with them. They just do not have the interests or the values demanded by marriage or the willingness to assume its responsibilities.

Of all these unmarriageables, one might even ask if they *can* marry. *Can* they make commitments? Are they ever really married in the sense of being committed? "The marriage of the psychopath. . . , of the dependent personality with the childlike need of a parental figure to support him, of the homosexual who seeks a cure through marriage—are these," Jack Dominian asks, "marriages in any sense at all except for the morality of the ceremony?" and answers that "to call them marriages is to delude everyone." But we do call them marriages and we do delude everyone, including the victims themselves.

Sweeping everyone into the married population is worse for women than for men. We know that the unmarried men who could be swept into marriage are likely to be "bottom-of-the-barrel" types; but the unmarried women could be "cream-of-the-crop." It is conceivable that the net effect on the social indicators of bringing the superior women into marriage would offset the negative effect of bringing in the poorer—in the marital aptitude sense—marital prospects. What effect an increase in marriage would have on the marriage gradient itself is something worth watching. For the present, and until we have explored all the angles, the first trend listed above deserves only a qualified plus; it is more likely to be beneficial for men than for women, even questionable for women.

An increase in the number of marriages among those with no aptitude for it would mean that we could expect more divorce to counter any decrease in divorces expectable on other grounds. When such people show up in divorce records or marriage counseling clinics or family welfare case loads, a common reaction is that we ought to make marriage harder. Marriage should not be open to just anyone, that we should not let people like that get married in the first place, that we can carry democratization too far; marriage should again be viewed as a privilege for those who can manage it.

As a matter of fact, from time to time legislators, churchmen, or others who confront the breakdown of these marriages do call for laws making marriage more difficult. There should be legal impedimenta. . . .

True, but alas, not at all feasible. We are no longer dealing with seventeenth-century villagers; and the implementation of any policy forbidding people to marry would involve such a tyrannical apparatus that most of us would shrink from it. It might even be argued—as it was when racial intermarriage was forbidden—that the civil rights of the person who wanted to marry these individuals were being violated. Moreover, there would be difficulties from a practical point of view. Diagnosis of marital disabilities is not, like the diagnosis of venereal disease, simple, a matter of a few minutes in the laboratory. Cleckley tells us that in the case of the sociopath, for example, it takes years of irresponsible behavior before the pattern of the illness can be traced and diagnosed; and by that time the sociopath has married and made many people unhappy.

Further, what alternatives would there be for those forbidden to marry? No question about the future of marriage is more thought-provoking than this. What *are* the alternatives to marriage? What could take its place? Marriage is a cheap way for society at large to take care of a lot of difficult people. We force individuals— a wife or a husband—to take care of them on a one-to-one basis. If or when these caretakers refuse, we are left in the lurch. Marriage is a nice way to parcel individuals out for individualized care and support, but if we did not have such care and support available, what alternatives would there be? Without alternatives, forbidding marriage would be punitive and unjust.

We cannot, in all fairness, impute blame to handi-capped people. We cannot look upon them as criminal or as deliberately destructive. It is not their fault that they cannot function well in our institutions, but neither is it fair to force their care on husbands and wives. Until we can devise some kind of design for living which is appropriate and suitable for those for whom marriage cannot work, we will have to use makeshift measures. So-called protective communities, such as those being experimented with for men and women with more recognizable handicaps, suggest themselves; or communities like Synanon with strong leaders trained to deal with the needs of dependent people; households in which people who need support can secure it without the abrasiveness inevitable in marriage, or with the abrasiveness deflected, rechanneled, or therapeutically managed.

Short of such communities, we may have to settle for better education in mate selection so that love could be given a modicum of insight, if not of sight; and for those disturbed people who, according to Edmund Bergler, have an unerring "instinct" for one another, we may just have to grit our teeth and be prepared to deal with the consequences the best we can. Until we learn what to do for and about these handicapped people, there will be, in the future as in the past, mil-lions of miserable men and women trying despairingly to make a go of marriage with partners who, if it had been possible to prevent it, should never have married in the first place.

All this discussion is based on the expected trend to-ward increasing marriage, "other things being equal." Glick and Parke, however, warned us that "the future patterns could actually veer off in new directions not anticipated in the projection." And so, indeed, this trend seems to be doing. The marriage rate, which had been going up since the early 1960s, began to falter at the end of the decade, and by the early 1970s, it was leveling off if not beginning to decline. There were, for instance, proportionately more single young men and women in 1970 than in 1960, the decline being especially notable among twenty-year-olds. A few months, even a year, do not necessarily portend a trend; the new figures might be only random fluctuations in a continuing upward trend, or the result of recession, which traditionally has a dampening effect on the marriage rate.

It might, however, also be that the marriage rate is in for a decline a decade earlier than anticipated. The statistics may be telling us something important about the future of marriage—what, for example, the easier availability of abortion might be doing to the marriage rate of young women, or what effect the new life styles might be having. The increasing practice of living in households of unrelated individuals, to be commented on presently, suggests that early marriage, and perhaps later marriage as well, is not so attractive to young women as it once was. And it may be that the message of radical women decrying the pressures to marry is getting across—that young women, therefore, no longer feel marriage to be the only tolerable career for them, that many find unsanctioned relationships preferable to marriage.

If those refraining from marriage include a considerable proportion of both men and women not suited for marriage, their exclusion from the married population would have a benign effect.

These conjectures may be too heavy to hang on so slender a thread as an incipient decrease in the marriage rate. Still, I am inclined to take that chance. I do believe that the marriage rate will tend to go down, the slack to be taken up by other forms of relationship.

teen-age marriage

The decline in teen-age marriage augurs well for the future of marriage. It will also help to reduce the birthrate. If the public interest calls for a moderation of the birthrate, as indeed it does, then, on the basis of past evidence, policies which encourage girls to stay in school and delay marriage are advisable. Delayed marriage has been one of the standard means advocated for controlling the birthrate, recommended, in fact, by Malthus himself. It has been found that the earlier women begin to bear children, the more they are likely to bear over the childbearing age.

The decline is a good omen, too, for marital stability. The hazards of teen-age marriage have long been recognized. Even in times and places when youthful marriages were common, it was recognized that marriages among those too young had a bad prognosis. For if people marry very young they are unformed, they have not achieved an identity, they really do not know who they are or what they want. When or if they do mature, they may find that they do not really suit each other after all.

Quite aside from immaturity, teen-agers tend to apply different criteria in mate selection. The young man is attracted to a young woman for precisely the qualities—cuteness, flirtatiousness, flightiness—that will not make her a good wife; the young woman is attracted to the kind of young men—the rock singer, the motion picture star, the unconventional—who do not make the best husbands. Understandably, therefore, teen-age marriages are notoriously unstable, showing the highest divorce rate at every duration of marriage.

But here again, a caveat is necessary. For, unexpectedly, too long a delay before marriage is not much better than too precipitous a marriage. Although we have always known that it was more than usually hazardous in terms of stability to marry too young, we used to think that marriages of older partners were assured of more stability. Apparently, however, this is not entirely so among first marriages. It is about as hazardous to wait too long to marry as it is to race into marriage too early. The optimum age, measured in terms of stability, Paul Glick has shown, is twenty-four for men and twenty-two for women. Marriages in which the partners are younger than these ages are, as we have just seen, more vulnerable to instability, but, surprisingly, so are marriages in which the partners are older than these ages. This is a novel and unexpected finding.

The reasons for the greater vulnerability (especially in the third to the fifth year) among the marriages of men marrying in their thirties or later are not so immediately understandable as the reasons for that of teen-age marriage, and they have not received half as much research attention. It may be that marriage has relatively less appeal to them; otherwise they would not have waited so long. It may be that their expectations are unrealistically high; otherwise, again, they would have found a mate earlier. It may be that the age difference between them and their wives is too great for marriage as it is now conceived. It may be that they are too set in their ways. They may represent an intermediate type between the married and the never married. Or there may be some other reason not yet discovered. Some might argue that the extra decade of carefree bachelorhood was worth the extra hazard of instability.

As expected, the situation is more complicated for women.

the age at which women marry

The third trend listed above, a rise in the age at which women marry for the first time, may or may not be benign. As among men, so among women, teen-age marriage is more vulnerable to divorce than later marriages. But stability is only one criterion to use in judging age at marriage. Others have been applied, especially by those interested in the career patterns of women. Their emphasis has been on the effect that age at marriage has had on preparation for professional life rather than its effect on marriage. Early marriage has been seen by some as an escape from the search for identity—as, in effect, a cop-out. If women could wait until they had completed professional preparation before they married, they would be in a better position to integrate their work and marriage roles.

There is, indeed, evidence that girls sometimes marry because that seems the best or only tolerable alternative. As we saw in chapter 3, the more income a young woman has and the better her job, the lower is the marriage rate in any one year. These facts suggest to me that young women often marry as the only thing they feel they can do. Given interesting work and/or suitable income, many would no doubt be willing to delay marriage—with, presumably, benign effects on the future of marriage.

But this way of looking at the third trend is based on past conditions when quite different conceptions of marriage and motherhood prevailed. Perhaps a different conception should guide our thinking now, a new conception of the total life history of women. Students of career motivation in women have found that, in contrast to young men who can plan their lifetime careers with some autonomy, women between the ages of around eighteen to twenty-four seem to be suspended. They cannot make career commitments until they know who they are going to marry. That crucial question has to be answered before they can go ahead with any other plans. At this time in their lives they are enormously preoccupied with having babies. Counselors tell us that young women students cannot think beyond marriage and the early years of motherhood. Girls may *know* that motherhood alone is no longer a lifetime career, but they cannot *feel* that way about it.

Perhaps we should not try to fight this compulsion. Perhaps we should not nag them to make career decisions during the almost obsessional preoccupation with marriage and motherhood. Perhaps we should take advantage of what they are really interested in, and come to look at the early years of marriage and child-bearing as "just a stage" or "phase" of their development through which women pass quite young and outgrow, a more or less transitory occupation which, once over, frees them for a major, serious, adult commitment, and leaves them ready to attack in earnest the problems of the almost half a century of mature life ahead of them.

It is, I think, interesting to note in passing that this book on the future of marriage now finds it essential to examine, however cursorily, how marriage can be made to adjust to the career patterns of women rather than, as always in the past, the other way round, that the questions raised are not in terms of "marriage versus career" or "the working wife" but rather in terms of plans for a whole life with both in mind.

age differences between husbands and wives

The decrease in the difference in age between husbands and wives, the fourth trend mentioned at the beginning of the chapter, will reduce widowhood by bereavement and thus enhances the prospects of marriage. There will be fewer lonely older women. It will also be a plus in that it will lengthen the post-parental stage of marriage that, as we saw in chapter 4, is one in which there is a rebound, at least in middle-class marriages, to the level of satisfaction of earlier years. Conversely, however, greater longevity may mean that marriages which would once have terminated in bereavement will now terminate in divorce instead.

One might ask if it is not just natural for men to be older than their wives. No, in fact, it is not. There is no "natural" age difference between spouses, one way or the other. If one is looking for beauty and sex appeal, then someone between, let us say, eighteen and twenty-five is the most suitable mate, regardless of one's own age or sex. If one is looking for economic security, then someone who has accumulated a substantial competence, regardless of one's own age, is desirable. To the extent that it is "natural" for a young woman to want to "look up" to her husband, the present practice of a few years in the husband's favor is natural; even a few years gives him more experience, so that he can hold his own with her. Actually, as we shall presently see, there is no unequivocal evidence that the direction of the age differential makes much difference, although the size of the difference might.

Aristotle was of the opinion that the ideal was for a man of about thirty-six to marry a girl of about eighteen so that he could train her to run his household according to his standards. To this day there are young women who prefer as husbands established, successful, older men to untried younger men. And rich, elderly men, including royalty, have often taken young wives. Youthful beauty and sex appeal were luxuries that rich men could afford. Among the British peerage in the sixteenth, seventeenth, and eighteenth centuries, the husband was rarely less than four years older than his wife. But among the yeomen, Peter Laslett tells us, the brides in the seventeenth and eighteenth centuries tended to be older than the grooms.

Property could operate to influence age differences in another way also. In Ting Hsien, China, for example, brides from rich families, E. A. Wrigley tells us, were older than their grooms because wealthy families, anxious to ensure the male line, married their sons off at the earliest possible age; they could afford the bride price. Sons of the poor families had to wait.

Although the tendency in the United States is for a smaller and smaller difference in age between husband and wife, when an adjustment has to be made, it is the girl, expectedly, who makes it. Thus, since the pattern is still for the husband to be a few years older than the wife, girls who have reached the marriageable age twenty years after a great upsurge in the birthrate, such as occurred in the 1950s, have to wait a few years for their male partners to catch up to them.[2] The age at marriage for young women rises. Twenty years after a downward trend in the birthrate, the reverse process occurs. We can expect, therefore, that—ceteris paribus again—the age at which women marry will go down again in the 1980s.

If one were not influenced by the love-or-money choice, it would make sense to have an older wife and a younger husband, since in our day women tend to outlive men. But the preference of men for younger wives persists, a preference few recognize as genuinely contrary to the interests of women. Thus, a recently divorced man of fifty advertises for a woman in her thirties or forties to share a beautiful new life with. Beautiful for him while it lasts, no doubt, but if he marries a woman of thirty-five, what she will get, Inge Powell Bell reminds us, is eighteen years of widowhood. The statistical chances are that she will be with him as long as he lives; so why should he bother about what happens to her afterward?

There is some evidence, it should be noted, that despite popular belief to the contrary, marriages in which the bride is older may have some advantage over those in which the groom is older. In Finland, for example, Paave Pieponen tells us that "the rate of divorce is smaller than expected in those cases where the husband is younger than the wife." He was puzzled as to how to explain this unexpected finding, so contrary to folk (male?) wisdom. He suggested that either unwitting or deliberate nonconformity to age-role expectations might explain it. "It may be that individuals who enter into such marriages are in some way psychologically selected; the men may be submissive and the women dominating. It may also be a question of conscious deviation from the behavior dictated by age-role expectations, which in turn leads to a successful marriage." If the second explanation is correct, there is an important lesson for us: people who have enough courage to be themselves and to deviate from "age-role expectations" have better prospects in marriage than those who are too timid to trust their own leanings and thus have to depend on conventional patterns for support.

divorce and separation

The fifth projection listed above is equivocal. It is true that marriages are more stable among those with higher incomes, more years of schooling, and higher occupational levels. If, therefore, we wish to improve marriage in the future, one good way to start would be to improve these factors. Still, when we look at the actual trend in the divorce rate, we note that, despite improvements in all these elements, it has been rising—after a fairly stabilized period—since 1965. This disparity raises the suspicion that the relationship between marriage stability and income, schooling, and occupation may have been only temporary. Their effect may itself change over time.

So far as income is concerned, there is little doubt that the elimination of poverty would vastly improve the stability of a large proportion of marriages. Paul C. Glick has shown that in the first half of the 1960s the probability of divorce among white men was twice as high among those with less than $3,000 income as among those with incomes of $8,000 or more. And during the early years of marriage, divorce was three to five times greater in the poverty bracket than in that of $8,000 and over. If getting rid of poverty were merely a matter of providing income, we could do more to stabilize marriage by providing this income than by any other single measure.

The relation between marital stability and occupation is not so easy to assess. We know, as Charles Nam has shown, that the lowest-level occupations are on their way out; their elimination may be expected to reduce the incidence of unstable marriages. But whether increasing the proportion of white-collar occupations will have the effect of increasing the proportion of stable marriages is still moot. The "intervening variable" of schooling has to be taken into account, and here the crystal ball clouds up, for education is the most equivocal of the three factors with respect to the future of marriage.

Nothing seemed better established by classic research than the stabilizing effect on marriage of education. Yet, on the basis of trends in the first half of the 1960s, no such clear-cut relationship between years of schooling and divorce showed up. In fact, for those white men with less than eight years of schooling, the probability of divorce was only half as great as the probability for those with thirteen to fifteen years of schooling. Those with eight to eleven years of schooling did no worse than those with sixteen or more.

It was not only marital stability that the old research had found to be related to education, but also a wide variety of other aspects of marriage as well. Kinsey and his associates, for example, had found educated men more monogamous than less educated men in the early years of marriage, but just the reverse in later years. They also found differing patterns of sexuality among men with different levels of schooling. And blue-collar marriages, usually involving partners with fewer years of schooling than white-collar marriages, have been reported by Komarovsky, Rainwater, Veroff and Feld, among others, to be different in many ways from white-collar marriages. The trend among the better educated, for example, has been in the direction of the companionate. Educated women want more contact with their husbands; merely formal role performance is not enough for them. They want their husbands to talk to them more, to share their leisure time with them. Deprivation of this kind of companionship, taken for granted in the old concept of marriage, can easily be construed as "mental cruelty." Even more, women educated in the modern manner are less inhibited in their interest in power; their college-educated husbands, even in the conservative 1950s, were having difficulty dealing with this situation.

Education today, further, is no longer the same as it was in the past. Changes occurred in the 1960s especially which challenge the validity of projections based on earlier findings. For education has come to mean something quite different from what it meant earlier. The young university students are not the same as the students who turned up in the earlier research. In the past, education was associated with conformity to the standards of the establishment; the kind of education young people received in college tended to be conservative. Today the avant-garde who are fighting these very standards come from the ranks of university students.

A national survey reported in 1969, for example, that almost twice as many college students as noncollege youth would welcome more sexual freedom. Considerably more college than noncollege youth favored abortion. Many more noncollege than college youth strongly disagreed with the statement that "sexual behavior should be bound by mutual feelings, not by formal and legal ties." Almost an eighth of college youth were revolutionaries or radical reformers; about a tenth of the noncollege youth were. Students were being advised by Roxanne Dunbar and Vernon Gizzard of the radical avant-garde not to enter family situations; those who already had should leave if possible, or at least find ways to reduce the traditional responsibilities of marriage.

Does the kind of education to which university students are exposed today, then, have the same effect as the kind received a generation ago when the old research was done? We are learning that governing an educated population is not at all the same as governing an ignorant one. The church is learning that dealing with an educated membership is not the same as dealing with an ignorant one. And men and women are learning that living with educated spouses is not the same as living with uneducated spouses or as living with those educated in the old-fashioned manner.

It is true that as yet the radical young constitute only a minority of all youth. Are they, as they were once called, a prophetic minority? Will their ideologies and life styles finally come to prevail? And if they do, what will they do to marriage? Which curves will they redirect? the proportion of the population married? the birthrate? the divorce rate? the nuclear household? This will be something to watch. I believe that the patterns of the university and college avant-garde will spread to all educational levels—not suddenly and traumatically, but gradually, in a sort of trickle-down fashion. They will be the first to work through the "bugs" in the new forms of marriage. By the time the new forms have been shaped to fit the modern world, they will no longer seem so radical after all.

their own households

That "nearly all married couples now maintain their own household" seems such a banal statement that one wonders why Glick and Parke even thought it worth mentioning. Of course they do. The individual household for every married couple is the final outcome of a long history. We can now write finis on that trend. Mission accomplished.

But is a household of their own for every married couple really to be taken so much for granted? Even if it is today, is it to be the wave of the future? Should it be? Or is it now an anachronistic hangover from the past, a vestigial survival no longer suitable, remaining only because we don't know how to get rid of it? Is the isolated household that demands so much of so many women really desirable? In view of the pathogenic effect of housekeeping on wives, some married couples are beginning to question whether it is desirable.

Except for demographers, we hardly speak of households any more; we speak instead of "life styles." But whatever we have in mind, and whatever the term we use to describe it, the facts it refers to are the least glamorous imaginable, as unrelated to love and romance as anything could be. And one of the most shocking discontinuities in the lives of young lovers, male as well as female, occurs with the discovery that human beings have to be fed, kept clean, provided with sleeping quarters and sanitary facilities, and all the other humble services that daily living demands and that are taken for granted. What do all these practical problems have to do with this marvelous relationship between us? they say. All too much, alas, they soon learn. For marriages do not operate in a vacuum; they have to be lodged somewhere or other. Meals do not just automatically and by themselves appear on the table three times a day; clean sheets and towels do not grow in the linen chest; dishes do not wash themselves nor does dust independently disappear.

A great deal of thinking about the future of marriage centers as much on the kind of facility to house it in as on the nature of the commitment itself, and rightly so, for the two are intimately intertwined. It makes a great deal of difference in the relationship if its locale is a private home or an open, freewheeling commune. Most marriages are embedded in a household; the history of one reflects the history of the other; the future of one is part of the future of the other. "Life styles"—living arrangements—are as relevant for the future of marriage as "sex styles"—forms of sexual relationships.

Along with the democratization of marriage described in chapter 6, another process was also going on— namely, the gradual stripping down of the household, so that what began with a fairly large number of people —as high, Laslett has shown, as perhaps a dozen in a seventeenth-century London bakery—ended up with fewer than three in England and Wales at the beginning of the last third of the twentieth century. So also in

America, where a household which averaged almost six members in 1790 was down, Parke tells us, to 3.28 in 1967, and was projected to be possibly as low as 2.81 by 1985. The implications for marriage are both direct and indirect.

The large households were not kinship establishments as so often fantasied, houses filled with uncles, aunts, cousins, even grandparents. Three-generation households were rare; people didn't live that long.[3] The large households were peopled by servants, journeymen, and apprentices, as well as by relatives and children. In fact, they were little industrial establishments in which families and workers lived. We customarily think in terms of industry being taken out of the home by the Industrial Revolution. It might as well be viewed as the home being separated from the factory. Houses devoted exclusively to family living and not to industrial production are, as I have pointed out elsewhere, what is new, for the large household that characterized at least the more prosperous families in preindustrial times melted away. A kind of "nuclear fission" took place.

Little by little, the nonkinship members surrounding the married couple were stripped away. First the workers left; journeymen set up their own establishments. Then the apprentices left. The departure of the servants came later with an impact, one might add parenthetically, almost traumatic and with an effect on marriage not even yet fully assessed. By throwing the entire burden of housekeeping and child care on wives it cut deeply into other commitments, as we noted in chapter 3 above.

The traumatic effect of moving the family out of the workshop was masked for a while because increased longevity meant that at least some of the vacancies left in the household were filled by grandparents. But the three-generational households had a relatively brief history, often occurring in the United States primarily among immigrant families.

Now a two-way fission is taking place in the nuclear

family, one at each end of the adult age range. Not only
do the parents of married couples tend to live in households of their own, but so, too, are the young[4]—including late teen-agers—tending to leave the parental roof.
(See table 36.) There are, of course, repercussions on
all three generations, benign in two of them, indeterminate as yet in the other one.

The result is favorable on the whole for the oldest
generation, for it is generally agreed that the movement
of the older family members out of the households of
their married children into households of their own—
one of the goals of the Social Security Act a generation
ago—is a good thing for them; they feel more independent, and there is less opportunity for intergenerational hassling and in-law conflict. The repercussions
are favorable on the whole for the middle generation
also. Removal of the older generation reduces occasion
for in-law difficulties. The departure of children from
the parental roof may also, as suggested by the data in
chapter 4, be benign. We have already referred to the
difficulty parents and young adults have living together.
As a result of nuclear fission at both ends of the age
range, the married partners are left alone in their homes
from the late forties on, a phase in the natural history
of the marriage that can be one of the best. It must be
added here that the spinning off of family members
from the household does not mean that family ties are
necessarily abrogated. Contacts continue, Marvin Sussman has shown, and obligations remain fulfilled.

But what about the fissioned-off youngsters themselves, the young men and women between eighteen and
twenty-four? Where are they? How are they living?
What kinds of households are they a part of? What are
their life styles?

Some of them, of course, are married. Some of them
are on college campuses. Some of them are among the
million or so runaways waiting in detention homes for
their parents to come and claim them. But many of
them are spending the interval between leaving the

parental home and marriage in one of the most interesting and fast-growing phenomena of the times, households of unrelated individuals.

Such households have been increasing several times faster than have households of families, as have the proportion of young adults living in them, the increase being faster among young men than among young women but substantial among both. These households are not the notorious "hippie pads"; they appear in the census records as group quarters or as boarding houses. They do, however, include some of the unconventional households. Such households of unrelated individuals may, for an increasing number of young people in the period between leaving the parental roof and marriage, constitute the wave of the future.

Some of the young people are living alone and, presumably, liking it. They include the well-paid young people for whom the real-estate industry has been so ready to build luxury apartment buildings.

For others who find it impossible to live under the parental roof but for whom none of the above facilities is possible, it has been seriously proposed that special living quarters be designed. During the years when they are too old to be comfortable in a two-generation household and not yet ready for the commitment of marriage, there should be provision for a kind of "halfway" house to accommodate them. It can be cogently argued that it is a good thing for young adults to move away from the parental home, not only to avoid intergenerational conflict but also to help them develop independence, or at least to reduce dependency, especially in the case of young women.

On the surface, then, the sixth trend looks benign. But, as in the case of the others, it is not necessarily or unequivocally so. Among young families, especially those with small children, the isolated household is becoming anathema to many of the women on whose shoulders the weight of its maintenance rests. They answer the question raised at the beginning of this section

—"Is the isolated household that demands so much of so many women really desirable?"—with a resounding no. And they answer the question "Is it now an anachronistic hangover from the past, a vestigial survival no longer suitable?" with an equally resounding yes. And enough other people agree with them to provide evidence for a new, as yet only incipient, trend toward what I have labeled "nuclear fusion."

nuclear fusion

We have retained the old idea of the private, isolated household long after its original function as an industrial unit has passed away. All the nonfamily members departed long ago to do their work elsewhere, and so did the head of the household himself. Only the housewife remains, stranded. Everyone else's activities have been removed; only hers have remained. What reason is there to retain the isolated household as a design for living? Shouldn't we now think of it as merely a relic or as just transitional to something better? Shouldn't we be seeking new ways to supply privacy without exacting such a high price from women in the form of isolation and house care? It is argued that such privatized living is humanly artificial.

It is perhaps even harmful. Some animals, we are told, object to isolated male-female units of living. Man, in his characteristically anthropocentric way, has tended to house males and females in zoos together in one-pair units. It is apparently not necessarily congenial to the animals themselves. Some, Alan S. Parkes tells us, do not even mate under these conditions.

It is quite obvious that isolated human pairs can function very well from a reproductive point of view, but that they are always better off in every other way in this design for living is open to question. At least many young people are asking questions and seeking answers in other living styles. And marriage in the future will depend to some extent on what they come up with. A number of ideas are in the works.

In some cases, for example, cooperative households have proved successful, at least over a short period of time. The term *commune* is sometimes applied to such households; but that term has been so widely and indiscriminately used as to become almost meaningless. It has been applied to transient, unorganized hippie pads as well as to well-organized cooperative households of quite square couples. We prefer, therefore, not to call the kinds of "nuclear fusion" we are talking about here *communes*.

The cooperative household may overcome two of the difficulties of marriage: the burden of exclusive responsibility for the provided role on the part of the husband, and the exclusive responsibility for the care of the children and housework on the part of the wife.

Cooperative households may be viewed matter-of-factly as similar to any other kind of consumer cooperative; they lower costs and improve quality. Here is an example, as described by Carl Bernstein:

In a rambling frame house . . . John and Nina live in serenity with thirteen other people, among them their three-year-old daughter Mary, and her brother, Philip, two. Two other children live in the house . . . , the sons of the home's other principals, Dave and Myra. The remaining seven adults in the house of fifteen are two unmarried couples, two single men and one single girl, all in their late teens and early twenties. . . . John, Nina, and their two children live on the $45 a week he collects in unemployment compensation [as of 1969] and a small stipend. . . . "Before we moved here . . . we were always scrounging on $200 a week," John says. "You can't make it on $45 a week in the real world, but in this world you can, with four people. And there's been no drop in quality. In fact there's a richness that was never there before. Now we eat eleven different cooking styles, so meals become rather special; there are never any TV dinners or eating out of cans. Before, we were cramped into a tiny apartment. Now we're on the park and have plenty of space. I can't think of anything we don't have." . . . Adds Nina, "I've never felt so free. I wanted more kids. Now, with the other two, who are like our own, we don't need any more. John and I have complete freedom to go off. We don't need baby sitters. We can walk off and just take a ten-minute stroll together. We couldn't do that before."

This seemingly idyllic example of nuclear fusion had only a short life span. It was terminated not by any intrinsic flaw in the design but by the most serious threat to any such kind of establishment—the mobility so characteristic of American life. The members were dispersed when they got jobs in other parts of the country.

In another cooperative household, described by M. S. Kennedy, ten people lived in a house renting (in 1971) for $300; in still another, eleven residents paid $90 each for both board and room in a six-bedroom house. On the side of costs, then, cooperative households relieve the burden of the provider. And the pattern in so many of them of wives' sharing the provider role relieves the husbands of the entire responsibility of even these lower costs.

There is usually little difficulty in getting the husbands in these cooperative households to share cooking. Housework and child care may offer more problems, but in one report on cooperative households in Washington, D.C., the author, M. S. Kennedy, found that "a man who wouldn't do housework and baby-sit would be looked at askance." In one two-family cooperative household, the wife in one couple was paid for her housekeeping and child-care services. Even the fact of her being paid could not, however, overcome the intrinsic hardships of the housekeeping and child-care services she performed. "The same elements were there to make her edgy. . . . [Her] theme was the problem of being the 'put-upon one.' "

These young middle- and upper-middle-class couples are engaged in one of the most important experiments having to do with the future of marriage. They are learning by trial and error the hazards involved and how to deal with them. For example: you can't make a fetish of household furnishings, according them an undue priority in your scale of values; you have to have a personality suited for this style of living, that is, you have to be a "more or less open, sharing person, willing to work it out in T-Group fashion"; you have to be flexible, able to "give and bend"; there has to be a passionate belief in "the ultimate right to privacy"; everyone must have his or her say on controversial matters.

Some cooperative households are rural. In one kind, there is reported to be a regression toward the seventeenth-century household: "the larger communes," E. L. Hagerty reports, "tend to take on a kinship structure closely resembling the extended family. There is usually a patriarch, better known as a guru, who is the spiritual leader and teacher rather than the authority figure. Members frequently refer to each other as brother and sister." All household chores are shared, as is child rearing. The successes of this form of nuclear fusion have not been impressive.

I believe that the cooperative household has a future. In time, we will learn the optimum number of people who can happily and cheerfully live together. Too few may be as uncongenial as too many. If there are only a small number, the demands made on them may be too great, for there is emotional security in numbers. The fourth or fifth person, informants told M. S. Kennedy, takes some of the emotional heat off of the second and third. "When one couple is having a fight it's better . . . [in a cooperative household] because there are more distractions to get you out of it." There is also a kind of safety in numbers, for "with more people pulling their ego-oar it is more difficult for any one person to 'take over' than with two people struggling for dominance, and unacceptable behavior is jumped on and quelled more readily." But if the number grows too large, cliques, isolates, coalitions, and confusion may undo whatever benefits living together provides.

In time, we will also learn how to build for such households. Here much of the experimenting is being done in Scandinavia. There, experimental "megafamilies" or groups of from thirteen to a hundred families design their own community or neighborhood in order to combine both privacy and shared facilities. In one near Copenhagen, the buildings are planned to provide both maximum communication and privacy. In another the houses are fairly expensive, ultramodern Danish in design, sharing a swimming pool, outdoor kitchens, workshops, game rooms, and sun terrace. There is a teen club, kindergarten, playground, and it is hoped in the future, even a zoo. In another, there is a less expensive megahouse. The architect describes the interior of this two-and-a-half-story building covering two acres as "something like a monastery." The private quarters are deliberately made small in order to encourage sharing the larger common rooms. This decision was arrived at after long discussions between the "privatists," who would have preferred larger family rooms, and the "collectivists," who preferred the common-room idea. One of the major lessons drawn from Scandinavian experience has been that housing itself is a fundamental influence on intergroup, including interfamily, reactions—and, of course, on marriage also.

The kind of marriage people are going to want in the future calls for the kind of household conducive to achieving it. This Scandinavian model comes closest to what some young suburban mothers I know are searching for. Hemmed in by what is possible rather than free to create what is desirable, they would settle for a neighborhood of their own in which each would have her own house but in which there would be a shared facility also, a neighborhood in which they could share their responsibilities, their mutual aid—and their thoughts and feelings.

Meanwhile, we will have to call on all our available scientists, architects, and technologists to design for us living arrangements that provide as much privacy as couples want without too much isolation. (See table 37.) As long as our present stock of housing survives, the kinds of households that are possible are limited.

This depressing fact, however, need not deter us from thinking about the future. Home economists are, in fact, already preparing possible specifications for the different kinds of households that we can expect in the future, as illustrated by table 37 from Michigan State University. They foresee no less than nine kinds of living groups, ranging all the way from single individuals at one end to neighborhood groups with mutual aid and common interests at the other. They even foresee groups in which the sexes would be segregated, an experiment tried without success in China during "the Great Leap Forward."[5] That we are even thinking in these terms suggests that the trend toward nuclear fission may be in process of reversing itself. A kind of counter process may be going on. Nuclear fission may be leading to nuclear fusion.

If we try to evaluate the several trends and projections sketched by Glick and Parke for the future of marriage, we do not come up with clear-cut and unequivocal decisions. The uncertainty results in part from the uncertainty of some of the trends themselves, but some of it comes from the nature of the effect that they will have. This is the way I add it all up:

Projection	Effect on Husband's Marriage	Effect on Wife's Marriage
Almost everyone will marry	+	?
Teen-age marriage will decline	+	+ but also?
Rise in age at marriage of women	+	+ but also?
Decline in age differential between spouses	+	+
General improvement in:		
Income	+	+
Occupation	+	+
Education	?	?
Own households	?	−
Nuclear fusion or cooperative households	(+)	(+)

Like everything connected with the future of marriage, the effect of trends on the wife's marriage is more complicated than the effect on that of the husband. If marriage remains structured as it has been, the increase in the proportion married is not necessarily benign for wives; if it is modified; it may be. If provision can be made for women to have their children young and then proceed in a normal and acceptable way to professional or other careers, youthful marriages may be a good thing; but if we are going to continue to punish women for the time taken out to have babies, later marriage may be preferable. The effect of increasing education is equivocal as yet, among women as among men. The trend toward more and more households of their own may be negative for an increasing number of women. But if some kind of cooperative living arrangements can be devised, such a trend would be positively benign.

In chapters 5 through 8 we have been looking for the future of marriage largely in historical trends and statistical projections, hugging the research data fairly closely. Interesting or at least relevant, all this undoubtedly is even useful and perhaps necessary, but admittedly not wholly satisfying, not near enough to the longings of the human heart. Examining trends and projections tells us only what we may expect, "other things remaining the same." But why should everything remain the same? young people are asking. Why should we just stand here? Why don't we *do* something? Actually, the well of ideas for things to do is running over. There is no lack of prophets to supply them.

It is to them as much as to the scholars and scientists we have to look for a glimpse of the future of marriage. Not that prophets necessarily tell us what the future of marriage is "really" going to be like. But they do tell us what people want it to be like, and what, if they have anything to say about it, it will be like.

3
hopes and fears

chapter nine

male prophets and prophecies

diversity

The men discussed in this chapter do not constitute a homogeneous band of reformers marching under a single banner. They are, rather, a diverse assortment, with blueprints ranging all the way from advocacy of such conservative options as cooperative households to advocacy of such radical options as the legitimization of homosexual marriage. There is, thus, no single leader whom all proclaim and follow. Some of the male critics of marriage, as distinguished from parenthood, like Gore Vidal, see it even today as "no more than a ceremonial vestige of a bygone era." Other observers, like Kenneth Boulding,[1] see no fundamental change in marriage in the future. Between these extremes there are many degrees of acceptance or rejection of marriage as we know it today. Few want to abolish marriage altogether; most agree that some kind of mating is essential for the happiness of most people. Although they recognize that marriage can be the most destructive kind of relationship, they grant that it can also be the most creative and constructive. To minimize the first and optimize the second, most feel—with varying degrees of commitment—that new forms of organizing marriage are called for. But even when the proposals for such new forms of organizing the relations between the sexes are most unconventional, they represent a male bias and are designed to serve male fantasies and dreams.[2] I do not dismiss such fantasies as trivial.

Some of the men discussed here—the utopians and science-fiction writers, for example—are satisfied to dream and write about optimal ways to organize the relations between the sexes; others are eager to get on with the future and they experiment with ways to implement their fantasies. The first are more theoretical, the second, more pragmatic. Both share the male bias.

the utopians

Not because they can teach us anything about the future of marriage today but because they can teach us about the future men dreamed of in the past, we begin with the utopians; for utopias are age-old vehicles for social criticism.

Strangely enough, most writers of utopias—practically all of whom have been men—have paid remarkably little attention to marriage. That in itself is revealing. Their eyes were usually riveted on more abstract structures like the state or the economy. Marriage, apparently, did not seem all that important in comparison or as open to criticism. But whatever their general orientation, with respect to marriage and the family, even the most unconventional have been extremely male-oriented.

In Sir Thomas More's *Utopia,* for example, "the wives minister to their husbands," to whose house they go upon marriage. In Campanella's *City of the Sun,* boys but not girls learn all the sciences, and there is community of wives. In Etienne Cabet's *Voyage en Icarie,* though there is strict equality of the sexes in education, still there is no mention of women in positions of importance. Ignatius Donnelly, nineteenth-century advocate of violence and revolution, was still quite conventional in his attitude toward the relations between the sexes. And as late as 1905, H. G. Wells, extremely liberal in ideology, nevertheless viewed women primarily as mothers, and in his *Modern Utopia* there were sanctions to assure permanence of unions.

One conception of a utopia that has attracted a good deal of attention from modern young people is B. F. Skinner's *Walden Two*. Men and women in this community are equal and entirely free, but marriage remains. There is "free affection" but not "free love." Morals are strict. People marry young, and women become mothers early. Husbands and wives live in communal dormitories, either sharing one room or living in separate rooms. Aside from the emphasis on early motherhood for women, how could anyone take exception to this conception? Actually, Skinner's major interest has to do with the control of human behavior. He is less interested, for example, in the question, Should the family be strong or weak? than in the question, How may desired behavior be generated and maintained? Child rearing, as an aspect of "behavioral engineering," is his major concern. The "freedom" of his utopia is freedom from "negative reinforcement" but not from manipulation by "positive reinforcement."

One gets the feeling from the writings of most utopians that even when they had taken a determined stand on equality of the sexes, they could not really envision it; they betray themselves in one way or another. Women may enter professions, but they must be professions appropriate for women. Their work is still women's work. The girls may be educated along with boys, but they are not given adult male responsibilities. Women are still primarily mothers. The one great exception is the aristocratic Plato—who, it has been noted, is always on his way back from wherever it is we are running toward so fast—and he had a foolproof gimmick: a series of tests so rigorous that only true grit could survive them. His *Republic,* I am convinced, could only have ended up as a matriarchate.

social-science-fiction writers

Utopias are almost by definition desirable. In social-science fiction, the social criticism may take the form of either utopias or "dystopias." Skinner's *Walden Two* is an example of a social-science-fictional utopia; Aldous Huxley's *Brave New World,* of a social-science-fictional dystopia. Not advocacy but warning is the dystopian's aim.

A burgeoning literature of social-science fiction[3] has included both utopias and dystopias. William Kenkel's résumé of references to love and marriage in this literature concluded that there was a discouraging lack of idealism in it; there was, he found, rather, "with distressing regularity, twentieth-century greed, hate, and violence . . . projected to be even more pronounced in the future than in the present." A pervasive male bias was rampant in the books he examined. In one, Paul Anderson's *Virgin Planet,* for example, serial marriage was conceived entirely from the male point of view. William Kenkel sketches it like this:

Marriage as an enduring relationship did not exist. The system involved three marriages throughout one's lifetime. For the male the first marriage was to satisfy sexual urges, the second was for reproduction of the species, and the third was for mature companionship. The order of kicks, kids, and companionship was altered for the women so that their first marriage was for children and the second for sexual enjoyment. Accepting the fact that the sexes experience the height of sexual drive at different times in the life cycle, a young man of about sixteen years of age first would marry a woman twenty-eight to forty years of age. They would continue this relationship up to ten years. At about age twenty-six the male would establish a relationship with a girl about sixteen years old. In this relationship reproduction would be encouraged, for the girl was young and healthy and the male fully mature. During the decade of this marriage, the couple would have a few children, rear them and lavish them with affection until they were six years old, and turn them over to the state. When men and women reached age forty or thereabouts, they would again change partners, this time emphasizing companionship, mutual tastes, and shared interests. The writer of this story saw many advantages in the system of three marriages. A young man could prove his masculinity in a direct, biological way when his sex drive was at the height of its intensity. He could then spend his time on socially useful activities instead of trying to prove his manhood at football, juvenile delinquency, or the surreptitious use of alcohol or drugs. Anxiety over masculinity and its resultant fear of homosexuality, about which we are hearing more and more, should be reduced.

The women, twenty-eight to forty, would no doubt be delighted to serve as substitutes for football, delinquency, and alcohol in the lives of these sixteen-year-olds in exchange for an abundance of sexual satisfaction. Who needs companionship before the age of forty?

A gathering of playful utopians and scientists, practically all male, in a jolly "think-in" sponsored by the producers of a movie, came up with their own facetious group-think version of an ideal or optimal society. As reported in the press by Tim Matthews and Roy Perrot, adolescents in this utopia were to be given complete sexual freedom and instruction by "ambivalent" Sapphic women. (This suggestion was reported as coming from a woman.) In order to free nonreproductive sex from guilt feelings and from socially divisive tendencies, it was to be given religious sanction. One possibility: let all girls become temple maidens of Astarte (this reportedly from Dr. Bruno Bettelheim). Or how about saturnalia, "an eminently respectable institution" (Herman Kahn speaking). Or a religion of Eros, combining Darwin and psychoanalysis, with ritualized fertility cults (this, according to the press, from Max Lerner). Incest and homosexuality are acceptable. "Marriage as we know it, all agreed, was quite impossible for utopians;

it hinders self-realization, excessively compartments the community's sexual drive, and creates traumatic situations when in difficulty. Instead a system called 'pair-binding' [to run for about seven years] was cordially recommended by the group." Children were to be reared by the community as a whole, as in Israeli kibbutzim, and encouraged to break away from their pair-bonded parents at puberty.

The participants in this playful conference were ready to admit that they had not come up with anything new. One member chided the others for constructing nothing more than "Boy Scoutiana, a world of superficial flatheads." He wanted shame and guilt back in the picture. Even so, not one of the creators of this optimal society would care to live in it. A nice place to visit, they seemed to conclude, but that was all. Without a transcript of the actual discussion we have no way of knowing how much of the press report represents bona fide suggestions and how much idle chitchat. Does it really make that much difference which it was?

experimental communities: a prototype

Not all prophets limit themselves to daydreaming or to fantasying. Many, past and present, attempt to put into practice the ideas they propound in the form of actual communities. The nineteenth century was replete with them. Only one is discussed here, primarily as a sort of bench mark to show how little new thinking is being offered today. Few modern reformers have caught up, for example, with John Humphrey Noyes.

The injection of religion into sexuality in the optimal society referred to above, however playful, showed a great deal of insight. For the actual experience of experimental utopian communities in the United States, in the nineteenth century, even those with the most radical forms of marriage, or of nonmarriage (for some enjoined celibacy), showed that only those with powerful religious undergirding succeeded for any length of time. In the case of one of the most successful, the Oneida Community, "complex marriage," a regulated form of promiscuity strictly based on Scripture, replaced conventional marriage. Paul had placed women in the same category as other property, and since all kinds of property were to be abolished at the advent of the Kingdom of Heaven, sexual exclusiveness had also to be done away with. People were to take the New Testament injunction to love one another literally, not by pairs, but en masse. If marriage as now conceived forbids the partners to love others, that was contrary to biblical teaching. Implementing the Pauline doctrine thus involved the abolishment of conventional marriage altogether.

John Humphrey Noyes, the great leader of the Oneida Community, found marriage as structured in the world about him wholly contrary not only to the Bible but also to human nature and to nature, and the source of about every human ill:

The plea in favor of the worldly social system, that it is not arbitrary but founded in nature, will not bear investigation. All experience testifies, the theory of the novels to the contrary notwithstanding, that sexual love is not naturally restricted to pairs. Second marriages are contrary to the one-love theory, and yet are often the happiest marriages. Men and women find universally (however the fact may be concealed), that their susceptibility to love is not burnt out by the honeymoon, or satisfied by one lover.[4] On the contrary, the secret history of the human heart will bear out the assertion that it is capable of loving any number of times and any number of persons, and that the more it loves the more it can love. This is the law of nature, thrust out of sight and condemned by common consent, and yet secretly known to all.

The law of marriage "worketh wrath." It provokes to secret adultery, actual or of the heart. It ties together unmatched natures. It sunders matched natures. It gives to sexual appetite only a scanty and monotonous allowance, and so produces the natural vices of poverty, contraction of taste and stinginess or jealousy. It makes no provision for the sexual appetite at the very time when that appetite is the strongest.... This law of society bears hardest on females, because they have less opportunity of choosing their time of marriage than men. This discrepancy between the marriage system and nature is one of the principal sources of the peculiar diseases of women, of prostitution, masturbation, and licentiousness in general.

Quite a bill of particulars against monogamy! It would be hard for any contemporary prophet to top the cogency of Noyes' critique or the boldness of his solution.

The Oneida Community was one of the few that actually showed more than a merely pro forma concern for women—the bookkeeper was a woman—and protected them in their relations with men. No one was obliged to receive the attentions of anyone she or he was not attracted to and the responsibility for controlling conception was placed squarely on men. The Oneida Community was one of the most successful of all the experimental communities.[5] And much of its success was attributable to its strong religious underpinning.

The nearest modern analogues to the religious bonds of the nineteenth-century communities are, I suppose, those of the collective, a group of people bound to one another in a common ideology, but also in a common task. Working together on a common project seems to divert attention from too great concentration on the sexual complications of living together.

to each according to his taste: currently proposed options

If the results of social-science research were more fixed, and if our criteria for what we wanted in marriage were more unequivocal, there would be a fair amount of consensus with respect to the future of marriage. As it is, there is the widest, not to say wildest, diversity among the visions of those who look to the future. On one side we have those who see ever-greater privatization of the family with consequent greater intensity of relationships, and on the other, those who see declining privatization, greater communalization, and less intensity. Sometimes both greater intensity and greater communalization come from the same source. Thus, for example, Richard Farson tells us that:

. . . the family will . . . become a rehabilitative agent, a buffer against a very complex and demanding world in which family members constitute our only advocate, the only people who are *for* us. So we shall depend upon them increasingly. Furthermore, in one sense, the family may be one of the few places in the world of the future—one of the last places—in which we can find privacy. As such, it will be a safe place for expressing our aggressive and hostile impulses. So family life will be highly emotional, intimate, infantile, aggressive, hostile, and irrational. . . . We can expect a great deal more emotionality and intimacy, a broader range of emotional expression. This will come about simply because people everywhere are increasingly demanding it; they are no longer content to live composed, serene, calm, bland lives. They want more of both ends of the continuum—emotionality and serenity—and the family will become the matrix for such experience.

Marriage, in brief, will be able to accommodate and reconcile the two conflicting human wishes, for security and for excitement.

On the life-style aspects of marriage, Farson sees "more communal living; more extended kinship patterns; more of the experimental communality that is now developing." There is no necessary inconsistency here, for practically all agree that the future will offer a wide variety of options so that each marital pair can select the kind of relationship and life style that suits it best. There is recognition of the fact that since life in the modern world demands and creates diversity in human beings, provisions must be made for accommodating this diversity. Or suffer the consequences.

Thus James R. and Lynn G. Smith, members of the Sexual Freedom Movement, tell us that we must develop family structures and policies "with new and hopefully expanded means of sexual fulfillment worthy of rational adult human beings. What we must do is make room in our society for a genuine plurality of social forms. The professionals in medicine, welfare, education, and social science must respond with a sympathetic, informed, or at least genuinely tolerant view, in order to cope with this often ignored aspect of the struggle toward personal and social freedom. Our belief is that nothing less will do if we are not to have a literally sick and very confused and fragmented society . . . in less than a generation." The rest of this chapter is devoted to a consideration of some of the proposals for these new structures.

life styles: communes and cooperative households

The term *commune* applies to a life style, not to a form of marriage. It has come to be used in such a general way that without some qualifying word or phrase it is almost useless as a descriptive term. Thus, although group marriages involve living together in communes, not all communes involve marriage of any kind or have any relevance for marriage. Some communes do include married couples who retain their conventional monogamous relationship. Some may also include a set of assorted individuals of one sex or both sexes among whom liaisons form and dissolve but who are not in a seriously committed relationship to one another or whose commitment, if there is one, is implicit or merely a vague, unformulated, even unarticulated one. Any of these relationships may be exclusive for as long as it lasts; or, again, it may not be. But these relationships can hardly be said to constitute marriages. Some communes may discourage such pairing, everyone being "married" or at least informally committed to everyone else. Some communes consist of members erroneously called communal swingers, who are idealistic revolutionaries looking for a genuine new social order. There may be enormous preoccupation among them with working out genuine and human ways of relating to one another. But the relevance for the future of marriage of such communes is derivative rather than direct. In brief, a commune is merely a pattern of living, a life style, a household. The relationships within it may vary from strict conventional monogamy to essential promiscuity.

In the nineteenth century, members of experimental rural communities came to them with rural skills and some, even, with capital, so that they had at least a base on which to build. Modern rural communes rarely have these assets. That so many communes fail is no reflection on the blueprints.[6] The reality rarely seems to produce as much pleasure as the dream. It is more fun and more satisfying to read and dream about such modes of living than to live in them. They may be fun for a year or two for the young; but for the long haul the benefits do not seem to many to be worth the costs. We won't really know, though, until the acid test comes: what happens to the children.[7]

The commune life style may not have much of a future so far as marriage is concerned, but that does not mean that it does not have any future at all. For those who find our technological society truly intolerable, who are incapable of long-term commitments, who find true individualized intimacy impossible, who are basically dependent—for all those, in brief, who should not, both for their own sakes and the sake of others get married —some kind of commune would be an optimal solution. No one member would have to carry the entire brunt of taking care of them; they would be a joint responsibility of the whole group, and they would, in turn, help bear the weight of the others. Even individuals who are among the most creative but who, for lack of marital aptitude, cannot adjust to the demands of marriage might find a place in such communes. They are not everyone's dish of tea, of course, any more than the privatized home of conventional marriage is, but just one of several possible alternative options.

Communes might also be a suitable solution for the young people engaged in nuclear fission. They might be congenial for those who find it impossible to live at home but who are not yet ready to assume the responsibilities of a household on their own.

Women have a hard time in communes, as in so many of the male-designed options, fighting the preconceived ideas about sex roles which the young men bring with them. Unless strong regulations are laid down, they are likely to find themselves saddled with the household chores as ruthlessly as in any conventional household.

The most conservative option for the future is the cooperative household. It is like any other kind of consumer cooperative; it can lower costs. In this respect it supplies one way in which the husband's marriage can be improved, the easing of his financial burden. The case of John and Nina described in chapter 8 illustrates how such arrangements work. The only real modification in their marriage was in its living arrangements; for John and Nina were "like a lot of other people who live very conventional lives." (Cooperative households also make possible cooperative child care arrangements, a plus on the distaff side.)

Cooperative households do have a future. But until we learn how to build for them they will be seriously handicapped. And until the researchers have ferreted out the hazards for marriage of this life style as doggedly as they have the hazards of the nuclear family we will have to depend on the costly trial-and-error experiments of pioneering couples to teach us how to live in them. I rate the future of this option high.

But help with the provider function is by far the easier of the two improvements men want in marriage. The other, it will be recalled, has to do with sexual varietism. And here the story gets a bit more complicated.

swinging

If the cooperative household is conservative on the commitment side of marriage—with respect to both permanence and exclusivity—and avant-garde on the life-style side, swinging is just the opposite, conservative on the life-style side and avant-garde in its commitment, especially with respect to exclusivity. All the studies, whether by psychologists, sociologists, or anthropologists, agree that most participants are middle-class, even suburban, couples, living conventional lives in their separate, isolated households, at some pains to keep their activities hidden from their conventional neighbors. Some are even churchgoers. In their life style they are indistinguishable from their fellow suburbanites. It is only in their sexual activities that they are radical. Even so, they are not all that avant-garde in their marriages.

In one sense, in fact, swinging is the simplest and least revolutionary modification of marriage as it is now structured that achieves both security and at least sexual excitement. It violates none of the marital vows: the partners remain committed to each other, they do not forsake one another, they continue—so they say—to love and cherish each other. All they do is share one another with other sexual partners. To the charge, in fact, of L. James Grold, a psychiatrist, that swinging is part of "our consumer ideology with its concepts of planned obsolescence, replaceability, disposable containers, and discardable spouses," they reply that it is quite the opposite: swinging spouses do not discard each other. Indeed, they claim that their marriages may even become improved and stabilized by swinging.

The middle-class nature of swinging couples shows up in all the samples studied. A company president, a

mathematician, a lawyer—the most commonly represented profession in one sample—a realtor, a student,
an artist, a retired navy chief, a computer salesman, an
office supply salesman, an engineer, a restaurant manager, a marine private, and a sales manager were reported in one sample. Most are young, married four to
five years, and most have children. Most of the women
are housewives, with, perhaps, an occasional teacher.
They take their middle-class prejudices with them into
their activities; the selection of partners at parties resembles middle-class dating procedures. By and large,
the same kinds of race, age, and class criteria for selection prevail. (And the same kind of wallflower heartache, male or female.)

The largest concentrations of swingers are in the San
Francisco-Los Angeles area, the New York-Boston-
Washington area, the Chicago area, and the Texas-
Louisiana-Mississippi area, tied for fourth place with
the Miami area of Florida. The juxtaposition of "concentration" with "area" is not accidental, for swingers
must be prepared to travel fairly great distances to
rendezvous with other couples, one more indication of
their relatively affluent background. Strangely enough
and hard as it is to believe, despite this almost arche-
typically middle-class background, the image that male
swingers have of themselves, Gilbert D. Bartell found,
is one of cosmopolitan members of the jet set, the
beautiful people.

Homogeneous as they may tend to be in class background, however, swingers are not at all homogeneous
in other aspects of their common activities. They vary
among themselves, as all other groups do. Charles A.
Varni distinguishes three kinds; hard-core, egotistical,
and recreational. "Hard-core swingers . . . want no emotional involvement with their partners, and, with little
selectivity, swing with as many couples as possible.
They are seen as being generally cold and unfeeling by
other swingers. . . . Egotistical swingers do not seek
emotional involvement with their partners . . . [but they]

are usually fairly selective. They want purely sexual experiences. . . . Swinging is viewed as a distinct and separate part of their lives and they have no social relationships or friendships with their swinging partners. Recreational swingers emphasize the social aspects of swinging. They are members of fairly stable groups, enjoy both party and one-couple situations, and engage in nonswinging activities with one another. . . . [But] significant emotional involvement with the partner is neither needed nor desired. The emphasis is on the sociability and sexuality of the experience."

Sometimes only two couples are involved; sometimes three or more. If there are more than three couples, swinging may take the form of a "free-for-all group orgy." "The party situation," Varni tells us, "resembles any other weekend social gathering in a private home." A wide variety of sexual activities are acceptable, including sadism, masochism, and homosexual relations, usually between women.

Couples learn of available participants in several ways: newspaper advertisements, personal referrals or "matchmaking," and swing clubs. In Los Angeles, Carolyn Symonds found, the process has become institutionalized, even commercialized. Numbered automobile bumper stickers are issued by one organization designating the owners as swingers so that they can be identified on the highway. A central registry handles telephone calls. Some nightclubs cater to swingers.

L. James Grold finds the motives for engaging in swinging to include sheer marital boredom; desire for reassurance about masculinity (participants do not always get it) or femininity; hope for mending disrupted marriages; the excitement of the forbidden; and sheer "adventure . . . without any commitment."

The effects of swinging on marriage are reported by researchers—a psychiatrist, a sociologist, and an anthropologist—to be, on the whole, benign. The psychiatrist: "for . . . individuals sensitive to each other's needs, swinging develops into a highly pleasurable sharing ex-

perience adding variety to their lives. They discover not
only heightened desire and love for each other but also
that their ability to give and receive sexual satisfaction
increases with greater experience." The sociologist:
"the most often reported positive effect was greater love
and warmth between the [eight] couples. Learning new
sexual techniques was often mentioned as was rejuve-
nated or improved social life." The anthropologist:
". . . it is a form of togetherness. . . . The couple may
now spend more time together searching for new contacts and pursuing leads for parties, bars, and other
compatible couples."

On the other side of the ledger are such costs as
these: Many men, Bartell reports, find that they cannot
live up to their own sexual expectations, and many
women still suffer the pangs of the wallflower, selected
by few men. Jealousy, the hazard of venereal infection,
and mechanistic sex are also negative effects. Grold
found that for some couples "reality catches up," the
"pseudo-intimate bubble bursts," and "loneliness and
emptiness may penetrate once again." For some, swinging takes on an addictive character, they engage in it
more and enjoy it less. For others it becomes only a
sometime thing; they are in and out of the swinging
world. In one club, Varni found, "a six months' membership qualifies them as veterans." Only the Bartell
study included the dropouts among the subjects. One
couple dropped out because of fear of venereal infection; one because they found other swingers to be
"kooks," racists, fascists; some found that it took too
much time; and one couple found that they could not
cope with the anxieties it aroused.

Although the long-time effects of swinging on marriage cannot as yet be measured, one thing is certain:
if the female prophets have anything to say about it,
swinging as here described will not prevail. The completely male orientation of swinging, not only of the
participants themselves, but also of at least some of the
researchers, is revealed by one of them, Gilbert D.

Bartell, who believes that Women's Liberation is among the complex developments that encourage swinging. It is hard to imagine anything wider of the mark than this incredible statement, especially from a man who concluded from his own research that "most male swingers are, in effect, bartering their women." The kind of sexuality embodied by swinging—impersonal, mechanical, uninvolved—is precisely the target of the Women's Liberation Movement, anathema to its members. They decry it; to them such a relationship is degrading. That some women come to accept, even seek it, is, to them, one more illustration of the degradation heaped upon women by our society.

One of the most interesting results of all the research on swinging, in fact, is the light it throws on the reactions of the women involved. Almost always it is the husband who initially suggests that the couple engage in swinging.[8] The wives react with varying degrees of disgust and anxiety. Then there is either a gradual or a sudden about-face on her part, often to the surprise and even discomfiture of the husband. (We have already had occasion in chapter 5 to note this interesting phenomenon among nonconventional marriages in which the wives took seriously the theory of sexual freedom so persuasively argued by their husbands.) Most of the wives, Varni tells us, "after a convincing process (facilitative or threatening) on their husbands' part, agreed to try swinging one time in order to please the man." Their fears were not realized, and they came to accept, even desire, the new relationship. But for many, it is interesting to note, it was the social rather than the sexual aspect that was important. They even confessed that they faked climax. "The jaded women may pant a little too boisterously for realism," to please their partners, here no less than in the marital bed. But, ah! they enjoyed being desired. "Where else," one exclaimed to Dr. Grold, "could I have so many men desire and make love to me and have it be so totally acceptable to my husband?" James and Lynn G. Smith conclude that "women are better able to make the necessary adjustments to sexual freedom [as to almost everything else about the marriage] after the initial phases of involvement than are men, even though it is usually the case that the men instigate the initial involvement."

Impossible as it is as yet to evaluate the impact of swinging as here described on the future of marriage, its very existence does constitute a serious assault on the commitment to exclusivity involved in conventional marriage. The Smiths conclude that sexual permissiveness and plurality do not produce marital instability; monogamy is not essential; and swingers are not necessarily neurotic or pathological. They do not claim that swinging is the wave of the future for everyone. In the gross form presented by the researchers, in which the sexual relationships are mechanical and lacking in warmth, it is not likely to attract a wide following. The Smiths estimate that it will attract 15 to 20 percent of married couples under optimal conditions, but all who sample it will not accept it for any length of time.

the intimate network

There is another form of swinging that does not conform to any of the types discussed above. Varni calls it "interpersonal swinging." It is more idealistic, less crass. "Interpersonal swingers, unlike the other types, desire and emphasize close emotional relationships with their partners. They are seeking intimate and viable friendships with couples with whom they can share themselves both emotionally and sexually. The sexual aspect of the relationships is not felt to have primary importance and they expect to engage in social and recreational activities with their partners. Many interpersonal swingers emphasize openness and honesty as basic values. They almost always prefer one-couple situations. Most of their friends are also swingers."

When they achieve permanence in their relationship, the result is what has been called an "intimate network." Larry and Joan Constantine tell us that such a network consists of "a cluster or chain of families, maintaining separate domiciles and family identity, but coupled by intimate relationships between families. If today's model holds, families in intimate networks will maintain contact, continuously, meeting in various combinations from a few times a year to every few weeks. In most cases, intermarital sexual intimacy is an intrinsic element."

The intimate network retains the separate, isolated household. It does not, therefore, relieve the husband from the financial support of the family nor the wife from responsibility for the household. But it does introduce sexual varietism into the marriage, and avoids the perils of constant interaction in a common household. It presents the best of both worlds, stability and security combined with variety of sexual partners, together with the worst of one of the worlds, exclusive responsibility for the provider and homemaker roles on the part of husbands and wives. Such intimate networks do not represent much of a threat to marriage, but certainly more of a threat than swinging does.

Although there are no bona fide studies of such intimate networks in operation, John Updike's *Couples* describes a set of relationships which seem to approximate them closely. They may arise quite accidentally, according to the Constantines, and occur more frequently than we know. The Constantines see intimate networks as the most likely candidate for an acceptable marital option for the future.

serial polygyny

Some male prophets do not see the sexual varietism men crave supplied all at the same time but in the form of a succession of partners. A generation ago, the name *serial polygamy* was given to this pattern. And it is not at all unusual today. In 1967, for example, among white men, Glick and Norton found that 16 percent were living in a second marriage twenty or more years after their first marriage, and 2 percent in a third. Thus almost a fifth had engaged in serial polygamy. Young prophets today speak of serial monogamy or—unlike the old term, which included more than one husband as well as more than one wife over time—serial polygyny, which includes only several wives. We have already noted in chapter 5 the suggestion for limited commitments at marriage—for, say, three, or five, or seven years—a pattern that fits the serial polygamy blueprint. Here exclusivity but not permanence is emphasized.

geriatric marriage

Most thinking about marriage has to do with young people. But the future of marriage is going to involve more and more older people too. And, because of the greater longevity of women, which reduces the proportion of men so drastically in the later age brackets, polygyny is being seriously proposed for them. No generation has improved more as compared with the past than those we label "old" today. And as medical care continues to improve, so will their health. The women especially are wearing well. But they are lonely. Walter C. McKain is, therefore, on the basis of his study of retirement marriage, a strong proponent of geriatric marriage:

The excess of females in the older age brackets means that many widows will never have an opportunity for remarriage. ... In 1985 the excess of aged females will reach 4.5 million. Currently, the ratio of widows to widowers is four to one and three-fourths of the widows are sixty years of age or older. If companionship and some degree of sexual activity is important to these women—and there are those who say that sexual desire may increase after the menopause—pressure may develop to change our marriage customs.

Such a change has already been suggested by Dr. Victor Kassel. . . . [who proposes] a form of polygamy which would permit any man past sixty to marry from two to five women in the same age group. He believes that a genuine interrelated family group would emerge and that this new form would have advantages over the present family pattern which condemns a growing number of older women to celibacy in their later years. It would enable one man and several women to pool their financial resources. It would insure a better diet and provide more hands to care for any member of the marriage group who became ill. In addition, it would lead to better grooming and more cheerful dispositions. And most of all, it would serve to eliminate the loneliness and neglect that has accompanied the disappearance of the consanguineal family.

Acceptance of such a pattern will require overcoming much conventional thinking which tends to discount sexuality after, let us say, sixty-five or even earlier. Some have believed that a man has just so many orgasms in his system, and that they were, likely as not, all used up by the age of sixty or thereabouts. A man who fathered a child in his later years was the object of humorous, albeit admiring, comment. Horrendous tales of men who died in the act circulated sotto voce. Women, obviously, became sexless before the age of fifty.

Kinsey and his associates punctured the myths in the 1940s, as did Masters and Johnson in the 1960s. Both men and women retain sexual interest much longer than had once been believed. Why should they be deprived of any sexual contact in their sixties or even seventies? Marriage among the elderly has come to be accepted by just about everyone. The Social Security Administration even modified its rules in order to facilitate it. But polygyny? That will take a little longer to digest. "Plural marriage will be acceptable, if at all," McKain correctly predicts, "only after some venturesome older persons test the plan and suffer the abuse that is almost certain to accompany their actions." This is one male-designed option for the future that would benefit women as much as men.

In the marital options so far discussed, the commitment to the relationship was for permanence if not for exclusivity or for exclusivity if not for permanence. But some proposed options demand neither.

ménage à trois

We have moved away from both the conventional household and the conventional marriage with the three-member relationship. Its proponents, the Constantines, look to it as a kind of custom icebreaker, getting us used to totally free sexual expression as well as to communal-type life styles. Reflecting the bias of all the male prophets, the stablest and the most preferred form of the triangular relationship consists of one male and two females. And the most desirable one is a triad in which one woman remains attached, thus providing security, while the other is, so to speak, a floating concubine. Such an arrangement provides a good deal of sexual variety for the male partner. As in the case of swinging, it is usually the husband who initiates such a relationship; the wife accedes. The Constantines describe one such relationship which involved a couple and another girl:

...though an actual marriage never emerged, the three people became, and remain, very intimate. The involvement was initiated by the husband and a girl with whom the wife was already close. The wife initially reacted very favorably to her husband's sexual expression of his feelings for the girl. At later times the husband appeared to her to have a preoccupation with their threesome and this threatened her somewhat without apparently causing actual jealousy of the other girl. The key in this relationship was sharing and mutuality. Except for the first sexual encounter, both husband and wife participated together in all dimensions of the relationship. Both feel their own (two-person) relationship has deepened as a result.

But what, we wonder, about the other woman? What did she get for supplying the "permanent emotional subsidy"—as the woman quoted below put it—for this marriage?

Most of the descriptions of ménages à trois are written by men, and they have a rather idyllic flavor about them. A secure wife and an available outside partner look just fine to men. But here is a personal document supplied by a woman who was the other woman, and the arrangement doesn't look all that good from her point of view:

Dear Albert,

I was enormously disturbed at the reaction to my request to be let out. I fell asleep at about 8:30 and after a couple of hours of sleep I lay awake trying to put the pieces together. It's always difficult to communicate in a face-to-face situation because the other person always distracts the logic of what you have to say. So I am writing this out in order to get it all said and to clarify it to myself as well as to you.

First about the management angle, which you refuse to accept. This is what I mean. Here is a situation in which I am involved but in which I have no say. Sort of like emotional taxation without representation. Events take place, situations arise, decisions are made which affect me and yet I have absolutely nothing to do with them. It's like a child who watches his parents quarreling, feeling involved but helpless. The situation last November was one thing. The situation today is quite another. I think two things made me come to the conclusion I came to last week. One was your reaction to Ann's involvement with Harold. The other was the bargaining between you two, the raising of the ante, as you put it. Either this was a serious offer or it was an amusing game. In either case it made my own position untenable. If it is true as you seem to think that your marriage is going to need a permanent emotional subsidy then the design for living will have to be something like a ménage à quatre or à trois. The outside person or persons will have to have a responsible relationship and not be just satellites orbiting around the marriage. (Having Harold in the household is the kind of thing I mean, genuine community living in which all four of us lived together.) I think that if you really think this through you will agree with me. It is just impossible for a person to be involved in a relationship and yet to have no say in it. . . . I kept wondering last night why I should feel guilty, defensive. . . . I am extremely fond of both of you. I wouldn't hurt either of you on purpose for anything. This [moving away] was not an aggressive move on my part; it was purely defensive. I have so many emotional obligations to people . . . that I just can't let myself become involved in a situation where I have so little control. Before you deny the basic premises of my logic, think hard; at least try to examine them as though they were correct even if you don't accept them. . . .

Albert and Ann, without the "emotional subsidy" provided by the woman who wrote this letter, did finally divorce.

There must be some ménage à trois in which there are two men and one woman. But they do not show up in the literature.

"multilateral" or "group" marriage

The term *multilateral marriage* has been proposed by the Constantines to supersede the commoner term, *group marriage*. With this model we have taken a further step away from the conventional household, and scores of steps away from the commitments of conventional marriage. A multilateral marriage consists of three or more members who commit themselves to one another and consider all to be married to one another. What distinguishes it from merely a social group or, presumably, from a cooperative household is that the bonds are genuinely intimate and affectionate. The hope is that the commitment will be permanent, but permanence is not prescribed. Provision is made for opting out. There is no commitment to exclusivity.

Theoretically, the multilateral marriage answers all the difficulties of the marriages of both husbands and wives. It provides sexual varietism but also security; it relieves men of sole responsibility for the provider role, and women of sole responsibility for the child-rearing and housekeeping roles. The sexes may share roles or reverse them: "house-husbands can raise children while wives pursue careers." Less child-rearing responsibility rests on any given pair of shoulders. "In fact, children are potentially the major benefactors, thriving on the enriched environment and multiplicity of adult models."

As in other male blueprints, multilateral marriage gives lip service to egalitarianism. But in the ten such marriages observed by the Constantines, leadership did tend to emerge and it always seemed to be a male who was the leader. One man in a four-person marriage advocated expansion in order to increase the competition for leadership. With three rather than two men, he argued, competition for dominance would be less likely to constitute a problem because with three contenders, no one man could succeed so easily in dominating the group. Funny that it did not occur to him that one of the two women already in the group might compete for domination as well as a third man brought in for that purpose.

As in conventional marriage—or, in fact, any in-group—much depended on the initial choice of members; they had to be compatible and not looking for marital therapy. "The near ideal psychological makeup is rare," would seem to be a mild understatement. "Multilateral marital aptitude" is undoubtedly a good deal less common than even ordinary marital aptitude. When suitable couples were found, they were, in effect, "dated" or "rushed." If they passed this initial screening, they might be invited to trial membership. Since, as distinguished from those communes which include a wide variety of unattached individuals as well as pairs, the multilateral marriages in the Constantine sample took in members only as couples, complications arose. One member of the prospective member-couple might be ready for sexual relations with others before the partner was. Such lack of synchronization in readiness and differences in pace among prospective members were recognized, and experiments for dealing with them were undertaken. Unanimous acceptance of new members, not a mere majority, was prescribed.

Once in, integrating the new members was enormously involved and complex; and the more members there were, the more complicated it became. "Sensory overload" appeared when there were six members; and one group had to import a family therapist every week to help them cope with the interpersonal complexities which bogged them down.

All this and sex too. For sexual varietism does not come easily. How can spontaneity and fairness be optimized? How can freedom and control be reconciled? To keep sex under some kind of control, there were four ways of allocating partners: group sex, rotation of partners, free choice of partners, and a split form of the free-choice arrangement. The group pattern was usually most feasible in a three- or four-member relationship; it became increasingly difficult with more members. The fixed-rotation pattern usually involved several days or a week. It obviated the necessity for constant decision and assured everyone of partners. But these gains were at the expense of spontaneity and sexual preference. Free choice sounds ideal. It maximizes freedom and spontaneity. But in practice it became extremely involved. "Merely finding out preferences can take time, and it is often difficult to obtain spontaneous and unprocessed answers to the question 'Who do you want to sleep with?' Spontaneity becomes a mere slogan." And what about the hurt of the member who is low on the totem pole of desirability? Spontaneity for one may mean rejection for another. An alternative as yet untried was to have the men go to their rooms and let the women surprise them. But one woman protested that she might want to be surprised sometimes too; she suggested that the sexes rotate choice responsibility. Well, obviously, you can't have everything.

There is no simple, all-purpose solution to the problem of partner selection. Having assigned partners costs spontaneity; free choice costs possible rejection. Even the "surprise" solution involves deciding who is going to surprise whom. One could collapse with exhaustion by the time one dropped into bed.

Homosexual relations were permitted in the multilateral marriages the Constantines studied, but they were not common, especially among men. Where they did occur, however, they constituted a critical weak spot. Casual involvement of men with one another did not threaten one apparently stable group. There was, in brief, no standard way to deal with homosexual ties nor any documented evidence of their effect on the group.

The Constantines are under no illusion about the prospects of this option for the future. As yet it has been able to survive only in restricted parts of the country, in California—it goes without saying—and the eastern seaboard. It is not likely to be widely accepted soon. It requires not only people of a certain psychological makeup, but also matching the right people among them. If it is hard to find one congenial partner for a conventional marriage, it is far harder to find two congenial partners—congenial, in turn, to both pairs of spouses. Multilateral marriage aggravates and highlights the problems of two-person marriage: one has to adjust to the idiosyncrasies of at least three other members. Still, the Constantines tell us, if multilateral marriage exaggerates the difficulties of conventional marriage, it also enhances the potential for happiness.

Even granting that one could make a good case for multilateral marriage, if the problems are as complex as those the Constantines report, it would take all the time of both the husbands and wives to make them succeed. In conventional, two-person marriages, only the wife is required to invest so much in marriage. How many husbands would be willing to?

So much, then, for present-day male dreamers and experimentalists. There is something rather stale, unimaginative, unexciting, and quite déjà vu about the array of options they offer us. We have heard it and seen it all before. Men like John Humphrey Noyes were thinking and acting more radically in the nineteenth century. Many of the modern male prophets seem so hung up on their male biases that, try as they may, they keep coming up with the same old stuff. Nor have they come to terms with the spirited nature of the women they are going to have to live with, whatever the form their marriage may take, women who do not share their biases and who are far more in tune with the tenor of the times.

The women prophets are zeroing in on the crucial problems and coming up with far more interesting answers.

chapter ten

female prophets and prophecies

My own choice among prophets are those to be found among young, avant-garde, radical women. Like all prophets, they rub our noses in our hypocrisy and expose the injustice of our merely ritualistic virtues. I take especially seriously the radical women of the Female or Women's Liberation Movement. And when I think of the future of marriage, I look to them for hints about its general form. I see them capable of bending the most determined curves and projections. They no longer see marriage as the goal of every women; some even talk seriously of celibacy. They envision totally different kinds of relationships between men and women, in marriage or out of it. These women are, I think, going to exert an enormous impact on the future of marriage. They have, in fact, already done so.

The evils against which these women protest are not the same as those the men protest. Their blueprints for the future may coincide with those of men at some points, but by and large they are different, designed for different ends, to achieve different goals. Their targets are not only all the disabilities structured into the wife's marriage by biblical tradition, legislation, or common law, but also by the male morality and values which govern her marriage. The very nature of the relationship between the sexes itself, as well as the formal structure, is what they seek to change—and not only the sexual aspect of that relationship but also the personal, the psychological, and the psychosocial. Female "personhood" and autonomy loom large among their goals.

They have an extra load to carry. The generation of their grandmothers was the generation of the great female emancipators; one reads their writings with astonishment at their radical slant. But the generation of their own mothers was the one stricken by the Freudian orthodoxy, the devastating orthodoxy which took the form of what Betty Friedan has labeled "the feminine mystique," and which imposed on the twentieth-century woman a style of thinking and feeling appropriate perhaps for the nineteenth century but not at all for the twentieth. Radical women have had to recapture the ground they lost during the 1950s and move beyond.

Considering how male-biased the male prophets were, how lacking in sensitivity they were to women in their blueprints for the future, how complacent, how certain for their own broadmindedness and understanding of women and of what women wanted or ought to have, one should not be surprised that the first women prophets felt that they had to shout terribly loud to make themselves heard. Nor should one be unprepared for the urgency they felt to find words to reflect back to men how they looked to women: "male chauvinist pig" was a rough approximation. It took something shocking to shake centuries-old foundations as firm as those underpinning the relations between the sexes, in or out of marriage. They began to write as no women had ever written about sex or men before. Marriage would never be the same again.

It would be possible for me to state what the female prophets were saying in my own dispassionate voice, and, however briefly, I will. But that leaves out a great deal of their message, its passion and its anger. These emotions were as much a part of the message as the

words themselves were. The words, after all, only tell us
what we had always known, that men were strong and
aggressive and powerful and women passive and dependent, and their marital roles were cut to fit. What
the female prophets did was to say the same things with
a totally different accent, emphasis, and interpretation.
Was this the way things *had* to be? They left us non-
plussed—as they intended to leave us. I choose, therefore, to let the women speak for themselves as much
as possible.

they learned about women from . . .

A great many men have been learning about the
future of marriage since the message of the female
prophets first burst upon an unbelieving and astounded
world in the late 1960s. Men rubbed their eyes in
astonished incredulity. It had to be a joke, a put-on.
It had to be a cute device of female losers making a bid
for their attention—just a replay of the same old female
ploy. Nothing a good screwing couldn't cure.

They were wrong, far more wrong than they had ever
imagined. These women were not cuties playing a new
version of an old script. They were performing according to a script no one had ever heard before, the script
of the future not only of marriage but of all relations
between the sexes, before and after marriage.

The first that some young men learned about the
future of marriage came long before they even con-
templated marriage, at the premarital period we used
to call the dating or courtship stage. The young woman
was not letting the young man chase her until she caught
him. She was refusing to act in expectable ways. And,
believe it or not, she was actually turning him away. It
was bewildering. The men were understandably per-
plexed, even angry. They felt rebuffed. Women had no
right to treat them like that. Instead of welcoming him
eagerly, the woman feels "a quick hot flush of anger,"

Dana Densmore tells us, "when the arrogant male strolls in, sprawls himself down without inquiring whether she is busy, or about to leave, or enjoying a bit of solitude to think, assuming with total confidence that nothing could be as important as his attentions, that he is doing her a favor by taking her away from whatever he interrupted. He is already talking as he walks in, greeting her jovially, perhaps with a good-natured compliment or two. . . . She is a woman and he assumes from that that she will be uncritical, admiring, and kind. . . . This man, whom once she would have called a friend, . . . is showing insolent disregard for her privacy."

The first some other young men learned about the future of marriage was when the women they were dating rejected their chivalrous gestures. Dana Densmore, in "Chivalry—the Iron Hand in the Velvet Glove," analyzes the process:

Men often accuse women of desiring equality but still demanding chivalry. But the reaction to a rejection of a chivalrous gesture will usually reveal the gesture as a power play, important to the ego of the chevalier. He may whimper or squawk or speak in heavily patronizing tones behind which lies a barely veiled threat. . . . "Now you're going too far," he may say. "You're being ridiculous, oversensitive." Or he may allege that you've hurt his feelings. . . . "What *right* do you have to deny me something that gives me such pleasure?" . . . His insistence, after he has been firmly refused, . . . means he is getting a very significant benefit from it. . . . The reward is psychological, a feeling of superiority. . . . Spending money is a way of expressing power. . . . It is a maxim that you never get something for nothing. When a man does another a favor a feeling of anxiety is set up until the debt is paid off. . . . We are all concerned about "being bought," about setting up generalized obligations, the means of repayment of which we don't know in advance. In the case of women, they are "bought" by the instances of this practice and they don't know what's expected of them in return, a very uncomfortable situation. "Just your charming company," the man might say. . . . For him to pay for her, which is an indirect way of *paying* her, for her charming company, she must give him something in return, something he isn't also giving her. . . . Perhaps what is required is that she play up to him particularly; let him have his way in making plans; let him dominate conversation; encourage him to talk about his projects, listening attentively and admiringly, not boring him with her projects or expressing contradictory opinions or better ideas.... And suppose the woman doesn't understand that this "charm" really is adequate repayment (sometimes it obviously isn't, as when a man expects sexual privileges as a return on his financial investment). Or suppose she has too strong a sense of self, or just too much self-respect to *be* all that charming. She is then left with the uncomfortable feeling that she owes something she can't repay. ... Chivalry, then, makes equals unequal.

That is a hard lesson for a lot of men to learn. It isn't true, of course, he reassures himself, but if she feels that way, it might as well be true. And puts *him* in an embarrassing spot.

The first inkling by still other young men of the future of marriage came when the young women refused to hop into bed with them and remained firm in their refusal, immune even to the horrendous epithets: Frigid! Lesbian! To the young man who felt smugly avantgarde himself, Dana Densmore replied, "Mr. Smug Liberal, I've tried your delicious masochistic sex and it nauseates me to think about it. I'm a person, not a delectable little screwing machine equipped with subroutines for ... listening to all the pompous drivel you want to pour out to impress me."

The first yet another young man learned about the future of marriage he learned from Hilary Langhorst when she refused to marry him at all. Why, he wanted to know? She sat down to explain:

...It is clear that I can not communicate my ideas to you at this time. First, you must take my anger seriously. Now you can only reject it as a threat to your humane position. It seems as if I had attacked your honesty. You refuse to see that your way of understanding me is one strong factor in pushing me to express this oppression, to react against men.... We are not suited to be a "couple," but this fact does not leave me unaffected. A woman must continually face judgment.... Your judgment, despite your intention to accept me as Hilary, determines me to be a functional failure. The "good" woman, the woman used by a man, is allowed to survive happily because she contributes to the sex system. . . . If I were your woman friend, I could behave as a more detached and intelligent form of mother. Instead, I am Hilary, who must refer you to her personal history and to analyses other women have made from their lives. . . . I have lost my envy for a marriage. Godard and Bergman have explained what can be learned from it, and the public's response of boredom to such a film as *The Married Woman* is the most direct proof that it is not necessary to participate in marriage to be an emotionally educated human being. . . . Now love, tailored to marriage or an affair, only keeps women isolated, dependent, and inferior in personality. As there is no possible equality in any presently conceived relationship of woman to man, or in any functioning relation of the people to the controlling class, love must exist as some greater or less perversion of human awareness. The bitter flavor of this observation is not the result of my knowing you or any other individual, but is a summation of my total perception of men, beginning with my father, his God and his Reality. . . . You don't respect the experience from which I make my analysis. . . . It is evidence of your lack of trust [in my ability to] come to an understanding of my life that is not derived from some authority. Your measurements simply confine me, kindly and surely, to that segregated, man-sustaining ground-floor squatter's camp of the Great American Tenement.

Surely there never was a Dear John letter of this caste.

And the first some husbands learned about the future of marriage was their wives' request that they share responsibility for the household. Roger Burton, for example, learned about it from Gabrielle:

"Roger?" I said.
"Yes, dear?"
"I'd like to talk about something."
"Yes, dear?"
The house is there for the benefit of everyone in the family. The responsibility for it should be divided. At one time in my life, I volunteered to assume everyone's responsibility. It's time for me to be moving on. This will necessitate everyone's reassuming his personal responsibility for the functioning of this house. At this point, you explain that you're going back to school to become a brain surgeon, or write full-time (that's

me, saying that), or you're going to raise the kids REALLY without cluttering it up with diverse other full-time gardening, cleaning, or maintenance jobs. . . . Whoever uses it, takes charge of it.

Roger agreed: that the house does benefit all of us; that a benefit implies a responsibility; that if I didn't want to be Queen of the Castle anymore, I should have a right to abdicate; that I hadn't shown great aptitude for housework and eight years was a reasonable trial; that I had a right to try something else. . . . We proceeded to make a schedule.

Easier said, of course, than done. And no doubt a few husbands, to prove how broadminded and understanding they were, agreed, as Roger did. But their hearts were not in it.

Taken alone, none of these items—and many more like them—seems to be all that important for the future of marriage. But they add up. Girls not falling all over themselves for the attentions of young men? Young women rejecting the chivalrous gestures of their dates? Young women not only declining sexual relations—a very old pattern—but actively belittling them? Young women turning down marriage for heaven only knows what reasons? Wives asking for a wholly new definition of sexual roles and functions in the household? Strong clues, I believe, to the future of marriage.

Since the female prophets are not at all a homogeneous or standardized or stereotypical set of women, they do not all espouse all the same points of view on all issues. Each approaches the basic issues of marriage in her own way, giving it her own stamp. If a prism can fracture white light into a range of colors, so, analogously, can a figurative prism fracture the female prophets into an indeterminate array ranging all the way from fiery ferocity to lyric tenderness. At one end, Betsy Warrior, arguing like Jonathan Swift, that man is an obsolete life form and ought to be wiped out or, as an alternative, preserved only in zoos; at the other end, Ellen O'Donnell, who asks of her lover:

Let Me Eat Cake!

Make me a gift of words, love.
For every day
Frost, Emerson or Whitman.
They are poetry's bread and butter.
On Sundays a feast from the Rubiyat
Or the Song of Solomon.
Speak the words woven for Isolde
before you bed me down.
The line to the heart
comes from the ear,
for when I'm steeped in grief
diamonds and pearls are cold.
I cannot be true to stones.
The words of love
are my boundary.
When we're gray and misshapen
I'll warm to words of love.
As I demand the best in love only
You cannot afford to give me less.

what do you mean, "liberation"?

The nineteenth-century term *emancipation* implied
freedom from legal constraints. The twentieth-century
term *liberation* is subtler. It means freedom from psychological as well as from legal or political constraints,
freedom from the pressures, often unspoken, that as
persistently as and even more insistently than the
formal, verbal ones, force certain life patterns on
women.

To be sure, at the day-by-day level, some of the
specific, concrete, and immediate issues involved in
achieving liberation do deal with such commonplace
issues as abortion, birth control, child care, education,
paid employment, and the like. Some of the women
prophets share such issues with old-line feminists, male
and female; but other issues they make their own. The
specific bread-and-butter issues are far from being the
overriding and major ones. The critical form of libera-

tion for them is on a different plane. Of the many statements defining the word *liberation* as used by the women prophets, this editorial from a radical women's journal, *Women, A Journal of Liberation,* is especially relevant for a discussion of the future of marriage:

Liberation: A Widening of Choices. Liberation means choice among alternatives, something which has consistently been denied women. Women have been conditioned to accept passive roles in which all major decisions are made by nature or by men. The major choice in a woman's life is who her husband will be, and he then will determine all future choices. In another way, marriage can be seen as a way of avoiding the difficult and serious human choice of establishing an identity and purpose in life. To achieve liberation, each person must discover herself as an individual with significance in her own right. A woman cannot fulfill herself through her children or through her husband; she must do it alone. Identity comes only through making choices and liberation is the process of obtaining ever-wider choices for people.

Liberation meant, in this context, release from the restrictions imposed by stereotyped sex roles. It meant autonomy, belief in oneself, self-confidence, independence of rather than subservience to male-determined standards.

Liberation was not, however, liberation from men per se but liberation from what they labeled sexism. Thus, Laurel Limpus tells us, "when I speak of female liberation, I mean liberation from the myths that have enslaved and confined women in their own minds as well as in the minds of others. I don't mean liberation from men. Both men and women are virtually oppressed by a culture and a heritage that mutilates the relationships possible between them." In this sense, liberation was a far more profound desideratum than the more superficial issues of child care or abortion. It was a fundamental reorientation of the relations between the sexes.

As an experience, liberation was analogous to religious conversion. Men as well as women who came to scoff remained to pray. It happened not as the result of debate or of the marshaling of rational arguments; all the facts on which it rested had been common knowledge to almost everyone for centuries. What happened in the experience of liberation was the—sometimes sudden—restructuring of these facts. Even the most sophisticated, the most resistant, found themselves converted, "liberated."

the "idolatry" of marriage

Liberation as a widening of choices included alternatives to marriage. As related specifically to marriage, the women prophets were speaking out against the idolatry of marriage, the compulsion they were made to feel to get married, the oppressive stereotypes and put-downs of the unmarried woman.

We referred earlier to Rozanne Brooks's experiment which showed how erroneous the stereotype could be, but it persists as an almost punishing reminder of failure in the major enterprise of women, the achievement of marriage.

Understandably, therefore, women resisted admitting even to themselves that they did not want to marry because it was assumed that there must be something wrong with the unmarried. In the 1950s women had been convinced that not to get married was indeed a fate worse than death, for without marriage, one could not be completely fulfilled. College seniors were struck with "senior panic" if they did not have some kind of marital commitment before they got their degrees.

The marriages which the women prophets saw about them, even the so-called companionate marriages, did not look all that good to them. As they saw it, there was still no equality. They saw marriages that favored husbands; they saw marriage as an agency of oppression. They took a hard look at the marriages of their mothers, of their friends, even of their sisters in the radical movements. They were not impressed. They were, in fact, depressed. And came to feel oppressed. It looked to them as though marriage was for women one of the most oppressive institutions of the establishment. Some became virulently antimarriage. Some were not so much antimarriage as pro nonmarriage. Some were for marriage, but for a quite different form from that of the immediate past and present.

When we were discussing the 1970–1971 decline in the marriage rate in chapter 8, we warned against taking it too definitively. It could be just a random fluctuation rather than a change of trend. And even if it were a genuine change in trend, it might be only a response to the recession or to the availability of abortion. Or it could result from the "marriage squeeze," which results some twenty years after an upturn in the birthrate while girls wait for their male peers to catch up to them. We are suggesting here that it might also reflect a new attitude toward marriage itself, and thus adumbrate new alternatives for women.

antimarriage prophets

While male prophets were devising more varieties of marriage, some of the female prophets were arguing against it altogether. There were several bases for their stance. Some, like Roxanne Dunbar, argued against marriage because revolution was a full-time occupation, leaving no time for purely personal concerns. They called upon women to leave houses, brothers, sisters, father, mother, children, land, to give single-minded dedication to their salvation. It sounds absurd. Still, how does it differ, when you come to think about it, from the same rationale for celibate religious orders?

Other radical female prophets objected to marriage not only because of what they felt it did to women but also because, like their conservative opposite numbers, they saw it as a major support of the status quo. But whereas conservatives argued for strengthening marriage because they wanted the status quo protected and preserved, the radical women argued against it because they did not. They were against marriage precisely because, as Judith Brown put it, it did shore up and support the status quo:

The institution of marriage . . . is a potent instrument for maintaining the status quo in American society. It is in the family that children learn so well the dominance-submission game, by observation and participation. Each family, reflecting the perversities of the larger order and split off from the others, is powerless to force change on other institutions, let alone attack or transform its own. And this serves the Savage Society well.

Still others argued against marriage not only because it was conservative, but also because it was antirevolutionary in the sense that it deflected the righteous anger of workers against their exploiters. The wife who offered an emotional refuge to her husband from the jungle warfare of occupational competition was supporting a nonhumane system. Fran Ansley is speaking here:

Women serve as "lightning rods" for men's frustrations at other factors in their environment. This can be especially serviceable for the ruling class. Often it is the man of the family who experiences most directly the real power relationships in the society. (He sells his labor to a capitalist who then exploits him; he has a direct relation to industrial production; etc.) When wives play their traditional role as takers of shit, they often absorb their husbands' legitimate anger and frustration at their own powerlessness and oppression. With every worker provided with a sponge to soak up his possibly revolutionary ire, the bosses rest more secure. Chauvinist attitudes help to maintain this asocial system of tension-release.

But it is once more a case in which the woman pays. The mental health of men, their balance, is preserved by the ministrations of their wives, who salve the wounds inflicted on them by the outside world. The real beneficiaries in this framework are employers and exploiters of men against whom the aggression of unsoothed men would wreak itself. All is at the expense of wives, says Beverly Jones: "the inequalitarian relationships in the home are perhaps the basis of all evil. Men can commit any horror, or cowardly suffer any mutilation of their souls and retire to the home to be treated there with awe, respect, and perhaps love. Men will never face their true identity or their real problems under these circumstances, nor will we."

Some argued against marriage because it was so oppressive for women. They translated the material presented in chapter 3 into polemics. This was how Judith Brown saw it:

The married woman knows that love is, at its best, an inadequate reward for her unnecessary and bizarre heritage of oppression. The marriage institution does not free women; it does not provide for emotional and intellectual growth; and it offers no political resources. Were it not for male-legislated discrimination in employment, it would show little economic advantage. Instead, she is locked into a relationship which is oppressive politically, exhausting physically, stereotyped emotionally and sexually, and atrophying intellectually. She teams up with an individual groomed from birth to rule, and she is equipped for revolt only with the foot-shuffling, head-scratching gesture of "feminine guile." . . . Marriage . . . is the atomization of a sex so as to render it politically powerless. The anachronism remains because women won't fight it, because men derive valuable benefits from it and will not give them up.

Some argued against marriage because it did not provide a suitable unit for the rearing of children. "There is," said Roxanne Dunbar, "little reality in the human relations in this society, and least of all in marriage. Ask the children what they think of the institution which supposedly exists for their upbringing, their benefit. All the love between 'man and woman' in the world will not make that tiny unit any less lonely, any less perverted to the child who is raised within it."

A few, finally, fought marriage because they hated men. In reply to the "official" position against man-hating among the female prophets, one of them—

Pamela Kearon—made a plea for open recognition of its existence in the displaced form of hatred of other women: "there is no dearth of hatred in the world. I agree. . . . People do not react to oppression with Love. . . . When women take their hatred out on others, those others are likely to be other women. . . . If hatred exists (and we know it does), let it be of a robust variety. If it is a choice between woman-hating and man-hating, let it be the latter."

It is doubtful whether these antimarriage arguments had much effect on the marriage rate. But the fact that they could be articulated, whether accepted or rejected, cannot help but affect the future of marriage. The idolatry of marriage was finally being challenged.

prophets for nonmarriage: celibacy

Some of the women prophets were not positively and aggressively opposed to marriage. They were not fighting it. Their stance was one of non- rather than anti-marriage, a side effect of their groping for a way of life suitable for women not oriented toward men. Among some of them there was even a reevaluation of celibacy. In an age that was exalting sexuality, they were willing to come out in defense of celibacy.

We commented in chapter 9 on how wrong Gilbert D. Bartell was in assigning to the Woman's Liberation Movement any part in the explanation of swinging. Absurd as he was, Hugh Hefner—who prided himself on having liberated men sexually from the *Ladies' Home Journal* brand of sexuality—was nearer the mark when he accused the female prophets of antisexualism. They were anti *his* brand of sexualism. To the extent that men had appropriated sex, made it their own exclusive prerogative, their domain, claimed monopolistic ownership of it, taken charge of it, defined it for women, yes, of course, the female prophets admitted, they were antisexualists; but only anti-male-sexualist. The exalting of the woman's right to sexual fulfillment had proved to be only a gimmick to increase the power of men over women.

Dana Densmore, in "On Celibacy," notes the enormous emphasis being placed on sexuality as a roadblock on the way to liberation. The "supposed need" for sex had therefore to be "refuted, coped with, demythified, or the cause of female liberation is doomed." Usually "what passes for sexual need is actually desire to be stroked; desire for recognition or love; desire to conquer, humiliate, or wield power; or desire to communicate." True, "it gives a lift and promises a spark of individual self-assertion in a dull and routinized world . . . [and] compared to the dullness and restrictiveness of the rest of her life it glows very brightly." But at great cost. "Already we see girls, thoroughly liberated in their own heads, understanding their oppression with terrible clarity trying, deliberately and a trace hysterically, to make themselves attractive to men, men for whom they have no respect, men they may even hate, because of 'a basic sexual-emotional need'" that had been programmed into them. To achieve genuine liberation "we must come to realize that we don't need sex. . . . How repugnant it really is, after all, to make love to a man who despises you, who fears you and wants to hold you down! Doesn't screwing in an atmosphere devoid of respect get pretty grim? Why bother? You don't need it." Then the clincher. "Celibacy is not a dragon but even a state that could be desirable." Not a last resort; not an imposition; not a stigma. Not merely a negative withdrawal from sexual activity but a positive, active movement toward a goal.

Such secular advocacy of celibacy was not without precedents. A great early pioneer in women's higher education, Vida Scudder of Wellesley College, had once written a cogent, if less passionate, apologia for celibacy a generation ago. Yes, it had its drawbacks. But so did marriage. And, like marriage, it had its advantages. She may, she admitted, have missed out on "something . . . supremely precious" but, she was quick to add, "had it come to me, how much it would have excluded!" She had lived a satisfying and fruitful life. And, she had added, "I confess that married life looks to me often as I watch it terribly impoverished for women." Dana Densmore was merely picking up, after the hiatus of a generation, where earlier feminists had left off.

We have had occasion several times to note that not everyone had marital aptitude, and, conversely, that marriage is not the best design for living for everyone. There are people for whom celibacy *is* the best life style. It is as cruel to pressure them into marriage as it would be to pressure out of marriage those for whom celibacy would be intolerable.

At the other extreme from those who made the case for celibacy on secular grounds were the female prophets who invoked a religious sanction for it. "Some people," the poet Ellen O'Donnell reminds us, "were born with the secret of loving. As children they abhorred the violence of playmates with their toy soldiers, guns, and battles. They preferred the beauty in music, nature's collage, and the playmates in books at home. They were content to observe these things rather than reach out, trying to mold things to their will [for] in reaching out in physical love there is still the desire to mold the other person's energy under the guise of togetherness. If they were lucky they were allowed to enter cloisters. I think they joined these orders because the order existed rather than from strict religious expression. It does seem that celibacy would be worthwhile in order to preserve the quietness ('be still and know that I am God') needed for graceful loving."

The persistence of religious celibacy is evidence enough that for a substantial portion of the population it is not only a prescribed but also a desired life style. One young suburban housewife noted wistfully that she thought she was living in the wrong century. "I would have been completely at home in the medieval convent of a contemplative order. I can think of nothing I would rather do than sit and study and ruminate all day long." Even academia until not too long ago almost prescribed a monastic life style; Alice Freeman, first president of Wellesley, was severely castigated when she resigned to marry. There may not be many priests manqués in the executive suites of corporations, but there are doubtless quite a few nuns manquées in the kitchens and nurseries of suburbia.

No more than the revolutionary argument against marriage would the celibacy argument have a great impact on the marriage rate. Its impact would not be so much on the actions of young women, leading them to forswear marriage, as on their feelings about it. To those, whatever their number, for whom celibacy was a genuine preference, it would no longer be an impossible alternative.

nonmarriage: autonomy and upgrading the career girl

Other female prophets advised nonmarriage simply as a means for achieving autonomy. They advised women to remain single and, in Lisa Leghorn's words, "to deal with the problems of being a woman alone and free, living autonomously in control of their own lives." Liberation did not demand celibacy, but, marriage being what it was, abstention from marriage was vitally necessary. Nonmarriage might or might not involve celibacy; that was not the important issue. "Until we acquire enough self-confidence to realize that we should want no part of a relationship in which we are reduced to so few possibilities and such a low level of humanity, there is no shame involved with abstention from these kinds of relationships with men. At this point in history, this is the only way we can become total persons. We are working hard to overcome those weaknesses that we have acquired in the course of our personal and collective histories. Until men wake up and start to work towards overcoming their oppressive attitudes, it is certainly healthier for us to stay away. The excitement of now available opportunities for the self-respect that we gain is fantastic reward. This freed state of mind provides immense amounts of energy which can only allow a more constructive and progressive existence."

There were others, too, who were arguing to make available to women the "excitement" of new opportunities, for the female prophets were not the only ones who in the 1960s were attacking the idolatry of marriage and casting about for alternative life styles for women and for ways to ameliorate the status of the unmarried woman. The Women's Liberation Movement just happened to coincide with growing pressures to lower the birthrate. Not only women, but men also became interested in upgrading nonmarriage.

In the 1970s, the stereotype of the neurotic spinster, for example, was being attacked head-on by men as well as by women. Roberta Hornig tells of one man who suggested that reading primers should portray "Aunt Debbie" as pretty, holding down a good job, and having a "hell of a fine time." Instead of, as now, learning only one life style for women, that girls grew up to be mothers, Dick and Jane should learn about other alternatives. They needed a sexy Aunt Debbie, "who likes men and loves children . . . but mainly in small doses." Such an Aunt Debbie was not necessarily to be portrayed as the ideal woman "but as an alternative one, so that the unmarried career girl is not held up as a freak."

Another attack on the spinster stereotype—on grounds admittedly not congenial to the female prophets—was suggested by Helen Gurley Brown, who, protesting against the campaign of the women's magazines in behalf of "getting a man," pointed out that "single women are too brainwashed to figure out what married women know but won't admit, what married men and single men endorse in a body, and that is that the single woman, far from being a creature to be pitied and patronized, is emerging as the newest glamour girl of our times. She is engaging because she lives by her wits. She supports herself. She has had to sharpen her personality and mental resources to a glitter in order to survive in a competitive world and the sharpening looks good. Economically she is a dream. She is not a parasite, a dependent, a scrounger, a sponger, or a bum. She is a giver, not a taker, a winner and not a loser."

This is a bit overdrawn on the glamour side, to be sure, for as yet the truly exciting occupations are not open to women. But more of the so-called single professions ought to be open to nonmarrying women, Shulamith Firestone tells us. Actually, they have almost disappeared even for men: "the old single roles, such as the celibate religious life, court roles—jester, musician, page, knight, and loyal squire—cowboys, sailors, firemen, cross-country truck drivers, detectives, pilots had a prestige all their own: there was no stigma attached to being professional single." She quotes an economist, Richard Meier, to the effect that glamorous professions like, for example, astronaut, formerly assigned exclusively to men should now be opened to women as well. Why, one might ask, only the glamorous professions? (And wouldn't it be more sensible to encourage all women, regardless of marital status, to find congenial work? Shulamith Firestone is quite right in stating that "a single life organized around the demands of a chosen profession, satisfying the individual's social and emotional needs through its own particular occupational structure, might be an appealing [alternative to marriage] . . . in the transitional period." But the same kind of chosen profession could upgrade marriage also and serve equally well as a depressant to the birthrate.)

Nonmarriage in this career-oriented form does not mean celibacy. But sexual freedom is far from being a major, or even an important value, certainly among the women making blueprints for the future. Men might dream of more sexual freedom if that was their thing; but to women, sexual freedom had proved to be a great disappointment. Inside or outside of marriage, what they were seeking was better, not more, sex.

better, not more, sex

Our previous discussion of sex implied a stable relationship between the partners. Some of the liaisons proposed as alternatives to marriage for the future do not. In such often unstructured situations, sexual relations are different; they involve hazards for women not originally envisaged by advocates of greater freedom. Outside of marriage the vision of sexual varietism that looked so delectable to the male prophets came to look like a nightmare to many of the female prophets. It was not in their blueprints for the future.

The turn of the century had been a sexual revolution which liberated women from the Victorian attitude of compulsory frigidity. A process that I have called "re-sexualization" of the female body took place that was all to the good. The new viewpoint was regarded as a triumph, for women could now enjoy sexual relations as well as men. It proved to be more complicated than anticipated.

With no model of sexual relations based on their own sexuality rather than on male definitions of it to guide them, the first reaction of women was to imitate the male model of sexuality. That was the only way that occurred to them. They began to treat men as objects, as men had long treated them, so that now there were two treating each other merely as means for securing sexual gratification. That, however regrettable, was first seen as "natural," Judi Bernstein notes, "given that people are taught, in order to keep them alienated from one another, to treat other people as the object of their wants and needs and not as human beings." But imitating men they found to be a dead end; even worse, it was, they finally concluded, sick and destructive. "Women of high ideals who believed emancipation possible, women who tried desperately to rid themselves of feminine 'hangups,' to cultivate what they believed to be the greater directness, honesty, and generosity of men, were badly fooled," Shulamith Firestone tells us. " 'Emancipated' women . . . found that by imitating male sexual patterns . . . they were not only achieving liberation, they were falling into something much worse than what they had given up. They were *imitating*. And they had inoculated themselves with a sickness that had not even sprung from their own psyches. They found that their new 'cool' was shallow and meaningless, that their emotions were drying up behind it, that they were aging and becoming decadent; they feared they were losing their ability to love. They had gained nothing by imitating men: shallowness and callowness, and they were not so good at it either, because somewhere inside it still went against the grain."

The switch from the Victorian sexual ethos to the one of complete equality in sexual encounters had accelerated at such a rate that by midcentury it had become as mandatory for women to be sexy as in the nineteenth it had been for them to be frigid. Now, for example, they were being told in *Cosmopolitan* by Barbara Bross, a gynecologist, that "sexual abstinence in a normally constituted person is always pathogenic. We have been given sex organs to use them. If we don't use them, they decay and cause irreparable damage to body and mind. This is blunt, firm, indisputable, and true." So far as the female prophets were concerned, the new norm was no better than the old. It got to the point where men expected women "to be raving sex maniacs," complained Dana Densmore. "This frantic interest in sex is a reversal of our puritan mores; the reversal is of such fanatic proportions as to make one wonder which is worse—the disease or the cure." An anonymous participant in a talk session bemoaned "this obsession with frigidity and orgasms. Frankly I get bored with the subject."

As some of the unanticipated consequences of the new point of view became apparent, it came to be seen as an actual as well as a potential weapon against women. If a woman did not want to have relations with a man he could call her deviant; if she did, he could define his part as, in effect, sexual ministration to her needs not, therefore, calling, in addition, for tenderness and concern. "If you don't want to sleep with him, he assumes it's because you're hung-up and then you have to stay up the whole night anyway convincing him you're not! . . . It's almost easier to go to bed and get it over with." On the assumption that sexual relations were a fifty-fifty enterprise, women no longer had the right to ask for anything more: "women today dare not make the old demands," Shulamith Firestone pointed out, "for fear of having a whole new vocabulary, designed just for this purpose, hurled at them: 'fucked-up,' 'ball-breaker,' 'cockteaser,' 'a real drag,' 'a bad trip,' etc."

The new pattern of relationships were posited on a concept of female sexuality which did not conform to the facts. As long as the old status relationships between men and women remained, sexual freedom could be exploitative of women. They were still engaging in sexual relations to please the men, not themselves. They were still sex objects. All the women were getting was "sexual exploitation, pure and simple" for the new attitude toward sex served the interests of men, not of women: "the rhetoric of the sexual revolution, if it brought no improvement for women, proved to have great value for men. By convincing women that the usual female games and demands were despicable, unfair, prudish, old-fashioned, puritanical, and self-destructive," Shulamith Firestone notes, "a new reservoir of available females was created to expand the tight supply of sexual goods available for traditional exploitation, disarming women of even the little protection they had so painfully acquired." The camaraderie which the women had been led to take for granted had backfired. Neither the old Victorian nor the new liberalized point of view produced genuinely liberated women; each only bound them in a different way.

One of the most persistent themes—dogmas, in fact —of the new sexual morality, as Ira Reiss has shown, has been that the quality of the relationship defines its morality. If the partners have a warm and affectionate relationship, whatever they do is, in effect, all right. We noted that the teachings of the seventeenth-century divines that love justified marriage had been interpreted by young people to mean that love justified sexual relations outside as well as inside of the marital bond. But who, the female prophets were now asking, defines the quality of the relationship? Women, trained from infancy to please men, could easily be led to validate the male's definition of the situation as good. *This* relationship has honest; *this* partner really cared. So the male-defined relationship justified sexual relations.

Only gradually did it dawn on women that this path led to destruction. They found themselves in bed with men they did not care for, too well-socialized in the female role to let the men know how incompatible— often even loathsome—they were as sex partners. Here are excerpts from a female rap session in 1968:

At the risk of sounding naive . . . I've been listening to this for an hour and no one has mentioned love.

Love?

God, if I waited to fall in love, I'd be climbing the walls.

Yeah, forget love. If you even just like him. . . .

Forget like. I'd be happy if I could only respect the guy *a little bit.*

Respect—forget it. If you can even talk to him at all, you're lucky.

Even just small talk. About the morning orange juice.

If you can even stand to wake up next to him. . . .

. . . can stand having his head on your pillow!

(A shocked silence.)

Do you realize what we're saying? Not only have we been

sleeping with guys we don't love, but with guys we positively can't stand.

What are we doing it *for*?

Well (with a sigh), looks like we're back where we started. Doing it for every reason but the right one.

This is frightening. I mean, we shouldn't have to give up concern for good relationships to prove we're free.

These women were perceptive enough to recognize that in the new situation "men really aren't free either. . . . Sensitive men admit they're unhappy sleeping around. They feel cheap and empty too. [For] that Don-Juan-Playboy Mystique is just as false as its reverse, the Terrible Tramp. . . . Men are unhappy too in the role of empty conqueror."

The female prophets, in brief, were longing for a future with more than merely sexual contact between men and women. Outside as well as inside of marriage. Certainly for far more than mere orgasm. They were asking for a relationship with men which would make sexual relations meaningful; they did not want to be sex objects, conveniences. They wanted to relate to men on a level which would make the purely sexual relationship more than a merely physical one.

Some of the women even recognized that their ideas were precisely what all those old disillusioned fogies had been talking about. Shulamith Firestone was herself surprised to find how similar her charges were to the old clichés: "more and more women . . . find out too late and bitterly that the traditional female games had a point: they are shocked to catch themselves at thirty complaining in a vocabulary dangerously close to the old I've-been-used-men-are-wolves-they're-all-bastards variety." The position of women had come almost full circle. They were almost back where they had started but not on the same plane. They were not looking back to the old pedestal, although it is not unthinkable that some of the reluctantly swapped wives referred to in chapter 9 may have given it at least an occasional nostalgic glance. These women were looking, rather, for more than merely sexual way for men and women to relate to one another. Inside or outside of marriage, better, not more, sex was their hope for the future.

Not all, or even many, of the female prophets were either anti- or non-marriage. Most were pro-marriage, but not for marriage in its traditional form. Many paralleled the male prophets in their designs for the future of marriage. Thus, in an outline called "Is There Life After Marriage?" a group at Chapel Hill, North Carolina, proposed several alternatives to marriage, including: (1) trial marriage, renewable or not after a given period of time; (2) companionate marriage, designed not to have children; (3) marriage as now set up, but divorce by mutual consent and no financial responsibility for either partner toward the other, as in the commitment described in chapter 5; (4) group marriage; and (5) a "write-your-own-ticket" kind of relationship. Margaret Mead proposed a two-step marriage. Other proposals included provision for homosexual marriages and even for nonsexual unions.

"personhood" the goal

Whatever the form of the commitment, the goal of the relationship between partners sought by the female prophets was what they called "personhood." They were searching for a relationship in which the wife would not be a nonentity, in which she could retain an identity of her own, in which she was not absorbed. Some felt that this goal was better achieved without the formal commitment of marriage. As an illustration of the "write-your-own-ticket" alternative to conventional marriage, we offer here the case of Theodora Wells and Lee S. Christie, the mature couple whose commitment we presented in chapter 5:

We chose to live together rather than marry. I am Theo, forty-four, chronicler of the tale. My female sex-roles include:

daughter, daughter-in-law, wife, mother, stepmother, divorcée, aunt, grandmother, lover, and now—consort. Lee fifty-one, has almost as good a collection of male sex-roles. This is our position paper.

"Personhood" is central to the living-together relationship; sex-roles are central to the marriage relationship. Our experience strongly suggests that personhood excites growth, stimulates openness, increases joyful satisfactions in achieving, encompasses rich, full sexuality peaking in romance.

Marriage may have the appearance of this in its romantic phase, but it settles down to prosaic routine where detail invades ideas, talk scatters thought, quiet desperation encroaches, and sexuality diminishes to genital joining. Personhood is renewing of self, sex-roles are denigrating of self.

To us, personhood means that each person accepts primary responsibility for tending to his or her own physical, mental, emotional, sexual, and spiritual growth. It means bringing to the relationship two healthy, growing persons who want to share their strengths and who offer secondary support to each other's growth processes. Also, both persons bring human needs that can only be met with another, but they are not needy in the sense of having to make excessive or neurotic demands that the other must meet.

The female sex-role is least like personhood and therefore more denigrating than the male sex-role.

On the asset side, the "truly feminine woman" is warm, nurturing, likes to please others, soft, pliable, cooperative, pretty, good at detail, giving of herself, charitable, moral, and of religious spirit.

On the liability side, she is a bit helpless, not good with figures nor conceptual thought, moody and illogical, crying to get her way, dependent, needing approval and praise, biologically defective, and subject to "penis envy."

As a girl she is brought up to find fulfillment in "her man," rather than achieve something on her own. Her name is taken from her when she marries; she becomes simply "Mrs. Him." She is not to excel, if she expects to get married. (No one asks her if she wants to marry, because marriage is the only acceptable choice.) She learns to downgrade the capabilities of her mind, and to fail. Competing with other girls for the "best catch," she learns not to trust other women and so becomes isolated from them as potential friends with genuine persons.

After she marries, she is supposed to confine herself to her husband and no other men. This effectively cuts her off from friendships with the other half of the population. When babies come, her world is home, pets, children, and repairmen. Surrounded by material comforts, she is indeed ungrateful if she complains, and it proves that "you can't please a woman." If she settles cheerfully into her role, she proves that that is her "nature."

Any woman who does something on her own, who competes and excels, is subject to the charge of "not being feminine." The highest praise of all is "You think like a man!"

In short, the female sex-role defines woman by her sexual function of childbearing and nurturing "instincts." By performing sexual and maintenance services for the male, she "earns" her way as an economic dependent. At the same time, the male sex-role prescribes the man's obligation to be achieving and responsible. These patterns, which radiate out into all aspects of living, are held as cultural values to be transmitted by all our social institutions.

Lee and I are rejecting marriage, the most basic of these institutions. As a woman, I have been through every bit of the denigrating vicious circle, while working toward personhood. I choose to keep my own unique way because I must. Anything else is self-chosen insanity, now that I know what I do. The wife role is diametrically opposed to the personhood I want. I therefore choose to live with the man who joins me in the priority of personhood. . . .

We choose living together, and find ourselves designing a new pattern of man-woman relatedness. We appreciate the value of a long-term, continuing, growing relationship. As we see it, we are joined in a commitment-for-growth. . . . We've lived together for a period approaching two years, but we don't know how long we will stay together. We feel, however, that the freedom to rechoose each other whenever we want to reduces the risk of separation.

So much, then, for the alternatives to marriage, ranging all the way from celibacy to living together without the formal legal commitment. They should be enough to support the belief I expressed at the beginning of this chapter, that these ideas are bound to have an enormous impact on the future of marriage, that after the critiques of marriage made by these women, it would never be the same again.

Even granting this, however, by far the largest proportion of women are still attempting to achieve personhood within the bonds of conventional marriage. Not all agree with Theo that "the wife role is diametrically opposed to personhood." At least not necessarily so. They are trying to prove her proposition wrong by redefining wifehood as compatible with personhood. They have learned that they cannot do it alone. Many of them are learning how to achieve personhood by way of sisterhood, which, they are finding, is indeed powerful and far more radical and revolutionary than most of the other proposals for the future.

achieving personhood in marriage: sisterhood

Everything the female prophets were saying and doing was more or less revolutionary. And much of it was unspeakably painful. They were attacking the inertia, literally, of millennia, with weapons no more powerful than justice, all by themselves, one by one. They were therefore extremely vulnerable. The sheer weight of the system was against them. So where did all this power come from? How was it possible all of a sudden for women to stand up to men? Like Gabrielle, to their own husbands? Or, like Hilary, to their lovers? How could they say no, thank you—or rather, for that matter, just no.

It came from loyal and supportive contacts with other women who shared and therefore understood their plight. Husbands had always known such contacts to be subversive of their own interests. Plutarch's *Rules for Husbands and Wives*, for example, had included one to the effect that "the wife ought not to make friends of her own but in common with her husband enjoy his friends." Mirabel, in *The Way of the World*, specified that his wife was to have no conspiratorial friends. The Lysistrata model has been accepted as gospel, literally good news for men: women could not successfully organize because they were more bound to individual men than to one another by common interests. And that was the way it had to be.

They might attend bridge clubs, yes, and garden clubs, and sewing circles, and church groups, and take part in all the other activities that helped wives while away their time and thus free men from any responsibility for their leisure hours. Great. But that did not alleviate their dependencies or their loneliness or their basic psychological isolation. They carried their isolation with them. They took part in these activities always as private individuals, secretive about their personal relations, protective of their husbands, always on a very superficial level. To bare their souls would have exposed them either to shocked contempt or juicy gossip or, at least, humiliating pity. Or an implicit, Shut up; don't you know that's the way things are? So all her personal problems with her husband remained hers alone—and her fault alone. No matter how many contacts women had with one another they remained either competitors or separate individuals. Without mutual support.

Confidantes, yes. Lower-class women have traditionally resorted to female relatives, but mainly for emotional patching-up work, rarely for reasoned, rational analyses of their situation. And the outside world has always tended to be protective of the husbands, hostile to anyone who supported a wife in her grievances against them. Mirra Komarovsky, on the basis of her study of blue-collar marriage, is of the opinion that having confidantes with whom she could share her marital woes saved the emotional balance of many a wife and even, in some cases, made it possible for her to be content with her marriage. But men have been intuitively suspicious of such sharing. To them, as Willard Waller perceptively noted, "the secrets of marriage are among its important assets." Not the least, for husbands, maintaining the isolation of the wife.

Now the female prophets were tearing down the walls of isolation. Look, we're all in this together. It isn't just a personal problem between you and your husband. It isn't your fault. It isn't something the matter with you.

All women, Beverly Jones told them, carry around "a strange and almost identical little bundle of secrets." And it is *not* disloyal to divulge them. We need one another; no one of us can go it alone. And Judith Brown added that "if we are to . . . preserve our marriages, it will require group approaches." So a new form of organization among women sprang up. No longer bridge or book reviews or knitting, now it was their own consciousness of themselves as human beings that the organization was all about. In small groups married women found sisterhood. And it was powerful. It supported them, broke down their isolation, gave them respite from the constant demands being made on them. The essential isolation which had made them vulnerable as they faced the world, one by one, like the Greeks at Thermopylae, was at least partially breached. Gabrielle Burton describes her group:

In our group, we speak intimately of our personal experiences. . . . At our weekly discussions, we piece together these common parts of our experiences to recognize prevailing conditions that stifle us all. We carefully look at society to see what it has done to us and what we can do about it. . . . In the past, spouses, priests, economists, and sociologists told us what we were and what we should be. Now each of us is making that decision. However, one quickly realizes that there are no personal "solutions" possible. This is because it is not a personal "problem." . . . In the group we use a specialized way to talk to one another, called raising consciousness. This technique increases our sensitivity to the various forms of oppression in our lives. In order to adjust successfully to our conditions, most of us have had to develop elaborate blinders. Raising consciousness helps us recognize our blinders, let out our angers and frustrations so that we can take hold of our lives and rechannel ourselves. Ideally one raises consciousness to the point where one can and must change her life. . . . I have learned to think again through the weekly discussions. . . . Roger always used to say, "I think what Gabrielle means is . . ." Now I am able to make my thoughts intelligible all by myself. . . . Every woman in our group has made at least one major change in her life during the past year. We have returned to school, begun careers, severed oppressive relationships. Aspirations are sky-high, and we are fulfilling them. We don't have men come to our group. Many women find it extremely difficult to speak in front of men; they defer to them or are dishonest in their presence. Most men find it difficult to keep quiet and listen without presenting a defense or examples of how they are oppressed too.... Women are our main concern. We look at things in "her" focus. We concentrate on preserving our strengths and strengthening our weaknesses and working together as women. Someday, hopefully, everyone will be able to relate to anyone as people, not as men or women, or roles. Right now we are finding ourselves as women; we are discovering what that means.... This is a basic social change and it's happening right now.... We are learning to love and respect women and, in the process, to love and respect ourselves. We are also changing the world.

Gabrielle's marriage, in case anyone is interested, is one of the best on record.

Unless one has observed it in action, it is impossible to believe the change that such groups can have on a marriage. The weekly consciousness-raising group has a life span of about a year. To supply the recharging that may be necessary after that, Marilyn Terry, as well as others, has proposed that provision be made for "a room of her own," that is, a place where women could retreat from the exigencies of their lives when the pressures overwhelmed them, where they would not be at the beck and call of those around them, where they could stop for a little while being wives and mothers and be individuals in their own right. Women could move into such centers for a longer or shorter period of time during crisis periods of their lives or at times of great decision. They would be analogous in their protective function to such male prototypes as the "club" of the upper-class Englishman, but totally different in form, or analogous to the neighborhood pub of the lower-class Englishman, the first with its exclusion of women and the second with its separate "family entrance" to segregate women. The discovery of the power of sisterhood is one of the reasons why marriage will never be the same again.

Although commitment to sisterhood complements

rather than supplants the marriage commitment so that both partners can gain, such a benign consequence is not inevitable. Support from the group sometimes makes it possible for women to free themselves from oppressive relationships, something they would not have been able to do on their own. There are always stories floating around about the woman who divorced her husband after joining a consciousness-raising group, the implication being that it was the experience which was responsible for the divorce, not the quality of the marriage, as though such an outcome should be held against consciousness raising. Sometimes, on the other hand, the group is mainly a crutch that makes it possible for a woman to remain in a marriage despite its uncongeniality.

husbands

Husbands react to the new relationship in different ways. To some, the idea that their wives can achieve an identity on their own from other women rather than from them is threatening. The total dependence of wives on husbands for their identities has been, as much as their economic dependence for support, one of the husbands' most powerful weapons. Outside of her role as wife and mother, the wife had no separate, individuated existence. Achieving an identity, consciousness of herself as an independent human entity, reverberates through the marriage and transforms it in ways that disturb some husbands.

Some, like modern Plutarchs and Mirabels, forbid participation in consciousness-raising groups. Others ignore sisterhood; their lives are already so far apart from their wives, anyway, that they hardly even notice that something new has been added to the distance between them. Some, at first amused, become uneasy, especially if more or less drastic changes are called for —fewer valet services from the wife, greater input into the household operation from them, return of the wife to school or to a job.

Once they understand the liberation point of view, however, many husbands become as enthusiastic as their wives. They are delighted to be relieved of the full weight of their wives' dependencies, happy to find their wives individuals in their own right. The new relationship is far better than the old. It dawns on them that the game is more than worth the candle. Not easy, mind you. But being married to a lively women is far more rewarding to them than living with a compliant wife. Some even become envious; they covet similar liberation from their own isolation, imposed on them by the demands of their own careers.

My own blueprint for the future—the shared-roles marriage—depends on this new conception.

life styles

Important as the nature of the commitment between men and women was for the female prophets, the kind of life style suitable to women was equally so. For if the female prophets, as contrasted with the male prophets, were underemphasizing sex, they were playing up to a far greater extent than the men the importance of life styles, of ways to relieve women from the onerous burdens of the isolated household.

They rejected the way in which the nuclear family was supposed to live, the private, isolated household it was expected to maintain, and the standard division of labor and function it was supposed to conform to. Traditional patterns imposed intolerable burdens on women. Some kind of relief from them was a major goal.

Communal living? Perhaps. But certainly not according to the male blueprints which, though they might make generous provision for the sexual satisfaction of women, were not much concerned about other satisfactions. The female prophets dreamed of communes, if or when they did, with the idea of relieving women of the heavy weight of housekeeping chores. Unless they had that goal in mind, Beverly Jones pointed out, the woman in a commune was "likely to become a domestic slave for many rather than for one man. There should be absolute equality in all domestic work, child care, work outside the commune, and education."

A typical design for living approved among female prophets emphasizes ways to better the social relationships among family members; let the sexual relations take care of themselves. Here is one example, proposed by Beverly Jones:

Somebody has got to start designing communities in which women can be freed from their burdens long enough for them to experience humanity. Houses might be built around schools to be rented only to people with children enrolled in the particular school, and only as long as they were enrolled. This geographically confined community could contain cheap or cooperative cafeterias and a restaurant so that mothers would not have to cook. This not only would free the woman's time but would put her in more of a position of equality with Daddy when he comes home from work. The parents could both sit down and eat at the same time in front of and with the children, a far different scene from that of a conversing family being served by a harassed mother who rarely gets to sit down and is usually two courses behind. These geographic school complexes could also contain full-time nurseries. They could offer space for [musical] instrument, dance, and self-defense lessons. In other words, a woman could live in them and be relieved of cooking, child care for the greater part of the day, and chauffeuring. The center might even have nighttime or overnight baby-sitting quarters. Many women will be totally lost to us and to themselves if projects like this are not begun. And the projects themselves, by freeing a woman's time and placing her in innumerable little ways into more of a position of equality will go a long way toward restructuring the basic marital and parental relationships.

The young mothers I know long for some kind of neighborhood, though not necessarily organized around a school. They reject communes, attractive as the ideology is. They hesitate about cooperative living arrangements, though they do not reject the idea out of hand. A major roadblock is the absence of suitable housing for such cooperative living. What they dream about are blocks of houses in which congenial families with ideas like their own can live both their private and their community lives.

It is, we might note parenthetically in passing, a sobering thought that the future of marriage is severely restricted, at least so far as it depends on life styles, by the current supply of housing. Communal and cooperative life styles which release wives from the isolation they now suffer from can never take over as long as the present type of separate, individual dwelling units remains. They, in effect, embalm a concept of marriage and family characteristic of the past and stand in the way of a new conception more in conformity with this day and age.

the household: kinship surrogate?

Some of the female prophets want to go even further in "restructuring the basic marital and parental relationships." We said earlier that some young people today are thinking in terms of "nuclear fusion" rather than "nuclear fission," of a return to the large household rather than the preservation of the small family. The household would not, however, be a kinship unit but a group of people or "affinity group" selected for their congeniality rather than one based on blood ties. Before presenting one such blueprint suggested by Shulamith Firestone, let us examine the fate of the idea of kinship in our society and of the home as we have traditionally conceived it.

The concept of kinship, expressed in the folk saying "blood's thicker than water," was one of the most powerful ever created by the human imagination. It has

recognized for centuries that "kinfolk" do not necessarily love or even like one another; still brothers and
sisters recognize bonds among themselves even though
they may not see one another for years on end. Feelings
of responsibility to kin remain even when there is no
affection. A perfect stranger has a recognized right to
drop in on distant relatives with whom there has been
no contact for generations and have his claim to hos-
pitality honored. Recognition of the kinship tie is one
of the most extraordinary aspects of human history.
"Blood" has very little to do with it. It is a culturally
defined, not a biological, tie.

The last two centuries have seen a gradual attrition
of this remarkable phenomenon. We no longer take it
so much for granted. In fact, sociologists have to research it in detail in order to discover it and determine
to what extent it still persists. But the psychological
function served by kinship—that of supplying an unassailable and indestructible tie with a group of people
who had no choice but to accept you—remains. Is the
"affinity group" an adequate substitute?

At least some of the women seem to be groping toward a set of relationships that would supply the stability and security, if not necessarily the permanence,
formerly supplied by the family home. The new-style
marital commitments seem to make adequate provision
for the freedom that people crave; but do they make
enough provision for the security they also want?

Shulamith Firestone envisages a "stable reproductive
social structure" which she calls a "household" as a
surrogate for the old-style family unit:

This [stable reproductive social structure] I shall call a household rather than an extended family. The distinction is important. The word *family* implies biological reproduction and
some degree of division of labor by sex, and thus the traditional dependencies and resulting power relations, extending
over generations; though the size of the family—in this case,
the larger numbers of the "extended family"—may affect the
strength of this hierarchy, it does not change its structural

definition. "Household," however, connotes only a large grouping of people living together for an unspecified time, and with no specified set of interpersonal relations. How would a "household" operate?

Limited Contract. If the household replaced marriage perhaps we would at first legalize it in the same way—if this is necessary at all. A group of ten or so consenting adults of varying ages could apply for a license as a group in much the same way as a young couple today applies for a marriage license, perhaps even undergoing some form of ritual ceremony, and then might proceed in the same way to set up house. The household license would, however, apply only for a given period, perhaps seven to ten years, or whatever was decided on as the minimal time in which children needed a stable structure in which to grow up—but probably a much shorter period than we now imagine. If at the end of this period the group decided to stay together, it could always get a renewal. However, no single individual would be contracted to stay after this period, and perhaps some members of the unit might transfer out, or new members come in. Or, the unit could disband altogether.

There are many advantages to short-term households, stable compositional units lasting for only ten-year periods: the end of family chauvinism, built up over generations, of prejudices passed down from one generation to the next, the inclusion of people of all ages in the child rearing process, the integration of many age groups into one social unit, the breadth of personality that comes from exposure to many rather than to (the idiosyncrasies of) a few, and so on.

Children. A regulated percentage of each household—say one-third—would be children. . . . Responsibility for the early physical dependence of children would be evenly diffused among all members of the household. . . . Adults and older children would take care of babies for as long as they needed it, but since there would be many adults and older children sharing the responsibility—as in the extended family—one person would never be involuntarily stuck with it. . . . Enduring relationships between people of widely divergent ages would become common.

Legal Rights and Transfers. With the weakening and severance of the blood ties, the power hierarchy of the family would break down. . . . Women would be identical under the law with men. . . .

If the child for any reason did not like the household into which he had been born so arbitrarily, he would be helped to transfer out. . . .

[Adults could also transfer out but] the unit, for its own best economy, might have to place a ceiling on the number of transfers in or out, to avoid depletion, excessive growth, and/or friction.

Chores. The larger family-sized group (probably about fifteen people) would be more practical—the waste and repetition of the duplicate nuclear family unit would be avoided . . . without the loss of intimacy of the larger communal experiment. . . . Housework would have to be rotated equitably.

This blueprint does not specify the nature of the relationship between or among the adults in these households. Presumably, they might take a variety of forms. But, it is to be hoped, "all relationships would be based on love alone, uncorrupted by objective dependencies and the resulting class inequalities."

The importance of this dream for the future lies, it seems to me, in its recognition of a need not recognized by many of the other blueprints, a need supplied in the past by the home. The concept of a "home," which can serve as a firm, permanent, solid, stable base from which one can sally forth, confident that there is a secure place to return to, has not always been salient in the discussion of the future of marriage. In a world of increasing mobility and flux, the need for such an anchored base becomes even greater than in the past. The individual can tolerate a great deal of rootless movement if he knows that there is a place to return to. Until now the family home has provided this base. The prodigal son knew that he could return and that he would be accepted. But a variety of trends now operate to dissolve the whole concept. Fewer people are willing to return to the family home; there are fewer such rooted homes to return to.

Shulamith Firestone's household does not supply everything the family and the home once supplied to its members; the costs of which, she argues, were in any event too great. But it does fill in the interstices left unrecognized in most of the other blueprints. As in so much of the thinking of the female prophets, the emphasis is less on sexual relationships than on the care of children. Recognition is made of the fragility of the child's security when he has only his parents to depend on. With all his eggs in the one parental basket, his security hangs by a slender thread. The large household here envisioned would reduce the hazards implicit in such a relationship. In an analogous way we might say that it is hazardous for men and women to rely only on each other for the satisfaction of their dependency needs. In a large household like Shulamith Firestone's, one individual is not exclusively dependent on another individual; there are others to whom one can turn, male or female, if one's partner is not available for such support. Dependencies breed possessiveness, painful for both would-be possessor and possessed.

some of their best friends are men (even husbands)

This chapter has been built primarily around the dreams and hopes of women—for freedom from the pressure to marry, for interesting life styles outside of marriage, for communities built to relieve their load, for households designed for all ages and especially for children, and for commitments that permit them to achieve what they call "personhood." It is also about their fears —among them, mechanical sexual relationships. We end, not with equal time for men, but at least with a male statement of the women's case. Here is Richard Farson's way of putting it:

In the future we shall not think in terms of power relationships. The idea that one person is boss or that one person is the major influence will not be important: we shall find ourselves learning from our children. We shall find women increasingly making a place for themselves in the world and fulfilling themselves in such a way that they will refuse to be subservient to men. Now there is more prejudice against women than against any other group in our society. And though the prejudice is deeply entrenched—and though it is held by women even more than by men and though women may be the last "minority" to achieve equality—I am sure women will take their place as women in a world very different from the world that the women of today have grown up in.

If I have been sardonic with the male prophets and tender with the female prophets, it is because I believe the future of both the husband's and wife's marriages would be much better off if patterned on the designs of the women than on those of the men. Some men have come to agree. Says one husband, Harmut Zielke, "one thing I hope for . . . is a change in men's and women's attitudes [so that] instead of talking about one another as sexual stereotypes, we might [as in good marriages from time immemorial] come together as individuals and talk."

This is not, most people would undoubtedly agree, a bad prognosis for the future of marriage, but it is far more revolutionary than it sounds. Sexual stereotypes will be long in dying, in marriage or anywhere else. Individuals are hard to see behind the stereotypes, especially as the stereotypes mold the individuals. But now that we begin to see the problem, we can, hopefully, learn how to deal with it.

overview

The major ideas for the future of marriage presented in chapters 5, 8, 9, and 10, are summarized in the accompanying table. Throughout our discussion, we have distinguished between the commitment that constitutes the marriage and the life style that goes with it. In the chart below, the life styles (the privatized home, the cooperative household, the communal neighborhood or community, and the communal household) are in columns, and the kind of commitment specified in the marriage (permanent and exclusive, permanent but not exclusive, exclusive but not permanent, and neither permanent nor exclusive) are in rows. The several boxes or cells show the results of the several combinations of marriage and life style. The table is by no means exhaustive; it is intended to be only a suggestive synopsis.

options for marriage commitment and life style

Nature of the Commitment	Life Styles			
	Privatized Home	Cooperative Households	Communal Neighborhoods or Communities	Communal Households
Permanent and exclusive	Traditional form of marriage	See chap. 8	Swedish "mega-families" as in chap. 8	See chap. 9
Permanent but not exclusive	Ménage à trois, swinging	Group marriage, comarital relations (chap. 9)	Intimate networks	Group marriage, comarital relations (chap. 9)
Exclusive but not permanent	Limited commitments, informal relationships (chap. 5)	See chap. 8	Intimate networks	"Household" (chap. 10)
Neither permanent nor exclusive	Households of unrelated individuals	Households of unrelated individuals	"Free" communities	Communes and collectives of unrelated individuals

some questions and my answers

Chapter 1 ended with a series of questions. One question implied whether, anatomy being destiny, life was intrinsically so unfair to women that, as the psychoanalysts have taught them to believe, they should just learn to grin and bear it? Should they not therefore stop trying to do anything to improve marriage for wives and just settle for what they've got? The advice of the psychiatrists notwithstanding, the answer given by many young women today is a loud and resounding No! And I agree.

But the other questions asked in chapter 1 remain. What direction will changes, planned or unplanned, take? Will they be toward changing the husband's marriage more than the wife's, or vice versa? Will the two marriages converge or diverge still farther? If the wife's marriage is improved, will it cost the husband's anything?

Like the radical young women, I see the first order of business so far as the future of marriage is concerned to be that of mitigating its hazards for women. There is, it seems to me, no longer any reason why the costs of marriage should be so excessive for wives. So my answers to the second series of questions are that the direction of change will be toward improving marriage for women. I believe that the two marriages will converge and that in the long run, both will profit from the change, and that one way in which they will change—though by no means the only way—will be by more sharing of roles by both partners.

chapter eleven

the shared-role pattern

reasonable but not easy

Two of the major goals of the Women's Liberation Movement—better, rather than more, sex, and relief from the entire responsibility for child care and housekeeping chores—sound very modest indeed, and, to any except the oldest fogies, reasonable enough. But granting the legitimacy of their goals is not the same as finding ways to achieve them.

With respect to the first goal, there is not much that policy can do. Releasing men from the bonds of the male mystique and women from the thrall of ancient preconceptions are things that men and women, in and out of marriage, will have to achieve themselves. Education can help, as can the mass media, and also consciousness raising for both sexes.

But relief from the entire responsibility for child care and—so long as we still retain the isolated, privatized household—for housekeeping is a somewhat different matter, for to achieve this involves changing not only relations in the bedroom and the household but in the world outside as well. Bringing about changes here will call for change all along the line, in offices and shops and factories and hospitals and schools, in construction sites and laboratories and libraries, and in every other place where people work at jobs of any kind.

"a new kind of life style"

One way to achieve such changes proposed by Susan Brownmiller is "a new kind of life style in which a husband and wife would each work half-day and devote the other half of the day to caring for their childen." I like the idea very much. It seems to me to fit the conditions of modern life and to offer the best trade-off between security and challenge for both partners. With one stroke, it alleviates one of the major grievances of men (sole responsibility for the provider role) and of women (exclusive responsibility for housework and child care). It seems to me to be most in line with what is actually happening in our society. It is both the most conservative design for the future and the most radical.

shared, not reversed, roles

We are in such an intellectual bind when thinking about sex that we can think only in terms of polarities. Thus, when we think of change at all we think in terms of reversals. If men are not to be the providers, then women must be; if women are not to take care of children, then men must. But role reversal is not role sharing.

There is, of course, nothing inherently wrong with reversed roles, if that is what the partners prefer. A generation ago, Dorothy Canfield wrote a best-selling novel called *The Homemaker,* the story of a marriage in which the roles of husband and wife were reversed. The idea was to show that it was possible and not at all degrading to either partner. In 1965, as a matter of fact, such a reversal had occurred in the 15 percent of families of working mothers in which the husband was taking care of the children. From time to time we hear about real-life cases of such role reversals, although for the most part they are temporary: the husband is releasing the wife for professional training or education but intends to return to his own career later on.

Reversing roles, however, is not the same as sharing them. There undoubtedly are men who would enjoy household management—on a large enough scale it has long been an honorable male profession in the form of stewardship—as there are women who do. All power to them; there should certainly be no sanctions against such reversal. It is a legitimate option. But it violates some of the basic tenets of role sharing: that children should have the care of both parents, that all who benefit from the services supplied in the household should contribute to them, and that both partners should share in supporting the household.

bona fide, not counterfeit, sharing

It is a truism in the literature on working wives that although the husbands of working wives do help with household tasks, all too often wives continue to have responsibility for running the household. They rush home from work, shopping on the way, in order to have dinner on the table by six. They clean and tend to the laundry and do whatever has to be done in the evenings or on weekends. This is not role sharing.

The husband may promise to do his share, and increasingly he does—or, at least, agrees to. But he can make his contribution so grudgingly as to force the wife to conclude that she would rather do it herself. Pat Mainardi has shown how such reluctant sharers of the burden manage to renege. She has translated all of their dodges. Eleven are standard:

"I don't mind sharing the housework, but I don't do it very well. We should each do the things we're best at." MEANING:

Unfortunately I'm no good at things like washing dishes or cooking. What I do best is a little light carpentry, changing light bulbs, moving furniture (how often do *you* move furniture?). ALSO MEANING: Historically the lower classes (black men and us) have had hundreds of years experience doing menial jobs. It would be a waste of manpower to train someone else to do them now. ALSO MEANING: I don't like the dull stupid boring jobs, so you should do them.

"I don't mind sharing the work, but you'll have to show me how to do it." MEANING: I ask a lot of questions and you'll have to show me everything every time I do it because I don't remember so good. Also don't try to sit down and read while I'm doing my jobs because I'm going to annoy hell out of you until it's easier to do them yourself.

"We used to be so happy!" (Said whenever it was his turn to do something.) MEANING: I used to be so happy. MEANING: Life without housework is bliss. No quarrel here. Perfect agreement.

"We have different standards, and why should I have to work to your standards? That's unfair." MEANING: If I begin to get bugged by the dirt and crap I will say, "This place sure is a sty" or "How can anyone live like this?" and wait for your reaction. I know that all women have a sore called "Guilt over a messy house" or "Household work is ultimately my responsibility." I know that men have caused that sore—if anyone visits and the place *is* a sty, they're not going to leave and say, "He sure is a lousy housekeeper." You'll take the rap in any case. I can outwait you. ALSO MEANING: I can provoke innumerable scenes over the housework issue. Eventually doing all the housework yourself will be less painful to you than trying to get me to do half. Or I'll suggest we get a maid. She will do my share of the work. You will do yours. It's woman's work.

"I've got nothing against sharing the housework, but you can't make me do it on your schedule." MEANING: Passive resistance. I'll do it when I damned well please, if at all. If my job is doing dishes, it's easier to do them once a week. If taking out laundry, once a month. If washing the floors, once a year. If you don't like it, do it yourself oftener, and then I won't do it at all.

"I hate it more than you. You don't mind it so much." MEANING: Housework is garbage work. It's the worst crap I've ever done. It's degrading and humiliating for someone of *my* intelligence to do it. But for someone of *your* intelligence. . . .

"Housework is too trivial to even talk about." MEANING: It's even more trivial to do. Housework is beneath my status. My purpose in life is to deal with matters of significance. Yours is to deal with matters of insignificance. You should do the housework.

"This problem of housework is not a man-woman problem. In any relationship between two people one is going to have a stronger personality and dominate." MEANING: That stronger personality had better be *me*.

"In animal societies, wolves, for example, the top animal is usually a male even where he is not chosen for brute strength but on the basis of cunning and intelligence. Isn't that interesting?" MEANING: I have historical, psychological, anthropological, and biological justification for keeping you down. How can you ask the top wolf to be equal?

"Women's Liberation isn't really a political movement." MEANING: The Revolution is coming too close to home. ALSO MEANING: I am only interested in how I am oppressed, not how I oppress others. Therefore the war, the draft, and the university are political. Women's Liberation is not.

"Man's accomplishments have always depended on getting help from other people, mostly women. What great man would have accomplished what he did if he had to do his own housework?" MEANING: Oppression is built into the system and I, as the white American male, receive the benefits of this system. I don't want to give them up.

This is not, obviously, the shared-role pattern.

Not all men, however, are as recalcitrant as Pat Mainardi's partner. Only the older ones seem so resistant. Among the younger men the new life style is taken in stride. Among those who opt for cooperative households, for example, old patterns are "bullied out of existence." In visits to several such households, M. S. Kennedy did not see a single man who "at least openly still thought of women as their handmaidens, assigned to certain tasks parceled out according to gender. On the contrary, a man who wouldn't do housework and baby-sit would be looked at askance." One man who was writing a book did his work at home and actually enjoyed doing the things "most housewives rebel against and most men never think of doing," a life style for men that such households "are making respectable."

In rural households, especially the poorly equipped ones, as such "intentional communities" tend to be, the going is harder for the shared-role ideology. Where there is a considerable amount of hard physical labor, the ancient allocation of function remains even among the radical reformers. They tend to be conservative. In one rural commune of twelve young men and women, for example, Kit Leder, one of the participants, tells us, "even though there was no society-dictated division of labor, even though we had complete freedom to determine the division of labor for ourselves, a well-known pattern emerged immediately. Women did most of the cooking, all of the cleaning up, and of course, the washing. They also worked in the fields all day—so that after the farm work was finished, the men could be sitting around talking and taking naps while the women prepared supper."

It takes a considerable amount of sophistication to understand, let alone accept, the logic and the justice of the shared-role ideology, and a considerable amount of goodwill to implement it.

shared parenthood

Sharing responsibility for the household is only one part of the new pattern. If female "personhood" is a goal of the Women's Liberation Movement, so also is male parenthood. When or if there are no children, role sharing is not too much of a problem. It is when there are preschool children that the real test comes, because sharing roles also means sharing the child-care and the child-rearing function as well as the work of the household.

Only recently has it begun to strike anyone as outrageous that the entire burden of child care should be placed on one parent alone, and that if she cannot assume it, the child-care center, staffed primarily by women, should take over. Round-the-clock child-care centers have been a major plank in women's groups for some time. Whatever official sanction they have achieved, however, has been justified not on the grounds of what they could do for children but on the grounds that they would make it possible for welfare mothers to take jobs. Child-care centers planned and run from the point of view of what they can do for children are indeed needed. But child-care centers that are run only to make it possible for women to work is another kettle of fish, and not nearly revolutionary enough, especially if they are run exclusively by women. That is why day-care centers are not a substitute for role sharing.

There is a considerable amount of concern expressed about feminization of boys by too much exposure to female caretakers and schoolteachers. Fathers are exhorted to spend more time with their children. Wives take this seriously, but fathers rarely do. Even when they grant the validity of the argument, they usually draw the line at child care. Pitching a few balls to their sons in the backyard on a summer's evening after work is acceptable; they may even go to an occasional sports event together. But serious care of infants and small children on a half-time basis? Well, hardly.

The respectable objection to the idea is that it would cost too much. A man can earn so much more doing what he does than the woman could in the labor force. Precisely; this is an unassailable argument under the present status quo. If the wife is to share in the provider role, she has to be free from discrimination in the world of work. She has to be trained to her optimum capacity, and given as good a chance as her husband to put it to use. Her time at work has to be worth as much as that of her—or anyone's—husband doing the same work. Now turn to the vast literature on sex discrimination in education, access to employment, and promotion. It explains why it is cheaper to assign child care exclusively to mothers. They aren't worth as much as fathers in the labor force.

This economic argument, however, is only the most respectable one, not necessarily the most powerful one. The most powerful arguments are rarely expressed or, for that matter, even recognized.

fears and nightmares

Some men would welcome role sharing enthusiastically as partial relief from the dull and unrewarding work that now takes forty hours of their lives each week. They would be willing to exchange half of those hours for work around the home, even for child care. But some men will fight it. They are the men who love their work—even, admittedly in some candid cases, more than they love their families. A sample of tycoons, for example, did admit to Stanley Talbot that they preferred to spend their time on their job than to spend it with their families. And B. F. Skinner, the psychologist, said on a television program that he had told his daughters that if he had to choose between saving his work and saving them, he would save his work. No hard feelings, he assured them, just a matter of priorities. Such men will not willingly surrender even one hour of their work. Still they are quite willing to ask women to do so, women who would like to spend as much time on work that enthralls them as the men do themselves. In such cases it is not so much aversion to housework or child care that is the stumbling block but the aversion to any loss of time from their work. This is a form of self-indulgence they are not prepared to curtail. It is very difficult for wives to persuade such careerist husbands that they are being paid twice over, once in the form of freedom from domestic cares and once in the form of rewarding work. Such husbands and wives will have to hassle out this one by themselves.

The counterparts of the work-intoxicated men are the thousands, perhaps even millions, of women who do not want to be anything but housewives. And of course that option should not be foreclosed. In cases where this is a genuine preference, so be it. Coercion could not be justified. Still the research evidence is that almost all women—as many as four-fifths in one study and at least a third of another—say that they would prefer to enter the labor force if adequate provision could be made for the care of their children, and even more would do so if the work was part-time only.

There are other fears that are aroused by the shared-role idea. Some men, like the informant in a 1969 Gallup poll, fear the loss of the comfort and services provided by a full-time housekeeper. "Women," he said, "should stay home and take care of their families. . . . A woman's obligation is still to make a home for her husband." The increasing participation of wives in the labor force may, further, have an impact on the husband's marriage by making independence more possible for wives, and, through independence, reducing the superiority which the structure of marriage has traditionally accorded to husbands. An income of her own improves the position of the wife in the marriage.

Others fear that role sharing will depolarize the sexes, robbing men of their masculinity and women of their femininity. If we are thinking in terms of maleness and femaleness rather than masculinity and femininity, we have no cause for alarm. I am convinced that women and men are intrinsically so different that nothing we do will obliterate or even reduce the differences. I do not think men have to worry that women will become unsexed or women, that men will. In fact, the freer we become in allowing both sexes to be themselves, the more the fundamental and ineradicable differences will show up. I think that women will find maleness better than masculinity and men will find femaleness better than femininity.

the brighter side

The other side of the coin is brighter. Right off, the sharing of the provider role by the wife relieves the husband of the sole responsibility for it, and immediately removes one of the grievances men have expressed against marriage as now structured. Not only does the increased participation of the wife in the labor force ameliorate the financial load the husband has to bear, but it also has benign effects on the wife as well. Her mental health is improved. She becomes less susceptible to the housewife syndrome in the form of symptoms of psychological distress. Less concentrated on her children, she is less likely to succumb to depression when the children no longer fully occupy her. Among educated women—and more and more women are going to be educated—work outside the home improves marriage. This is especially true of part-time work.

Employment seems to make it possible for disturbed women to hold out longer before they become mentally ill enough to be hospitalized. Taking the work of mothers out of the home has a tranquilizing and fulfilling effect on many of them which may ruffle, but at the same time salvage, their marriages. The nature of the job makes a difference, to be sure; wives who are very satisfied with their jobs are less likely to express marital dissatisfaction than those who are not.

Not the least advantage of the participation of fathers in child care and child rearing is the effect it has on them. If the nurturing quality in women is related to the function they perform in the care of children, it is an excellent idea to permit men also to come under this benign influence. It would mark a great advance in human relations if men came to have a chance to develop this nurturing quality as well as women.

the cash value of wives

One possible alternative to the shared-role pattern would be to pay women for their services as housewives.

I think it is a far inferior alternative, but it deserves at least passing attention.

Before the Industrial Revolution, most people lived in a so-called status world; that is, they did what they did primarily out of love and/or duty. When the Industrial Revolution took work out of the home, an increasing proportion of people entered the cash-nexus world, a world in which people did more and more things for cash rather than for love and/or duty. The world of the family was the last holdout against the cash nexus. There was never any question about paying family members for performing family functions or for asking for such payment. The status love and/or duty world continued there.

People who did work outside the home became part of the labor force, their work contributed to the gross national product; it therefore had economic value. Those who worked in the home were not part of the labor force; their work did not contribute to the gross national produce; it therefore had no economic value. Not, of course, that it did not have enormous social, psychological, and emotional value. There was always complete unanimity in the belief that the work of women in the home was priceless, invaluable. But it was not worthy of monetary payment. In fact, the law of some states even forbade money payment for it. Much of its value resided in the fact that it was not paid for, that it was not an exchange, not a monetary matter.

There seems, however, to be some kind of sociological "law" that more and more services that begin as role obligations become "favors" and, finally, paid services. Children used to do chores around the house as a matter of obligation; nowadays they expect to be paid to do the most onerous of them. Women used to drop by the homes of the elderly or the shut-in to bring a fresh loaf of bread; there are now professional agencies who can be hired to drop in on elderly parents to see that all is well. We used to take a bouquet of flowers to a friend; we now wire them. We used to listen to the woes of the miserable, for example; we now pay counselors to do that. Scores of little services that used to be taken for granted as tokens of human concern are now professionalized.

The same sociological "law" may even come to operate in the household. The services that the wife performs for her husband keep him in good shape for his job. If she did not perform them, employers would have to supply them—as, indeed, they do for workers in lumber camps, ships, mining camps, construction camps, engineering camps, and wherever else wives cannot go. The man who is traveling for his company is given a per diem allowance in addition to his salary to pay for the services of maid and cook which his wife supplies at home without payment except her keep. It is now being suggested that the services that wives perform in keeping the work force in good condition be paid for by the employers, perhaps by contributions to some fund like the social security fund. The payment would not be a family wage going to the husband; it would be a wage to the domestic worker, the wife herself.

I am not myself enamored of this design. It does not draw the father into the child-care picture nor relieve the mother of her entire responsibility for child care. It does not relieve her of one of the most serious drawbacks of the housewife role, its isolation. But I do grant that if half of the world operates in a cash-nexus world the half that does not is at a distinct disadvantage. If one wishes to overcome that disadvantage, he should either extend the cash nexus to the love and/or duty world or vice versa. Or find some better way, which I believe the shared-role pattern to be.

how feasible is the shared-role pattern?

All this talk about sharing roles assumes that it is feasible. But obviously it depends on the availability of jobs with flexible hours, and that, in turn, depends on the organization of industry. The shared-role model of marriage will not come because it improves the mental health of women or relieves stress from men or because it is good for children. It will have to have more hard-headed justification. It does have.

We have noted several times that the technologists have as much to say about the future—of marriage as well as other relationships—as anything else. They are now telling us that by 1990 a twenty-hour, four-day week could produce the same annual increase in gross national product as we now produce with a forty-hour, five-day week. With increased productivity, industry could afford to pay the same wages to workers for half time as presently for full time.

Hours of work are not determined by natural law laid down in the beginning of time. They are an insti-tutionalized matter, subject to change. The current direction of change is toward the four-day, forty-hour, three-day weekend week. Workers spend ten hours working during four days and then have the rest of the week off. From the point of view of marital role shar-ing, this is not a good kind of schedule. But as an en-couragement of experiment, it is good; it makes inno-vation more acceptable. The four-day week is profitable for many firms; in the automobile industry it has been seen as a way to improve quality control. And in some cases it improves productivity to such an extent that hours can be cut below the customary forty. The drift toward the four-day work week may be inevitable, al-though as yet only less than seven hundred out of the five million firms in this country have adopted it. But the number is increasing rapidly, and Riva Poor, who has studied the movement in detail, believes it "could herald a new era of innovation in which this particular innovation in work scheduling is only one. The rapidity with which the public has adopted this new idea could be a harbinger of increased receptivity to change and improvement."

To be sure, the first reaction to any radical innovation is that it is impossible, it just can't be done. Most of us are like the physicist who declared that it was impossible to throw a curve ball; then, when a pitcher finally did, he went to work to show how, of course, it was possible to throw a curve ball.

Large-scale rescheduling of hours of work in industry has been shown to be possible, even profitable. But how about service occupations? This is, indeed, a crucial question, for an increasing proportion of the labor force is engaged in services and a decreasing proportion in physical production. Different approaches may be called for. Interestingly, it is in the professional services that the most reassuring experiments are being reported.

In one marriage, a temporary reversal of roles had such salutary effects that it led to the shared-role pattern later on. The case of Steve and Marge Everett, reported by Jorie Lueloff, was an almost archetypical example of all the grievances that marriage can generate in women today. Both were about as conservative and traditional in background as one could imagine, both school-teachers, and both quite conventional in life style. There was one exception: Marge was willing to continue her teaching job while Steve went on for his master's degree: "I thought it was my duty as a woman to help him get ahead at a sacrifice to myself." At first Marge found the role of housewife delightful. Only later did she come to "resent the fact that he got his master's and there was no thought of my going for one." The birth of their first child marked the beginning of her disenchantment: "I had to take care of the kid all day and most of the night too. I had to clean the house just to see it get dirty again. I had to get all the meals. Worst of all was the isolation: "My world grew so small. . . . I lived through Steve's life." When Steve was given a sabbatical leave, the idea of role reversal was explored. "They had qualms about the psychological effects of a role reversal. They wondered what would happen to a male ego cut off from the competitive jungle and left at home to file recipes. Does a woman who becomes a provider also become an emasculator? And what about Andy and Anne, then at the impressionable ages of four and two? How would a little boy identify with a father who cooked breakfast while Mommy paid the bills? And who would be the female model for a little girl—a bread-baking father or a breadwinning mother?" In the end they decided to take the risk. There were rough times while each learned by experiencing them what the gripes of the other were. They learned that the kinds of behavior they objected to in the other were the result of the position they were in, not of personality quirks or sex characteristics. Anyone, male or female, who had prepared a meal for a given hour would be annoyed and irritated when it had to wait for a delayed homecoming. Anyone, male or female, who had worked hard all day at a demanding job would flop down and resist having to talk when he —or she—got home. Among the other benefits was the fact that Steve came to know his children better. The results were so successful that it was decided that Marge also should now return for her master's degree. Thus, in time, role reversal would result in role sharing.

Different in some details but almost identical in general import is the case of Ted and Sally Oldham, of Reston, Virginia, as described by Sandie North. Ted is an architect and Sally, an art teacher. As in the case of the Everetts, role sharing salvaged a badly threatened marriage. "Sally's sudden requirement for work sharing four years ago nearly led to a divorce. Both Ted and Sally had married with traditional expectations of each other. He would earn the living and she would keep the house. All that changed when Sally neared completion of her master's degree. 'We separated for nearly a year . . . because one day I realized I was fed up with the conventional husband-wife roles we were playing. I had been trying to fill the typical female mold with a spotless house I could never seem to achieve. But all the time I obviously was more interested in doing something else—teaching, eventually administering a museum.' "

It was during a year in Europe that they worked out the new design for living which salvaged the marriage. Ted began to assume some of the household and child-rearing functions—vacuuming, tending to the laundry, diapering the baby—and Sally returned to work. "The Oldhams could afford baby-sitters, but they think it far more important to let Ted share in Erin's growing up." On occasion he even takes the baby with him to work. "I enjoy being with her when I'm working. And I know as much about taking care of her as Sally does, so it's no problem." In this family, role sharing may turn to at least temporary role reversal when Ted takes a year off to engage in sculpting while Sally earns the family income.

There are even beginnings of experiments on the part of employing agencies. One approach is being made in academia, where part-time appointments are on the drawing board and are even being tried out. Such part-time appointments would be optional; they would have all the dignity, status, and fringe benefits accorded to full-time appointments—not as they so often are now, underpaid, last-minute emergency appointments to handle unexpectedly large introductory enrollments. They would be attractive enough to appeal to both men and women and to the top as well as to the lower ranks in the academic structure.

One example of this new concept in operation is that of William and Patricia Dean at Gustavus Adolphus College in St. Peter, Minnesota. They have a single contract with the college, both teaching part time, permitting them to be at home with the family and also providing the opportunity for each to pursue professional interests as well, he in the religion department, and she in area studies.

This is Patricia's statement: "We asked for the arrangement because of my problems in dealing with the pressures of home responsibilities, in addition to a job. We have two children, seven and two. The most sensible and just solution seemed to be for my husband to assume more of the family responsibilities, but he could not do so unless he were released from some of his teaching duties. Accordingly, a proposal was presented to the college for each of us to work part time, between us teaching a full load. The college was willing to endorse it as an experimental and potential solution to problems facing parents who both want to work. The college has benefited in this venture we believe because we each bring more energy to our courses as a result of the new arrangement. Although the experiment was undertaken as a solution to my problems, my husband has discovered some unanticipated advantages. He feels fresher in the classroom, has as much or more time for research as before, and has gained a more intimate relationship with his children. The preschool child, in particular, has benefited from the arrangement; he appears equally attached to both parents and has a lessened dependence on his mother. The elder child has the advantage of living with a more satisfied mother."

Here is William's statement: "First, I should admit that it is still disconcerting to deviate from a role I have always accepted as normal and to watch men drive off to work and see myself remain in the neighborhood with the women. But my positive reactions are more important. First, I have traded one course, of a three-course teaching load, for a morning's work at home. The loss of a course gives me about as much working time as I lose at home. I think I will have about the same amount of time for extracurricular research as I have previously had. Second, I find my professional working day less tedious, probably because it is now limited to a long afternoon and a couple of hours picked up in the evening or in the morning while at home. In retrospect, it seems that it was the third course, or the last three hours of work, that dried me out and drove down what productivity I may have. Third, I sense an unforeseen benefit in the new arrangement. I think a man who sees his children only in the evening or on the weekends has a more restricted experience with them than he may realize. I, at least, have felt a new kind of intimacy with my preschool child, partly because I am alone with him and partly because it is during the calm of the morning. I think, for example, of silently driving through the hills, on an errand in the morning, with my two-year-old son on the front seat with me, sucking his thumb and holding his blanket. Finally, a much anticipated benefit is the alleviation of my feelings of guilt. I do not have to live with the realization that my occupational responsibilities are forcing a capable and professionally trained woman to work full time on a house and children that are half mine. Nor must I see her work outside of the home while already working full time in the home." The male sociologists who, like Ira Reiss, "doubt very much if males in our society will change very drastically in their sharing of the mother and wife roles" may be projecting too indiscriminatingly their own biases.

The shared-role model of marriage does not tell us the nature of the commitment which the partners will make nor the style of household in which the marriage will be lodged. Their commitment might be a permanent one, or it might not be; it might demand sexual exclusivity, or it might not. It might occur in far-out kinds of relationships, or in quite conventional ones. The marriage described by M. S. Kennedy was housed in a cooperative household; the Oldhams' in an upper-middle-class suburban community; that of the Deans in a Middle-Western college town. The shared-role pattern specifies only the way in which the partners will allocate the day-by-day functions of providing for a home and maintaining it.

right on!

It is hard to remain avant-garde in our fast-paced age. Who, for example, would ever have dreamed that by 1971 a U.S. senator—Russell Long—would be advocating the admission of housewives into the social security system so that their work in the home, though not paid for in wages, would nevertheless count in accumulating retirement benefits? The idea represents a first step toward paying the housewife for her services.

Or who would have thought that in June 1970, a television program would be debating the question: "So that women may work and men share in family tasks, should unions demand that everyone be given the option to work full time or half time?" Or that the idea would be so favorably received? Neither studio nor national audience was a random sample of the public, but almost half of the first and three-fourths of the second voted yes. And so did the judge, Esther Peterson, a veteran of many union battles:

My vote goes to those who are working for a society where no one is forced into a predetermined role on account of sex; a society where men and women have the option to plan and pattern their lives as they themselves choose. This society will require many things: a new climate of opinion which accepts equality of the sexes while still recognizing human and biological differences; a society which provides day care and supplementary home services which make choice possible; a society where nonmerit factors in employment such as sex do not count; a society which provides a new concept of training for both young men and women with an eye to employment and social usefulness along with active parenthood. And most important, a society that provides a shortened work day and work week with adequate pay for all workers—thus permitting time for families to be together, or father to participate in family activities (including the care and raising of children) where both parents can develop to their fullest as human beings. It's a long way down the road, but it's coming.

Not, actually, as far down the road as one might think. The shared-role pattern was already being viewed in Sweden as the basis for policy. It was beneficial for children as well as for their parents, for it would let the child have two parents rather than, as now all too often only, in effect, one. "The greatest disadvantage with the male sex-role," the Swedish prime minister noted, "is that the man has too small a share in the upbringing of the children." Children suffer from lack of contact with the father. Contact of children with men was advocated not only in the home but also in infant schools, kindergartens, and regular schools.

Nor was this merely political palaver. It was a bona fide statement of policy. In 1968, the government of Sweden had already proclaimed that it was "necessary to abolish the conditions which tend to assign certain privileges, obligations, or rights to men. No decisive change in the distribution of functions and status as between the sexes can be achieved if the duties of the male in society are assumed a priori to be unaltered. . . . The division of functions as between the sexes must be changed in such a way that both the man and woman in a family are afforded the same practical opportunities of participating in both active parenthood and gainful employment." And, astonishingly, the prime minister of Sweden reported in 1970 that "Swedish trade unions and management organizations have worked out plans to make it possible for men to share the child care with women."

If this book had been designed as a work of art—as a novel, for example, or play or even symphony—this chapter would have constituted the great climax and denouement toward which the entire work had been tending. Now would come the great catharsis. Here all the conflicting strains and themes would find resolution. The tension, assiduously and cannily aroused by the preceding chapters, would be resolved. Here finally would be the answer: let husbands and wives share roles and they will live happily ever after. Finis.

But not so. I have appended this discussion of one of the blueprints for the future not because I view the shared-role pattern as resolving all the problems raised in earlier chapters, certainly not because I see it as a panacea. Such a view, however satisfying artistically, would be irresponsibly simplistic. A relationship as intrinsically tragic as marriage—tragic in the sense of embodying the insoluble conflict referred to so often here between incompatible human desires—cannot so easily be perfected. The shared-role pattern may solve some of its dilemmas, but certainly not all: not the nature of the original marital commitment itself; not the nature of the sexual encounter; not all aspects of life style. It can help. That's all.

4
as i see it

chapter twelve

toting it all up

does marriage *have* a future?

The answer to this question is an unequivocal yes. The future of mariage is, I believe, as assured as any human social form can be. There are, in fact, few human relationships with a more assured future. For men and women will continue to want intimacy, they will continue to want the thousand and one ways in which men and women share and reassure one another. They will continue to want to celebrate their mutuality, to experience the mystic unity that once led the church to consider marriage a sacrament. They will therefore, as far into the future as we can project, continue to commit themselves to each other. There is hardly any probability that such commitments will disappear and that all relationships between them will become merely casual or transient. The commitment may not take the form we know today, although that, too, has a future. But some form of commitment there will be. It may change its name; people may say they are "pair-bound" rather than married, but there will be such "paired" men and women bound to each other in one way or another. Still, I do not see the traditional form of marriage retaining its monopolistic sway. I see, rather, a future of marital options.

a future of options

Not only does marriage have a future, it has many futures. There will be, for example, options that permit different kinds of relationships over time for different stages in life, and options that permit different life styles or living arrangements according to the nature of the relationships. There may be, up to about age twenty-five, options for childless liaisons; for the years of maturity, stable and at least "temporarily permanent" marriages involving child rearing; for middle age and beyond, new forms of relationships, perhaps even polygynous ones. People will be able to tailor their relationships to their circumstances and preferences. The most characteristic aspect of marriage in the future will be precisely the array of options available to different people who want different things from their relationships with one another.

Traditional marriage will of course be among the options available, for there is little likelihood that lifelong commitments and vows of sexual exclusivity will be discarded entirely. For a long time to come, millions of people will prefer this form of marriage, whatever the costs. But it will not have a monopoly; it will not be the only choice open.

Some couples may even want to relate to each other in the nineteenth-century manner. They will wait to marry until the young man has established himself in a well-paying job; and the young woman will either go directly into marriage without ever holding a job of her own, or give up her job upon marriage and devote herself exclusively to her household forever after. Her husband will make all the important decisions, and she will accept them, glad to be free of the responsibility. Since an increasing number of married women do enter the labor force, however, this style of marriage will predictably be of declining importance.

At the other extreme, the future will permit free-wheeling relationships which will allow both partners a maximum of individuality and independence, relying wholly on emotional commitment, and limited only by their own feelings of responsibility. They may specify the length of their commitment, with an option for extension, if they so desire, as the proposed bill in the Maryland legislature specifies; or they may want only a partial commitment, spelled out in detail. Some may want specifications that strike us as outré and outrageous—separate households, for example, or weekend marriages. They may become matter-of-fact, quite acceptable choices for those who prefer them, with no raised eyebrows on anyone's part.

There will, in brief, be marriages in the future as different from conventional marriages of today as those of the present are from those of our forebears in the nineteenth century. Individual men and women will make different demands on their relationships. It is fallacious, then, even to speak of "*the* future of marriage." We should rather speak of "marriage in the future."

It is not, however, the specific forms the options will take that is important but rather the fact that there will be options, that no one kind of marriage will be required of everyone, that there will be recognition of the enormous difference among human beings which modern life demands and produces. It will come to seem incongruous that everyone has to be forced into an identical mold.

no promised utopia

In making this appraisal of marriage in the future no one should be led to ignore the increasing hazards that marriage will encounter. Options make great demands.

One of the oldest arguments against divorce is that, if people knew they had no choice, no way out, they would learn to live with one another, reconciled if not satisfied. Introduce the possibility of divorce and they become miserable. Offer people marital options and they are exposed to conflict. No matter which option they choose, they wonder if they should have made a different choice. Some will run from one to another in the hope that some other kind of relationship will be better. That possibility is a genuine hazard.

Any option that does not guarantee permanence is hazardous. We have already noted that the dissolution of an intimate relationship is painful, no matter what the nature of the original commitment. No form of marriage guarantees utopia.

I would also like to raise the question whether, in attempting to find the best, or at least optimum, trade-off between freedom and security, the swing has not moved too far in the direction of freedom. Do we have enough support from other institutions to serve as "back-ups" for individuals left stranded by marital bonds that are too fragile? We know how traumatic divorce can be. The nonrenewal of a marriage would be no less so. Would the household proposed by Shulamith Firestone supply the security not supplied by some of the options?

For good or ill, then, there *will* be options—a wide gamut of options, in fact. But are there not certain intrinsic limits to the forms that such options may take —in human nature, in the nature of societies, in the nature of culture?

are there intrinsic limits in human nature to the forms of marriage?

Is there anything about marriage that is demanded or prescribed by human nature, or even proscribed? Are some forms "unnatural" or contrary to human instincts?

Neither "human nature" nor any of our instincts demand any special form of marriage. Just how "natural" marriage is can be gleaned from the diverse forms it has taken and the enormous literature on how to come to terms with it that has been necessary.

The variety of ways in which husbands and wives can relate to each other in marriage, and have, is so staggering as to boggle the imagination. Human beings can accept almost any kind of relationship if they are properly socialized into it. Just as people learn to accept fasts, painful rites, scarification, sacrifices of the most difficult kinds as a matter of course, so also can they accept lifelong celibacy or lifelong virginity—and they do—if that is defined as their lot. Girls accept doddering old men as husbands if that is what their parents tell them to. Wretched, miserable, quarreling spouses remain together no matter how destructive the relationship if that is what their community prescribes. Almost every kind of relationship has occurred somewhere, sometime—monogamy, polygyny, polyandry, exogamy, endogamy, matrilocal residence, neolocal residence, arranged marriages, self-selection of mates, parental selection of mates, marriage for love, marriage for convenance. . . . There is literally nothing about marriage that anyone can imagine that has not in fact taken place, whether prescribed, proscribed, or optional. All these variations seemed quite natural to those who lived with them. If any of them offends our "human nature," we have to remind ourselves that "human nature" as we know it this moment in this country is only one kind of human nature.

Millions of words have been used to document both the naturalness and the unnaturalness of monogamy. To those who chafe at its restrictions, monogamy is just not natural. At least not for men. They suffer greatly under its restrictions. On the other hand, a long list of distinguished social scientists have found it completely natural, buttressed by the rock-bottom fact of sheer male jealousy. That was, in fact, Westermarck's position in his nineteenth-century classic study of the history of human marriage.

But not so, said a sociologist, Kingsley Davis. Monogamy produced jealousy, not jealousy monogamy. Jealousy was the result, not the explanation, of monogamy. It was needed as a major prop for that form of marriage. If monogamy as the monopolistic form of marriage is on its way to becoming only one of several alternative options in the future, jealousy in the traditional sense may be in process of attrition, as the experience of swingers and participants in comarital relationships suggests.

In fact, the kind of jealousy that would once have precluded any nonmonogamous relationship is hardly salient at all today. In Updike's *Couples,* for example, the sexually peripatetic characters experience no jealousy. Articles in the periodical press deal with sibling jealousy but scarcely at all with marital jealousy. It doesn't seem important enough to precipitate much popular discussion. At least that side of human nature does not seem to preclude any of the new options.[1]

It is true that some of the options proffered for the future by the avant-garde are contrary to the human nature characteristic of the century just past. But that was just the human nature characteristic of the last hundred years, not necessarily of today's or tomorrow's. For each generation in every age develops the human nature it needs to live in its culture. Victorian families created the kind of human nature that Freud revealed to us; intense emotions; men who could "hate like brothers"; powerful fears and jealousies. The human nature produced by modern methods of child rearing, Miller and Swanson tell us, will be less intense, flatter. And the jealousies, insecurities, and anxieties that plagued people reared under the patriarchal authoritarian model will be mollified. Marriage will not have to contend with them. The new kinds of human nature are not necessarily any better than the old on any absolute scale, just different, less intense, less Dionysian. Indeed, some young people today complain that they cannot feel anything deeply, or, in the case of others, feel at all. These are exaggerations; for it is not likely that all capacity to feel can be trained out of any generation, whatever the pattern of socialization may be. It is just what seems natural or unnatural that changes.

There is, then, nothing in human nature that favors one kind of marriage over any other, none more natural than any other. Whatever we are used to seems natural; anything else, unnatural. Still, whatever the form marriage has taken and however natural that form has seemed, it has had to be propped up; not only by a moralistic, but also a didactic, literature. Human nature was not enough.

There has been for centuries, therefore, a voluminous didactic literature, especially proliferated in recent decades, dealing with the problems husbands and wives have to face for which their "human nature" did not prepare them. How to be happy though married has been one of the most persistent themes of such books, as well as how to manage marital conflict; how to deal with money; how to handle disciplinary problems; how to get along with in-laws; and even how to perform sexually.

It is now becoming clear that the conventional wisdom of the past embodied in much of this didactic literature is not a good guide for the future, for it applies only to marriage as traditionally defined, and is not relevant to the quite different kinds of marriage with which modern men and women are now faced. For forces have been at work placing them in relationships they have just not known how to deal with, for which they had no inborn preparation, and with which the authors of the didactic literature were themselves equally unfamiliar. Some of the writing outrages modern women. Standards and expectations that may have seemed natural or suitable for the past are just not natural for the present.

The question raised here is, actually, unanswerable. We will never know if there is anything intrinsic in human nature that limits the ways the sexes can relate to one another because no one has ever survived outside of any culture long enough to teach us. We imbibe the sex-role behavior required by marriage in our culture long before we marry. We can, therefore, find no blueprint for marriage in pristine, "uncontaminated" human nature. Human nature seems to be able to take almost any form of marriage—or unable to take any form.

For although human nature may not place rigid limits on the forms that marriage takes, it can, and does, place limits on the happiness experienced in marriage. We have referred many times to the incompatible demands that human beings make on life, for excitement, freedom, new experiences on the one hand, along with security and stability on the other. But they cannot have it both ways. Any commitment, however desirable, imposes restraints. What seems to be reflected here is an inevitable part of the human condition: people shaking their fists at the restraints they need and know they must have. Marriage, whatever form it takes, is for most, therefore, a compromise between conflicting impulses.

Most people come to terms with this conflict. The price they pay for marriage seems to them inconsequential as compared with the value received. Some find the costs too high; they feel that they sacrifice too much in the form of independence, freedom, adventure. Some of the options proposed for the future are designed to minimize the intrinsic conflict. It is conceivable that they might succeed, at least to a certain extent. They can mollify some conflicts by making possible the dissolution of commitments which are clearly untenable, in which the cost of either security or freedom is too high for one or both partners. But even if there were no commitments required, or if commitments could be abrogated at will, some people would long for the security that they represent along with the freedom that would come in their absence. There isn't much we can do about that.

are there intrinsic limits to the forms of marriage in the nature of society itself?

If there are no known intrinsic limits in human nature to the forms of marriage, are there any such limits in the nature of society itself? Are there certain minimum demands that a society—any society—must impose on the sexual relations of men and women in order to survive? Freud answered this question affirmatively; Marcuse challenges Freud's answer for our times.

Freud's *Civilization and Its Discontents* made the classic case for the restriction of sexual activity on grounds of subsistence. Stated simplistically (and hence in distorted form), it says that we have to restrict sexual activity in order to get people to work. We have to pay for civilization with sexual freedom. "Civilization is built up on renunciation of instinctual gratification. . . . The existence of civilization presupposes the nongratification . . . of powerful instinctual urgencies. This 'cultural privation' dominates the whole field of social relations between human beings; we know already that it is the cause of the antagonism against which all civilization has to fight." Work is important not only because it provides subsistence but also because it curtails aggression, especially erotic aggression. "Work is no less valuable for the opportunity it and the human relations connected with it provide for a very considerable discharge of libidinal component impulses, narcissistic, aggressive, and even erotic, than because it is indispensable for subsistence and justifies existence in a society." Restrictions on sexual life are among the reinforcements that culture needs "in order to erect barriers against the aggressive instincts of men." Control of sexuality, which represents the pleasure principle, is required, in brief, in order to force people to work, or to face the reality principle.

With quite a different rationale, the Pauline view of the world arrived at the same conclusion. Those who subscribe to the antisex view of Paul point to the fall of Rome as a classic example of how sexual anarchy can destroy a great empire. Others point to the experience of the USSR, which found that the almost complete sexual freedom of the early years of the revolution was not compatible with the stern work discipline demanded by the new status quo. And it is interesting to note that in Orwell's *1984*, sex is downgraded, rendered disgusting; celibacy is advocated. The goal is to dirty if not altogether to kill sexuality, a goal practically achieved in the case of women. All this is part of the system to keep the Party in control and the people at work.

Herbert Marcuse now challenges this Freudian-Pauline point of view. In *Eros and Civilization,* he points out that the inevitable decline in the need for work in modern societies renders Freud's identification of civilization with sexual repression no longer valid. Since work is no longer so necessary, sexual repression itself is not so necessary as it was in the past. He argues, further, that it has not been so much the need for labor that has necessitated instinctual repression as the exploitative way in which work has been organized. ". . . the prevalent instinctual repression resulted not so much from the necessity of labor as from the specific social organization of labor imposed by the interest in domination." And, he concludes, work relations would be improved rather than impeded by freer instinctual relations: "the liberation of Eros could create new and durable work relations." This was the point of view of Aldous Huxley in his *Brave New World,* where sexual freedom was obligatory; the heroine is rebuked for her exclusive relations with one man for four whole months; promiscuity was the ideal. Huxley saw such freedom as a bribe to pay for greater repression: "As political and economic freedom diminishes, sexual freedom tends compensatingly to increase." Sex was, in effect, a reconciliation to servitude.

Every society to date has, then, had to have some system for regulating sexual behavior. But whether the same grounds will hold for the future is moot, and only tangentially related to marriage. For marriage is only one form that such control takes, and marriage is far more than merely a system of control for sexual behavior.

Marriage is necessary also as a kind of accounting system for keeping track of relationships, especially in tribal societies in which kinship was the basic principle of organization. If there was any order at all in such societies, it had to be based on kinship ties. Some form of marriage was demanded by the nature of such societies themselves if for no other reason than to keep tabs on mating and to prevent incest or to guarantee legitimate ancestry for children. Societies in which property as well as kinship is important need marriage also to regulate and conserve such property and its inheritance.

Even when blood is no longer much thicker than water (that is, in civil societies no longer, like tribal societies, based on kinship ties), marriage so far as we know has always been part of the structure. And although I would be hard put to prove it, I believe that the very nature of society—civil as well as tribal—does call for marriage of some kind or other. But not for any one kind. It is to the technological aspect of culture, I believe, more than to the nature of either human nature or of society itself that we must look for answers to the forms that marriage takes and the limits imposed on them.

are there intrinsic limits to the forms of marriage in the nature of culture itself?

Culture is usually viewed as consisting of two major components, "material" and "nonmaterial," including symbolic components, or an "institutional" and a "technological" component. The relationship between the two is basic. Institutions affect technology, and technology, institutions. At this point, the influence of technology on marriage is the focus of interest. For although the forms which marriage has taken have varied enormously, they have not varied randomly or capriciously. They have been related to the way in which the society made its living—that is, to its technology.

There is an almost inexhaustible literature documenting this relationship between marriage and technology. The maternal form of marriage, for example, went with the gathering, preplow, or digging-stick, stage of agriculture. The patriarchal form went with plow agriculture. And a more egalitarian form goes, allegedly, with industrialization—one sociologist, W. J. Goode, having shown that with industrialization marriage in all parts of the world tends to converge toward the form that prevails in the industrialized West.

In the transition from one form or stage to another, many hitches may occur. Thus, half a century ago—coincidentally, at the very time when the urban population first surpassed the rural—W. F. Ogburn, a leading sociologist, was already showing why there was something seriously wrong with the way marriage and the family were then functioning. He attributed the problem to what he called a cultural lag—a lag, that is, between the material or technological aspects of our culture, now industrialized, and the adaptive or institutional aspects, then still tied to the waning agricultural society of the past. "Women," he pointed out, "have not become satisfactorily adjusted to the new material conditions of the factory system. Their work as producers has largely been taken away, so that many are idle, or do work which is only slightly productive of substantial economic value; or else they go into industry under such chance conditions as they may find. . . . A somewhat wider life for woman outside the home seems desirable, since so many of the home occupations are now found outside the family. . . . Finally, the reduction of the economic function of the family together with other functions has rendered the marriage union of man and woman less stable. It is thus seen that the change from agriculture to the modern factory system has necessitated changes in the family organization. There is abundant evidence to show that the old agricultural family organization is no longer adapted to industrial life as seen in modern cities."

That was half a century ago. We were then just beginning to make the changes necessitated by the transition from rural to urban life. Many have now been made. Not only the working girl but also the working wife and even the working mother, have by now become an acceptable part of the social scene. Women are no longer restricted to the domestic role; a worker as well as a domestic role—the so-called two-role pattern—has become recognized.

A great deal of the thinking about the future of marriage today, however, is based on anticipation of a "postindustrial" society, a "technocratic" society, one no longer bound by the after-effects of the first Industrial Revolution, which Ogburn was analyzing. The great technological innovations that created the first Industrial Revolution had to do with production; increasingly, the great technological innovations that will influence, if not determine, the future of marriage, will have to do with consumption. Many proposals for the future of marriage thus posit an affluent society, a highly productive society that does not need the regimented industrial organization we have needed in the past, a society in which the performance of services will take precedence over the production of material goods. Work, as Marcuse argues, will no longer have the same significance as in the past. Nor, if he is correct, will sexuality have to be subordinated to it.

In addition to the technologies related to production, technologies such as those related to fertility control, genetic engineering, surrogate or artificial gestation devices, sperm banks, and preventive geriatrics will have an important effect on marriage in the future. Work, leisure, everything will be influenced by technology and will in turn exert a powerful influence back on marriage. The form of marriage, in brief, will be as much related to technology as to either human nature or the nature of society.

will marriage be any happier?

This, of course, is the $64,000 question. Granted that there is no prospect of utopia, will marriages be any happier? The answer to this question depends on the definition of happiness used. If one defines it in terms of adjustment, as so many of the early studies did, and asks, Will the partners in marriage in the future be better adjusted? the answer is, probably, No. Human beings have enormous capacity to adjust to almost anything and, in the past, have done so. But they are now raising questions. Adjust to what? To an old order, now passing? And adjust at what cost? Most women today "adjust" to marriage. But the cost, as we have seen, is great. *Should* they have to adjust to a situation that is detrimental to their mental health? *Should* men become reconciled to Henry David Thoreau's quiet desperation? If we think so, then marriage will not be happier, as the currently rising divorce rate shows. Wives and husbands are not adjusting to the situation they find themselves in. They want out. The desperation is no longer quiet.

The reason is not that marriage itself is becoming any worse. It is mainly because it is getting better and because we face a "revolution of rising expectations." After the macabre events of this century, it sounds incredibly naive that one can believe that human behavior—at least human marital behavior if not human nature in general—is improving; not steadily, not without occasional reversals, and not in everyone's marriage everywhere, but still, overall, measurably. We do not tolerate today forms of marital behavior that were matter-of-fact in the past; our standards—as measured

in terms of the grounds on which divorce is permitted
—are, as I have shown elsewhere, higher.

In reply to the question asked about marriage—
"How could anything that feels so bad be so good?"—
Richard Farson replies that precisely because marriage
is so good it leads people to make too great demands
on it, to expect too much. Just as revolutions do not
come in times of the most abject misery but rather in
times of better and improving prospects, so discontent
with marriage is expressed today not because it is so
bad but because it is better than ever. Young people
are replying, "But the good need not be the enemy of
the better." They want marriage to become better.

what can be done to help?

There has been increasing talk in recent years about
a "national family policy," a feeling that government
ought to do something about marriage and the family.
Not everyone agrees, and even those who do are not
very optimistic.

The analogy of longevity is relevant here. We know
that although science cannot as yet extend the life span,
it can make it possible for more people to live it out.
And so, in the case of marriage, policy may not be able
to improve the quality of the best marriages, but it can
make it possible for more people to have good ones.

However one defines happiness, some men and
women in the past under all kinds of regimes have experienced the best possible marriages—like, for example,
the Brownings or the Madisons—and some, the Abra-
ham Lincolns, for example, have experienced the worst.
For it is possible for happy marriages to occur under
the most inauspicious circumstances; it is possible for
unhappy marriages to occur under the most auspicious.
There can, for example, be both happy and unhappy
marriages when young people select their own mates;
but so can there be when parents do. There were happy

marriages when all the weight of the church and the state shored up the power of husbands; there are happy marriages when they do not. There were happy marriages when female sexuality was anathema; there are happy marriages today when it is not. What changes is the proportion of good marriages and the proportion of bad ones. What the future can do is to make it possible for more to have a chance at the best, to doom fewer to the worst. If there is to be progress, it will not be in the form of the relationship but in the relative frequency with which good relations have a chance to flower in the kind of world we now live in.

No regime can guarantee happiness, but some can make it easier to achieve. Any system, for example, that makes poverty the lot of many people is asking for bad marriages. We cannot tolerate the poverty that has rendered so many marriages miserable in the past when it did not entirely destroy them. People are going to continue to be able to make one another as wretched as they please; but the social structure is not going to go along with them by adding to their armory. There will therefore be fewer marriages as miserable as the most miserable of the past.

Policy in the future can also attempt to minimize the costs to women of their reproductive function. It can make the participation of wives in the world of work less difficult, more nearly equal to that of men in terms of cost. Industry can organize its working hours to make shorter hours for more workers possible. And all kinds of societal structures can become more flexible, more responsive to the needs of families rather than requiring families to respond to their needs. All of these would make it possible for marriages to pursue happiness with greater success. The probabilities for good marriages can thus be increased by auspicious institutions, and the probabilities for bad ones decreased. I think the trend today is in the direction of increasing the probability of good marriages and decreasing that of bad ones.

A marital utopia is not, however, in the cards. Though policy may make it possible for more people to achieve good marriages and though it may make the worst less wretched than in the past, there is no guarantee that foolproof happiness for everyone is in sight. No amount of tinkering with the social system, or even complete revamping of it, can overcome the inherent contradictions involved in marriage itself. Even if we eliminated all the extrinsic barriers to happiness, marriage would still fall far short of perpetual bliss.

Policy in the future, then, is going to make it possible for more and more people to achieve good marriages. But the quality of the best will be no better than the quality of the best in the past. The shape of the distribution of happiness in marriage will change; the mode will shift to the right. It will be possible for people to be as unhappy as in the past; but fewer will be. It will be impossible for people to be happier than in the past, but more will be able to achieve the top ranges.

needed: new social spectacles

Before we can even think fruitfully about policy, however, we have to know more about what is happening, and we are not well prepared to find out. We are not well equipped conceptually. In fact, for a great many of the role and status changes taking place all around us today we do not even have terms to help us think about them, or symbols to perceive them through, or rules to guide us in reacting to them.

One of the most common grievances expressed by young people today is the pressure they feel they are under to perform certain roles which they find uncongenial. The whole matter of roles is anathema to them. They believe that roles interfere with spontaneity, and force them into stereotypical behavior that does not really fit them.

One could argue that precisely the reverse is happening. Men and women are evolving a host of relationships with one another without corresponding clarification of their nature. One could even say that it is a major problem in our day that we do not have definitions for them, not to use as weapons against them but as tools to secure them.

As an example, while traveling around the world one runs into young couples living together who are not in the conventional status of marriage. They sometimes find it awkward to know how to refer to each other. She is not his wife; he is not her husband. "Girl friend" or "boy friend" does not convey the meaning of the relationship either. Nor does "roommate" or "housemate." "Lover" or "mistress" gives a misleading impression. "Companion" is not accurate. We have no term for this relationship, nor is there any clear-cut recognition of precisely what status it implies.

Nor do we have any term for the status of young people who want a friendly, even, perhaps on occasion, an intimate, but nonmarital relationship with members of the other sex. One might cite for example, the case of a young woman who lives alone and likes it. She has a job that she enjoys, and is not interested in giving it up or sharing it with marriage. But she likes men, enjoys their company, wants to maintain warm and friendly relations with them, would like a variety of men friends. She might, even, from time to time, invite one to spend the night or the weekend with her if the relationship was especially congenial. But she does not want to assume any responsibility for him; she does not want him to become dependent on her, make demands on her; nor does she want to become dependent on him.

Nor are all such women young. Here, for example, is Jane, who is in her forties. Full of zest, almost fully invested in her work with just enough left over for her relations with men, she does not lack for men in her life. But marriage is the last thing she wants. She does not want deep commitments. She does not need them from others. The three or four men with whom she has relations from time to time understand that they are not to think in terms of demanding love. If they become too serious she warns them, gently but firmly, that they are treading on forbidden territory. She has exorcised that most frightening of female bogies, fear of losing sex appeal. Men do not desert her. She may not be like Cleopatra, whose infinite variety time could not wither nor custom stale, but she has enough appeal to keep men interested in her. She is willing, within limits, to supply the dependency needs of men and to accept, within limits, emotional support from them when she needs it. But, no more than the younger woman, does she want to be the sole emotional support of any man at the expense of her own identity, nor does she want to force anyone to bear the load of her own dependency needs.

A quite new kind of woman is illustrated here; there may have been individuals of this mold in the past— there surely must have been—but not on so large a scale as now. We do not yet have a clear-cut definition of the statuses implied in the relationships they are forging, nor definitions of the expected kinds of behavior they call for. "It confuses some of the conventional types," says one such young woman, "when I show simple affection by, like a kiss. That's all I mean by it. Just warm affection. The proper ones stiffen. They get uptight and defensive. They're afraid I'm making advances to them. Actually I'm not. At least not advances toward *that*. Some are afraid I'm trying to trap them into marriage. Wrong again. The with-it men understand, though. They're on to it. They have learned or always knew that men and women can have nonerotic relationships that lead to nothing but more quiet understanding." Or, again, a woman writes to *Psychology Today*: "I'm not anxious for remarriage— would like sex with any of a number of men my age (late forties). They are too often the old double-standard type. Unless they could consider marriage, they don't see the possibilities."

In the absence of guidelines, we tend to try to fit these new kinds of relationships into the standard patterns, to which they do not conform. The men are therefore uncertain of the woman's position; she is uncertain of theirs. We are all uncertain about both. Once we have words for the new statuses, we can clarify their nature.

We may even come to devise symbols to tell the world what the nature of a relationship is. We are all familiar with the traditional symbols: wearing a fraternity pin to indicate a certain relationship, the engagement ring, and the marriage band, all to communicate clearly to others exactly what our status is. We now need other devices to indicate other kinds of commitment or noncommitment. The idea is that there would be a role—that is, an understood pattern of interaction—to guide people in their relations with persons in any particular status; for both sexes, obviously.

the "lag" in feminine human nature

The future does not hit everyone at the same time. Nor are all equally prepared for it when it strikes them. The avant-garde, already far into the future, find old patterns of marriage restrictive, uncongenial. But the rear guard, especially women socialized to conform to old patterns and well adjusted to them, are caught in a lag and find the demands of the new ones frightening. While some women are activists for the Lucy Stone League, others are still not even ready to step out as individuals in their own right. After so many years hidden behind her husband, Mr. William Jones, Helen is timid about her identity as Helen Smith Jones.

Some feel that although chivalry is pleasant, it costs too much. Here is how one woman put it, once she had tasted independence: "It is of course lovely to be protected, to have one's bags carried, cigarettes lighted, doors opened. But all these little amenities come high. They are paid for. Independence is a high price to pay for them. The protected person enjoys advantages but she is not in an enviable position. The serfs used to be protected too. And the Mafia's client." She was thoughtfully silent for a moment, then added: "The trick is to be independent without being so all-fired angry and hostile about it. The fact that you are beholden to no one doesn't license you to put others down."

For other women, however, independence is frightening. They have been socialized to buy protection at the cost of independence. They prefer a model of weakness and inferiority that leads men to surrender seats to them, to open doors, and to extend other favors. Any modification of the relations between men and women, and especially any modification of the permanent commitment in marriage, will therefore seem—and for many women, in fact, will actually be—threatening.

Throughout the discussion in this book we have referred again and again to the necessity for new patterns of socializing girls. In chapter 3, for example, we showed how we socialized girls for dependence in order to fit them for marriage as now structured, however anachronistic; in chapter 5 we noted that the new styles of commitment now being experimented with called for new styles for the socialization of girls, that it demanded preparing them for autonomy; in chapter 7 we discussed the changes in the socialization of girls called for in egalitarian relationships; in chapter 8 we suggested ways in which girls might be led to plan their lives for more than marriage and motherhood; in chapter 10, we presented some of the ideas for the socializing of women proposed by the Women's Liberation Movement; and in chapter 11 we pointed out that in order to implement the shared-role pattern, women would have to be trained to their optimum capacity. This recurring motif was neither incidental nor accidental. For there is little doubt that success in the kinds of marriage now being forged will call for a quite different character structure, in both sexes, but especially in women.

From the very earliest years, girls will have to learn that however large marriage may loom in their lives, it is not nirvana, that it does not mark the end of their

growth, that motherhood is going to be a relatively
transient phase of their lives, that they cannot indulge
themselves by investing all their emotional and intellectual resources in their children, that they cannot count
on being supported all their lives simply because they
are wives. They will have to prepare for loving autonomy rather than symbiosis or parasitism in marriage.

To help women achieve a better marriage we will
therefore have to prepare them for it in ways quite
different from those of the past. We used to think that
courses in "domestic science" or "home economics" or,
later, "family life education" were what was needed.
To prepare women for marriage of the future something
different will be called for. They will have to be prepared to become autonomous women, not economically
dependent; women whose economic dependence does
not weight every alternative in favor of remaining in a
marriage, regardless. The subject here is not the normal
dependencies intrinsic in any good marriage and equally
great for both men and women; it is the woman's extra
load of economic dependency added to the emotional
dependency that has to be lightened. A union between
a man and a woman in which, when it breaks down,
one loses not only the mate but also the very means of
subsistence is not a fair relationship. In the breakdown
of a marriage, a man loses a mate, a loss that may be
extremely serious; but he does not also lose his job. If
permanence is no longer to be guaranteed by the marital
commitment, women will have to achieve the independence required to mitigate—though it can never
eliminate—the trauma of the breakdown of the relationship.

no final solution

Are the new options that young people are now pro-
posing a final solution? If we come to terms with them,
can we then relax and close the book and say that we

have solved the problems of marriage? Will we be able to say that although we cannot make every marriage a happy one, we have at least guaranteed that we have made it possible for most to be happy? Alas, no.

Every generation is the last in the sense of most recent, but not in the sense of final, generation. There will never be an ultimate or last in the sense of final form of marriage. It will go on changing as the times and the people change and as the demands on it change. There is no Ideal Marriage fixed in the nature of things that we will one day discover, toward which we are groping, slowly finding our way, and which we finally achieve. Every age has to find its own. We are only now getting used to the idea that any form of marriage is always transitional between an old one and a new one. It was easier to get used to change in the past because it took a very long time, even centuries, to make the transition, to accommodate to new conditions. It took close to two hundred years, for example, for the thinking about marriage which began during the Enlightenment among a minuscule avant-garde to percolate down to the men and women in the street. It is less than a quarter of a century since the "two-role" pattern of marriage for women recognizing both her worker and her domestic roles, which was the accommodation to the urban industrial order, achieved official sanction. Such a fast pace of change is hard to come to terms with.

But we have no choice. Change is bound to come whether we like it or not. We might as well come to terms with it gracefully. And to those who show us the way, I would even add that I am grateful, glad that there are men and women willing to pioneer the path for those of us who are not willing to pioneer it ourselves.

Marriage is the best of human statuses and the worst, and it will continue to be. And that is why, though its future in some form or other is as assured as anything can be, this future is as equivocal as its past. The demands that men and women make on marriage will never be fully met; they cannot be. And these demands will rise rather than decline as our standards—rightfully—go up. Men and women will continue to disappoint as well as to delight one another, regardless of the form of their commitments to one another, or the living style they adopt, or even of the nature of the relationship between them. And we will have to continue to make provision for all the inevitable—but, hopefully, decreasing—failures of these marriages to meet the rising demands made on them which we can unequivocally expect.

And so now to the first order of business. To upgrade the wife's marriage. . . .

afterword

I have now, albeit reluctantly, closed shop on this book. I am finally surrendering to the imperative that some time or other one has to write finis. I have been re-writing this book so long that I am loath to stop now. Tomorrow, a research report will cross my desk that will illuminate an aspect of marriage quite new and arresting, and I will want to make room for it somewhere or other; or new legislation will pass, and the implications for the future of marriage will be so significant that some chapter will have to be torn up to include it; or one of my young women friends will reveal to me some new current in her experience that positively cannot be ignored. A book is an organic entity with a life of its own; it can take over one's life. Still, the time does comes when one must call a halt.

When this book was commissioned in 1968, it seemed to me one of the simplest assignments in my professional career. In line with my personal and professional bias, it was designed to be based entirely on research findings. I planned merely to put together in a systematic framework what had been reported in the research literature. I felt that I could do it in a few months' time, leisurely, without too much effort. I had, after all, been myself in the mainstream of sociological research on marriage for over forty years. I had been among its pioneers in this country. As early as 1932 I had published papers on the measurement of, distribution of, and factors in the success of marriage. In 1942, I had published a book on American family behavior in which I had discussed such topics, among others, as the equilibration of marriage, the nature of housework and its effects on women, and a shock theory of marriage.[1] I had researched remarriage, divorce, marriage among black families, dating, communication between the sexes, and the like. Writing a book on the future of marriage should present no great problems. In line with my habit, ingrained by years of professional experience, of never sitting down to write without a corpus of research at my elbow, when I began this book, I had at my side the research findings, hard and soft, and I was prepared to follow where they led.

Even the most perceptive reader, however, would never recognize that version in the present one. I have myself been surprised at the changes I have had to make in each successive draft in order to keep up with the world around me.

It is hard to realize how much has happened in our thinking about marriage in the last few years. Events that help us to understand the past and give us glimpses of the future have succeeded one another at a breathless pace. The Women's Liberation Movement, the concept of the no-fault divorce, the relaxation of laws on abortion, the four-day-work-week movement, the improvement and spread even to unmarried women and minors of contraceptive information, the movement for zero population growth, the proliferation of communes, the acceleration of the so-called youth culture, greater tolerance of homosexuality, are only among the most salient of these "random events." They are going to have enormous impact on the future of marriage. We are also in the throes of one of the truly major revolutions in several centuries with respect to child care as the insistence that welfare mothers go to work validates the whole day-care idea, shifting the child-care function out of the home. All of these events will in due time be faithfully traced to their historical roots by conscientious scholars, and will be shown to be the natural outcome of longtime trends. But to many of us who faced them as they occurred they have seemed revolutionary, and we have had to readjust all our thinking about the past, present, and future of marriage in the light they have cast.

Accommodating this book to take account of these "random events" was an interesting and stimulating intellectual enterprise. That aspect of the book's biography posed no problems. Not so, however, other aspects.

autobiography of the author

Any book is, in effect, an autobiographical record of its author while it was being written. This one is such an autobiography during the months I have spent thinking, rethinking, writing, and rewriting it.

Early in 1968 I became exposed to the Women's Liberation Movement in the underground press. My first reaction was purely academic; I saw it primarily as something interesting to study, as something I had a professional obligation to observe. When, after considerable effort on my part, I received an invitation to a consciousness-raising session, one of the young women there said that I "threatened" her. Sitting quietly on the floor in their midst, showing, so far as I knew, no disapproval at all, my academic objectivity, my lack of involvement, my impersonality, was giving off bad vibrations. This incident gave me something to think about, including my stance vis-à-vis research and also my discipline.

No target of the incredible flow of ephemera—mimeographed papers, articles, notes, newsletters—that circulated among radical women was more furiously attacked by them than my own discipline, sociology. A review of sociological writings did, indeed, support the contention that, with a few exceptions, they shored up a conception of marriage wholly out of phase with current trends. The most influential sociologist of the 1940s and 1950s, for example, when we were already accommodating marriage to the new industrial system by accepting the two-role ideology for women, was demonstrating to his own satisfaction and that of his followers that accommodating the family to the occupational world demanded that only one of the marital partners be in the labor force. The traditional specialization of functions in marriage was accepted virtually without challenge.

Radical young women were not the first to call to the attention of sociologists the fact that, despite our insistence on objectivity and our awareness of cultural relativity, we wrote and researched within a straitjacket. William Kolb, for example, had reminded us a generation ago that we asked, with respect to intermarriage, how did its success compare with other kinds of marriage instead of how could we help intermarriages succeed? We asked who made more of the adjustments in marriage rather than how we could make marriage better for women. We documented ad nauseam the dependencies of wives rather than how to overcome them. We did all this under the illusion that such formulations of research questions demonstrated our objectivity, a praiseworthy absence of value judgments.

Radical young sociologists are now forcing us to recognize that a value judgment is implicit in the choice of any research topic,[2] and young women sociologists are applying this tenet to research on marriage. The most painstaking report on the status quo is not value-free. "Social scientists," Arlie Hochschild reminds us, "write about what interests them. But these interests are socially conditioned, among other things, by sex." Even the research done by women has been from a male perspective. Why had we cared so little about what this research was telling us about the marriages of wives? Why were we so complacent about what it showed?

Why did the pathology—*pathology* is really not too strong a word—of the situation not move us? Why, in fact, were so many women blaming themselves for their plight? Why were we dealing with their problems so cavalierly? Or, even worse, if we took them seriously, why did so many prescribe a return to the feminine mystique?

"If we are to redress this unintended imbalance," Arlie Hochschild continues, "we will have to add to social science the woman's perspective. . . . It is not simply a matter of getting our heads straight; it's a matter of getting social science straight, of decolonizing it, of figuring out what is missing, what is an answer to a poor question or a dull, fuzzy answer to a fruitful question." She shows how research, or, in fact, lack of research, has served to maintain the disabilities to which women are subjected. "Some call it 'natural,' some call it 'oppression,' and some call it 'structured strain.' But more than labels we need better explanations" than research has so far provided.

Such a radical attack on one's "consciousness" is not easy to adjust to. Researchers in the academic tradition are not paid for their opinions. Indeed, they are rebuked for them by their professional colleagues. Opinions imply or constitute judgments, evaluation, and, worse still, feeling. The proper academic feels uncomfortable when pressed for an opinion on his findings, for statements not about their "statistical significance"—which in any event are mandatory for researchers—but for statements about their human meaning. The young woman in the consciousness-raising group who felt threatened by my objectivity sensed quite clearly that such objectivity was itself a value judgment.

I did not start out with the conviction that marriage was bad for wives. Nor did I expect this book to turn out to be a pamphlet on the destructiveness for women of marriage, with its "structured strain"—a result all the more remarkable because most of the facts had been generally known, some of them for a long time. I had reported many of them myself a generation ago. This time round, however, they looked different. The message of the radical young women had reached me.

No one book can reorient the public's thinking on a topic as emotion-laden as marriage. All that one could possibly hope to do is help turn attention to the "structured strains" built into the wife's marriage. I hope that this one can do at least that much.

tables

Today, it may no longer be necessary to apologize for the use of tables. We are more sophisticated than we once were, when it was considered witty to accuse those who used statistics of lying. Still, tables are not self-interpreting, and there are often several ways to read them. The text of this book in chapters 2, 3, and 4 shows how I have interpreted the following tables. But in all fairness I have felt it necessary to permit those who wish to challenge what I have said to look at the evidence themselves.

NOTE: In those tables where plus and minus figures appear, the figures are to be read as expectations. If the symptom occurs with more frequency than expected, it is plus; if it occurs with less than expected frequency, minus. A zero indicates that it occurs at about the expected frequency.

Table 1
HEALTH OF MEN BY MARITAL STATUS AND AGE, HEALTH DEFINED IN TERMS OF ABSENCE OF CHRONIC CONDITION OR RESTRICTED ACTIVITY

	Marital Status		
Age	Married	Never Married	(Percent healthy)
17–44	91.8	92.7	
45–64	80.0	73.0	
65+	48.8	47.4	

SOURCE: Unpublished table, National Center for Health Statistics. Data are from 1968 Health Interview Survey.

Table 2
SELECTED PERSONALITY DIMENSIONS AMONG MEN 30 YEARS OF AGE OR OVER BY MARITAL STATUS

	(Percent Scoring High)	
Personality Dimension	Married	Single
Depression	37	50
Severe neurotic symptoms	17	30
Phobic tendency	30	40
Passivity	50	66

SOURCE: Genevieve Knupfer, Walter Clark, and Robin Room, "The Mental Health of the Unmarried," *American Journal of Psychiatry* 122 (February 1966): 842.

Table 3
PROPORTION OF MENTAL HEALTH IMPAIRMENT OF MEN BY MARITAL STATUS AND AGE

	Marital Status	
Age	Married	Single
20–29	11.7	20.5
30–39	19.6	30.4
40–49	19.0	37.5
50–59	25.7	46.1

SOURCE: Leo Srole and associates, *Mental Health in the Metropolis* (New York: McGraw-Hill, 1962), pp. 177–178.

Table 4
SOME SELECTED SOCIOECONOMIC VARIABLES OF WHITE MEN BY MARITAL STATUS AND AGE

	35–44		45–54	
	Married, Wife Present	Single	Married, Wife Present	Single
Median years education	12.1	11.5	10.5	9.0
Percent with some college	21.2	20.6	17.7	14.7
Median income	$5,944	$3,913	$5,590	$3,440
Percent with income $10,000 and over	12.4	3.7	12.4	3.4
Percent with professional, managerial, or official occupation	26.5	20.2	25.0	17.4

SOURCE: United States Census, 1960: *Marital Status*, Tables, 4, 5, and 6.

Table 5

SELECTED SYMPTOMS OF PSYCHOLOGICAL DISTRESS AMONG
MARRIED AND NEVER-MARRIED WHITE MEN

Symptom	Married Men	Never-Married Men
Nervous breakdown	− .76	+1.00
Felt impending nervous breakdown	− .51	− .07
Nervousness	+ .31	−1.05
Inertia	− .76	+ .29
Insomnia	−1.17	+1.92
Trembling hands	− .23	− .52
Nightmares	− .75	+1.28
Perspiring hands	+ .55	−1.18
Fainting	− .11	+ .81
Headaches	+ .80	−1.96
Dizziness	+ .24	− .79
Heart palpitations	+ .02	−3.87

SOURCE: National Center for Health Statistics, *Selected Symptoms of Psychological Distress* (U.S. Department of Health, Education, and Welfare, 1970), Table 17, pp. 30–31.

Table 6

PSYCHOLOGICAL WELL-BEING OF MEN BY MARITAL STATUS

Happiness	Marital Status				
	Married	Single	Separated	Divorced	Widowed
Very happy	35	18	7	12	7
Pretty happy	56	63	55	53	56
Not too happy	9	19	38	35	37

SOURCE: Norman M. Bradburn, *The Structure of Psychological Well-Being* (Chicago, Ill.: Aldine, 1969), p. 149.

Table 7
MARITAL HAPPINESS OF MEN

Very happy	48
Above average	23
Average	26
Not too happy	2
Not ascertained	1

SOURCE: G. Gurin, J. Veroff, and S. Feld, *Americans View Their Mental Health* (New York: Basic Books, 1960), p. 102.

Table 8
SUMMARY OF STUDIES COMPARING HAPPINESS OF SINGLE AND MARRIED MEN

	Not too Happy		Very Happy	
Study	Single	Married	Single	Married
G. Gurin, J. Veroff, Sheila Feld, national sample, 1957	13	8	11	36
N. M. Bradburn, and D. Caplowitz, four rural Illinois communities, 1962	31	14	12	27
N. M. Bradburn, five urban and suburban communities, 1963	19	9	18	35
Genevieve Knupfer et al., San Francisco, 1962	21	7	16	39

SOURCE: Genevieve Knupfer, Walter Clark, and Robin Room, "The Mental Health of the Unmarried," *American Journal of Psychiatry* 122 (February 1966): 842. The number of cases were: *single men,* Gurin, Veroff, Feld, 82; Bradburn and Caplowitz, 42; Bradburn, 150; Knupfer, 101. *Married men:* 908, 794, 1,009, and 374 respectively.

Table 9
The Happiness of Husbands' Marriages

		Terman		
Burgess and Cottrell			Sample Studied	Random Sample
		Extremely happy	29.5	25.5
Very happy	55.4	Decidedly above average	36.8	29.4
Happy	24.7	Somewhat above average	16.3	13.1
Average	11.9	Average	12.9	18.2
Unhappy	5.6	Somewhat less than average	2.9	6.6
Very unhappy	2.4	Decidedly less than average	1.6	3.2
		Extremely unhappy	0.1	4.0

SOURCE: The Burgess and Cottrell data are from *Predicting Success or Failure in Marriage* (Englewood Cliffs, N.J.: Prentice-Hall, 1939), p. 39; the Terman data from Lewis M. Terman et al, *Psychological Factors in Marital Happiness* (New York: McGraw-Hill, 1938), p. 78.

Table 10
Health of Women by Marital Status and Age, Health Defined in Terms of Absence of Chronic Condition or Restricted Activity

	Marital Status		
Age	Married	Never Married	(Percent Healthy)
17–44	91.4	94.0	
45–64	80.9	83.2	
65+	57.6	65.5	

SOURCE: Unpublished table, National Center for Health Statistics. Data are from 1968 Health Interview Survey.

Table 11
SELECTED PERSONALITY DIMENSIONS AMONG MARRIED MEN AND MARRIED WOMEN 30 YEARS OF AGE AND OVER

	Percent Scoring High	
Personality Dimension	Married Men	Married Women
Depression	37	54
Severe neurotic symptoms	17	11
Phobic tendency	30	55
Passivity	50	74

SOURCE: Genevieve Knupfer, Walter Clark, and Robin Room, "The Mental Health of the Unmarried," *American Journal of Psychiatry* 122 (February 1966): 842.

Table 12
SELECTED SYMPTOMS OF PSYCHOLOGICAL DISTRESS AMONG MARRIED WHITE MEN AND WOMEN

Symptom	Married Men	Married Women
Nervous breakdown	− .76	+ .57
Felt impending nervous breakdown	− .51	− .18
Nervousness	+ .31	+1.05
Inertia	− .76	+1.00
Insomnia	−1.17	+ .60
Trembling hands	− .23	− .54
Nightmares	− .75	0.00
Perspiring hands	+ .55	+ .38
Fainting	− .11	+ .26
Headaches	+ .80	+ .97
Dizziness	+ .24	− .10
Heart palpitations	+ .02	+ .46

SOURCE: National Center for Health Statistics, *Selected Symptoms of Psychological Distress* (U.S. Department of Health, Education, and Welfare, 1970), Table 17, pp. 30–31.

Table 13
PROPORTION OF IMPAIRED RESPONDENTS IN MIDTOWN MANHATTAN MENTAL HEALTH SURVEY BY AGE AND MARITAL STATUS

Age	Married Men	Married Women
20–29	11.7	13.4
30–39	19.6	22.1
40–49	19.0	18.1
50–59	25.7	30.6

SOURCE: Leo Srole and associates, *Mental Health in the Metropolis, The Midtown Manhattan Study* (New York: McGraw-Hill, 1962), pp. 177, 178.

Table 14
SELECTED PERSONALITY DIMENSIONS AMONG WOMEN 30 YEARS OF AGE AND OVER BY MARITAL STATUS

	Percent Scoring High	
Personality Dimension	Married Women	Single Women
Depression	54	35
Severe neurotic symptoms	11	4
Phobic tendency	55	44
Passivity	74	57
Antisocial tendency	14	13
Lack of moral strictness	69	53

SOURCE: Genevieve Knupfer, Walter Clark, and Robin Room, "The Mental Health of the Unmarried," *American Journal of Psychiatry* 122 (February 1966): 842.

Table 15

PROPORTION OF IMPAIRED FEMALE RESPONDENTS IN MIDTOWN MANHATTAN MENTAL HEALTH SURVEY BY AGE AND MARITAL STATUS

| | Marital Status | |
Age	Married	Single
20–29	13.4	11.2
30–39	22.1	12.1
40–49	18.1	24.6
50–59	30.6	25.6

SOURCE: Leo Srole and associates, *Mental Health in the Metropolis, The Midtown Manhattan Study* (New York: McGraw-Hill, 1962), pp. 177, 178.

Table 16

SELECTED SYMPTOMS OF PSYCHOLOGICAL DISTRESS AMONG WHITE WOMEN BY MARITAL STATUS

Symptom	Single Women	Married Women
Nervous breakdown	− .86	+ .57
Felt impending nervous breakdown	−4.48	− .18
Nervousness	−3.04	+1.05
Inertia	−6.34	+1.00
Insomnia	−1.68	+ .60
Trembling hands	− .76	− .54
Nightmares	−2.35	0.00
Perspiring hands	−1.18	+ .38
Fainting	+ .09	+ .26
Headaches	−1.63	+ .97
Dizziness	−2.97	− .10
Heart palpitations	−3.43	+ .46

SOURCE: National Center for Health Statistics, *Selected Symptoms of Psychological Distress* (U.S. Department of Health, Education, and Welfare, 1970), Table 17, pp. 30–31.

Table 17
PROPORTION OF IMPAIRED RESPONDENTS AMONG UNMARRIED MEN AND WOMEN IN MIDTOWN MANHATTAN MENTAL HEALTH SURVEY BY AGE

Age	Single Men	Single Women
20–29	20.5	11.2
30–39	30.4	12.1
40–49	37.5	24.6
50–59	46.1	25.6

SOURCE: Leo Srole and associates, *Mental Health in the Metropolis, The Midtown Manhattan Study* (New York: McGraw-Hill, 1962), pp. 177, 178.

Table 18
SELECTED PERSONALITY DIMENSIONS AMONG SINGLE MEN AND WOMEN

	Percent Scoring High	
Personality Dimension	Single Men	Single Women
Depression	50	35
Severe neurotic symptoms	30	4
Phobic tendency	40	44
Passivity	66	57

SOURCE: Genevieve Knupfer, Walter Clark, and Robin Room, "The Mental Health of the Unmarried," *American Journal of Psychiatry* 122 (February 1966): 842.

Table 19
SELECTED SYMPTOMS OF PSYCHOLOGICAL DISTRESS AMONG
NEVER-MARRIED WHITE MEN AND WOMEN

Symptom	Never-Married Men	Never-Married Women
Nervous breakdown	+1.00	− .86
Felt impending nervous breakdown	− .07	−4.48
Nervousness	−1.05	−3.04
Inertia	+ .29	−6.34
Insomnia	+1.92	−1.68
Trembling hands	− .52	− .76
Nightmares	+1.28	−2.35
Perspiring hands	−1.18	−1.18
Fainting	+ .81	+ .09
Headaches	−1.96	−1.63
Dizziness	− .79	−2.97
Heart palpitations	−3.87	−3.43

SOURCE: National Center for Health Statistics, *Selected Symptoms of Psychological Distress* (U.S. Department of Health, Education, and Welfare, 1970), Table 17, pp. 30–31.

Table 20
SOME SELECTED SOCIOECONOMIC VARIABLES AMONG
NEVER-MARRIED WHITE MEN AND WOMEN 45 TO 54
YEARS OF AGE

Selected Socioeconomic Variables	Single Men	Single Women
Median years of education	9.0	12.2
Percent with some college	14.7	29.1
Median income	$3,440	$3,632
Percent with professional, managerial, or official occupation	16.4	31.6

SOURCE: United States Census, 1960: *Marital Status,* Tables 4, 5, and 6.

Table 21

SELECTED PERSONALITY DIMENSIONS AMONG MEN AND WOMEN
30 YEARS OF AGE AND OVER BY MARITAL STATUS

| | *Percent Scoring High* | |
Personality Dimension	Married Men	Never-Married Women
Depression	37	35
Severe neurotic symptoms	17	4
Phobic tendencies	30	44
Passivity	50	57

SOURCE: Genevieve Knupfer, Walter Clark, and Robin Room, "The Mental Health of the Unmarried," *American Journal of Psychiatry* 122 (February 1966): 842.

Table 22

PROPORTION OF MENTAL HEALTH IMPAIRMENT OF MARRIED
MEN AND SINGLE WOMEN BY AGE

Age	Married Men	Never-Married Women
20–29	11.7	11.2
30–39	19.6	12.1
40–49	19.0	24.6
50–59	25.7	25.6

SOURCE: Leo Srole and associates, *Mental Health in the Metropolis* (New York: McGraw-Hill, 1962), pp. 177–178.

Table 23
SELECTED SYMPTOMS OF PSYCHOLOGICAL DISTRESS AMONG MARRIED MEN AND NEVER-MARRIED WOMEN

Symptom	Married Men	Never-Married Women
Nervous breakdown	− .76	− .86
Felt impending nervous breakdown	− .51	−4.48
Nervousness	+ .31	−3.04
Inertia	− .76	−6.34
Insomnia	−1.17	−1.68
Trembling hands	− .23	− .76
Nightmares	− .75	−2.35
Perspiring hands	+ .55	−1.18
Fainting	− .11	+ .09
Headaches	+ .80	−1.63
Dizziness	+ .24	−2.97
Heart palpitations	+ .02	−3.43

SOURCE: National Center for Health Statistics, *Selected Symptoms of Psychological Distress* (U.S. Department of Health, Education, and Welfare, 1970), Table 17, pp. 30–31.

Table 24
MARRIAGE RATES FOR WHITE TEEN-AGE WOMEN BY INCOME

Income in dollars	Age			
	14–16	17	18	19
No income	30.4	178.3	331.4	380.9
1 to 999 or less	27.8	90.7	199.2	230.3
1,000 to 2,999	42.8	73.2	183.6	253.3
3,000 to 4,999	23.8	55.0	119.1	168.7
5,000 to 6,999	14.7	47.4	94.6	118.2
7,000 to 9,999	10.4	34.9	....	....
10,000 and over	....	....	....	....

SOURCE: United States Census, 1960: *Age at First Marriage*, Table 17, p. 159.
NOTE: The more income a young woman has, the less likely she is to marry.

Table 25

MARRIED RATES (PER 1000) FOR WHITE TEEN-AGE WOMEN BY OCCUPATION

	Age			
Occupation	14–16	17	18	19
Not employed	32.5	164.3	333.3	410.7
Operative	60.0	100.4	189.4	203.6
Service	23.1	69.9	120.5	135.8
Clerical	14.0	41.9	121.6	172.4
Sales	12.1	55.9	135.8	156.0
Professional	11.9	20.1	47.0	65.4

SOURCE: United States Census, 1960: *Age at First Marriage*, Table 17, p. 159.
NOTE: The better the job a young woman has, the less likely she is to marry.

Table 26

ANNUAL DEATH RATES FROM CIRRHOSIS OF THE LIVER AMONG WHITE WOMEN BY AGE AND MARITAL STATUS, 1959–1961

Age	Single	Married
15–19	0.3	0.3
20–24	0.4	0.2
25–34	2.8	1.3
35–44	7.2	6.8
45–54	12.2	15.7
55–59	12.1	16.3
60–64	13.3	17.5
65–69	13.7	18.0
70–74	14.7	19.3
75 years and over	16.7	22.7

SOURCE: National Center for Health Statistics, *Mortality from Selected Causes by Marital Status* (Public Health Service, Series 20, No. 8a, December 1970), Table 3, p. 40.

Table 27
Selected Symptoms of Psychological Distress among White Housewives and Working Women

Symptom	Housewives	Working Women
Nervous breakdown	+1.16	−2.02
Felt impending nervous breakdown	− .12	+ .81
Nervousness	+1.74	−2.29
Inertia	+2.35	−3.15
Insomnia	+1.27	−2.00
Trembling hands	+ .74	−1.25
Nightmares	+ .68	−1.18
Perspiring hands	+1.28	−2.55
Fainting	+ .82	−2.69
Headaches	+ .84	− .87
Dizziness	+1.41	−1.85
Heart palpitations	+1.38	−1.56

SOURCE: National Center for Health Statistics, *Selected Symptoms of Psychological Distress* (U.S. Department of Health, Education, and Welfare, 1970), Table 17, pp. 30–31.

Table 28
Psychological Well-Being of Women by Marital Status

Happiness	Marital Status				
	Married	Single	Separated	Divorced	Widowed
Very happy	38	18	12	11	14
Pretty happy	55	68	45	66	54
Not too happy	7	14	44	23	32

SOURCE: Norman M. Bradburn, *The Structure of Psychological Well-Being* (Chicago, Ill.: Aldine, 1969), p. 149.

Table 29
MARITAL HAPPINESS OF HUSBANDS AND WIVES

Happiness	Wives	Husbands
Very happy	45	48
Above average	20	23
Average	32	26
Not too happy	3	2

SOURCE: G. Gurin, J. Veroff, and S. Feld, *Americans View Their Mental Health* (New York: Basic Books, 1960), p. 102.

Table 30
SUMMARY OF STUDIES COMPARING HAPPINESS OF SINGLE AND MARRIED WOMEN

Study	Not Too Happy		Very Happy	
	Single	Married	Single	Married
Gurin, Veroff, and Feld, national sample, 1957	11	7	26	43
Bradburn and Caplowitz, four rural Illinois communities, 1962	15	11	27	27
N. M. Bradburn, five urban and suburban communities, 1963	14	7	18	38
Knupfer and others, San Francisco, 1962	12	10	24	39

SOURCE: Genevieve Knupfer, Walter Clark, and Robin Room, "The Mental Health of the Unmarried," *American Journal of Psychiatry* 122 (February 1966): 842.

Table 31
THE HAPPINESS OF WIVES' AND HUSBANDS' MARRIAGES

				Terman's Studies			
				Sample Studied		Random Sample	
Burgess and Cottrell Study							
Sample Studied	Wife	Husband		Wife	Husband	Wife	Husband
Very happy	51.8	55.4	Extremely happy	34.6	29.5	27.2	25.5
Happy	27.5	24.7	Decidedly above average	35.9	36.8	28.0	29.4
Average	12.3	11.9	Somewhat above average	14.7	16.3	10.1	13.1
			Average	9.2	12.9	16.3	18.2
Unhappy	6.0	5.6	Somewhat less than average	3.0	2.9	7.3	6.6
Very unhappy	2.4	2.4	Decidedly less than average	1.8	1.6	4.0	3.2
			Extremely unhappy	0.8	0.1	7.1	4.0

SOURCE: Burgess and Cottrell data from *Predicting Success or Failure in Marriage* (Englewood Cliffs, N.J.: Prentice-Hall, 1939), p. 39; Terman data from Lewis M. Terman et al, *Psychological Factors in Marital Happiness* (New York: McGraw-Hill, 1938), p. 78.

Table 32

MARITAL HAPPINESS OF HUSBANDS AND WIVES BY EDUCATION

	Education					
	Grade School		High School		College	
Happiness	Husband	Wife	Husband	Wife	Husband	Wife
Very happy	43	39	50	45	57	61
Little happier than average	20	9	29	22	30	17
Average	34	41	20	32	13	22
Not too happy	3	11	1	1	1	0

SOURCE: Joseph Veroff and Sheila Feld, *Marriage and Work in America* (New York: Van Nostrand-Reinhold, 1970), p. 377.

Table 33

MARITAL HAPPINESS OF HUSBANDS AND WIVES BY AGE

	Age					
	Young		Middle		Old	
Happiness	Husband	Wife	Husband	Wife	Husband	Wife
Very happy	49	49	56	49	50	38
Little happier than average	30	19	27	16	23	21
Average	20	29	22	33	24	34
Not too happy	1	3	1	2	3	7

SOURCE: Joseph Veroff and Sheila Feld, *Marriage and Work in America* (New York: Van Nostrand-Reinhold, 1970), p. 377.

Table 34

PROPORTION OF PARENTS AND CHILDLESS HUSBANDS AND
WIVES GIVING SPECIFIED MARITAL RESPONSES

Responses	Mothers (1)	Childless Women (2)	Fathers (3)	Childless Men (4)
Marriage is restrictive	48	35	39	34
Very happy	46	51	49	60
Problems in marriage	54	39	47	31
Feelings of inadequacy	8	9	9	3
Satisfaction with marital relation	42	52	42	46
Self-dissatisfaction	6	4	16	8

SOURCE: Joseph Veroff and Sheila Feld, *Marriage and Work in America* (New York: Van Nostrand-Reinhold, 1970), pp. 377–378.

Table 35
LOWEST AND HIGHEST POINTS IN MARRIAGE

Husband's Marriage

Pre-child	Negative feelings high; daily companionship high
Preschool	. . . .
School-age	General marital satisfaction low
Teen-age	Satisfaction with children low
Young adult	Satisfaction with present stage of family cycle low
Empty nest	Satisfaction with children high
Retirement	Positive daily companionship low; satisfaction with present stage of family cycle high; general marital satisfaction high; negative feeling low

---

Wife's Marriage

Pre-child	General marital satisfaction high; positive daily companionship high
Preschool	. . . .
School-age	General marital satisfaction low; positive daily companionship low; satisfaction with children low; negative feeling high
Teen-age	. . . .
Young adult	Satisfaction with present stage of family cycle low
Empty nest	Satisfaction with children high; negative feeling low
Retirement	Satisfaction with present stage of family cycle high; daily companionship low

---

SOURCE: Figure 2. Data on satisfaction with children from Wesley R. Burr, "Satisfaction with Various Aspects of Marriage over the Life Cycle: A Random Middle-Class Sample," *Journal of Marriage and the Family* 32 (February 1970): 36.

Table 36

PERSONS 18 YEARS OF AGE AND OVER PER HOUSEHOLD AND
FAMILY IN THE UNITED STATES, 1940 TO 1966, AND TEST
PROJECTIONS FOR 1985

Year	Persons 18 Years of Age and Over per Household	Persons 18 Years of Age and Over per Family	Col. 2– Col. 1
1940	2.5	2.5	0
1950	2.3	2.4	.1
1960	2.1	2.3	.2
1966	2.1	2.3	.2
1985	1.9	2.2	.3

SOURCE: Adapted from Robert Parke, Jr. and Paul C. Glick, "Prospective Changes in Marriage and the Family," *Journal of Marriage and the Family* 29 (May 1967): 254. The last column in the above table not in the source.

Table 37
FAMILIES OF THE FUTURE: SOME ALTERNATIVE STRUCTURES
DESIGNED TO MEET INDIVIDUAL NEEDS

Living Groups—
1. Single Individuals
   a. 1 male adult
   b. 1 female adult
   c. 1 non-adult (child)

2. Single adult with children
   a. 1 male or female with 1 child
   b. 1 male or female with 2 or more children

3. 1 Pair of adults +
   a. 1 male–1 female–0 children
   b. 1 male–1 female with one child
   c. 1 male—1 female with 2 or more children

4. Commune of Pairs
   a. 2 or more males, 2 or more females
   b. 2 or more males, 2 or more females with children of pair
   c. 2 or more males, 2 or more females, children shared

5. Communes—not paired
   a. 2 or more males—2 or more females
   b. (a)—all children within group
   c. (a)—children reared outside group (kibbutz-type arrangement)

6. Communes—Mixed Groupings
   a. Some pairs, some singles, children shared
   b. children with biological parents
   c. children outside group

7. Sex Groupings
   a. males in one group, females in one group
   b. males + children
   c. females + children
   d. (a) with children in separate sex group

8. Traditional
   a. one male, one female
   b. one male, one female, one child
   c. one male, one female, 2 or more children

9. Community or Neighborhood Groupings
   a. All family structures living in certain area, grouped in mutual helping roles
   b. (a) grouped according to interests, age, etc.

SOURCE: College of Home Economics, Michigan State University.

notes

introduction

1. In the second-generation Italian community, Irvin L. Child found that marriage was used by some as a way to escape the ethnic pattern of relations; their ideal for marriage was decidedly middle class: "Indications of desire to behave in accordance with the American pattern of family organization appear in a determination of the man not to dominate his wife but to have a relationship of equality with her." And Herbert Ganz found among the third-generation Italians in Boston that wives, who tended to stay in school longer and engage in white-collar work, were taking the lead in processes of change. Now Arthur Shostak tells us how blue-collar young men are being pressured into new family patterns by young women.

chapter one: the two marriages

1. For a discussion of the part played by communication in all relations between the sexes, see Jessie Bernard, *The Sex Game* (Englewood Cliffs, N.J., Prentice-Hall, 1968; New York: Atheneum, 1972). Chapter 10 deals with communication in marriage.

chapter two: the husband's marriage

1. As it turned out, Dr. Lee was advocating not less but more marriage. He was sympathetic, that is, to the idea of polygyny.

2. For an interesting discussion of Durkheim's analysis of divorce as well as of suicide in terms of marital norms, see Barbara G. Cashion, "Durkheim's Concept of Anomie and Its Relationship to Divorce," *Sociology and Social Research* 55 (October 1970): 72–81.

3. Comparing the married and the widowed does not entirely eliminate the selective factor, because marriage recurs after bereavement as well as in earlier years. Some men— probably the poorest and least desirable—do not remarry, so some kind of selection is operating even here. And since mortality is higher in the less privileged classes, the same factors that led to bereavement lead also to other dysfunctions in the surviving partner.

4. The same comparison as that made here between the married and the widowed could also be made between the married and the divorced, with essentially the same results. But marriages disrupted by divorce are different from those terminated by death, and the conclusions to be drawn from comparing them with intact marriages are different.

5. In teaching orders, the mortality rates for priests were not so unfavorable.

6. There is a strong selective factor here. One study that did not present data by sex showed that the "depression-prone" were less likely to marry, the "depression-resistant" more likely to. See H. J. Gross, "The Depression-Prone and the Depression-Resistant Sibling: A Study of 650 Three-Sibling Families: A Follow-up Note on Marital Status," *British Journal of Psychiatry* 114 (December 1968): 1559. Another study, again without a sex breakdown, corroborated the finding that depressives were less likely than average to marry. This was especially interesting, because in most of the cases the depression had appeared after the age of forty-five—at an age, that is, when practically all who are ever going to marry have already done so. Thus, even before they became ill, the depressives had selected themselves out of the married population. Would marriage have saved them from their depressive illness? See Alistair Munro, "Some Familial and Social Factors in Depressive Illness," *British Journal of Psychiatry* 112 (May 1966): 440.

7. In families with incomes in the brackets of $7,000 and over, wives' earnings were contributing on the average between a fifth and a fourth of family income. See Women's Bureau, *1969 Handbook on Women Workers*, p. 35. Wives were contributing 30 percent of family income or more in almost

half of the families with incomes of $10,000 to $15,000, and at least a fifth of family income in three-fourths of families with incomes of $15,000 or more (ibid., p. 34).

8. In another study of a similar but apparently more conservative sample, only 20 percent of the husbands said that they had experienced extramarital relations. See Ralph E. Johnson, "Some Correlates of Extramarital Coitus," *Journal of Marriage and the Family* 32 (August 1970): 451. Lack of opportunity might account for this low figure.

chapter three: the wife's marriage

1. Among women who become ill enough for hospitalization, marriage favors a good readjustment upon release. There is evidence that having a husband, regardless of the nature of the marital relationship, can be therapeutic, especially for women in lower socioeconomic classes.

... even the married patients who had been severely ill ... were significantly better adjusted than the unmarried patients who had the same degree of illness. ... The quality of the marital interaction did not necessarily relate to the quality of adjustment. ... As long as a patient was married it did not matter whether the marriage was stable and friction-free. ... It is the [sheer] presence of the husband and not the quality of marital interaction that predicts a good [post-hospital] adjustment (Andrew Ferber, et al., "Current Family Structure, Psychiatric Emergencies, and Patient Fate," *Archives of General Psychiatry* 16 [June 1967]: 659–67).

Another study of patient adjustment also showed family factors to be favorable, but the sexes were not analyzed separately (Ørnulv Ødegard, "Marriage and Mental Health," *ACTA Psychiatrica et Neurologica Scandinavica*, Supplement No. 80, Report on the 10th Congress of Scandinavian Psychiatrists [Stockholm, 1952]: 153, 160–61.

2. The income comparisons of unmarried men and women in the text and in table 20 are in terms of averages. But the disabilities under which women perform in the labor force are illustrated by the fact that only 1.9 percent of the single white women who had incomes were in the income bracket of $10,000 and over, as compared with 4 percent of the single men.

3. Even if a wife is working, a disparity in occupational status between her job and her husband's may make a difference to her. If her occupation is lower in status than her hus-

band's, she is more likely to show symptoms of anxiety (Lawrence J. Sharp and F. Ivan Nye, "Maternal Mental Health," in F. Ivan Nye and Lois Wladis Hoffman, eds., *The Employed Mother in America* [Chicago, Ill.: Rand McNally, 1963]: 309–19). When both are on the same occupational level, as among blue-collar and unskilled workers, the status differential does not exist and the anxiety symptoms do not show up.

4. Actually, in the earlier age brackets, twenty-five to forty-four, working women averaged more days of restricted activity or bed disability than housekeeping women, though in the later age brackets the reverse was true. (Data from an unpublished table by the National Center for Health Statistics.)

5. The members of the National Capital Area chapter of the National Organization for Women (NOW) monitored television programs, including advertisements, during the month of April 1971. Viewed through the eyes of these stern, no-nonsense monitors, the enormous pathos of the housewife comes through with a heart-sinking thud: young housewives who have to fortify themselves with pills to get through their day; housewives in a tizzy for fear that neighbors will catch them with their furniture unpolished; housewives cattily comparing the relative whiteness of their laundry; housewives being patronized by smug husbands. . . . Are *these* really the young women we saw in high school and college? Is *this* what they have been reduced to? Mrs. Millamant's "dwindling" was nothing compared to this. It might be mentioned in passing that advertising agencies were not pleased with NOW monitoring.

chapter four: their children

1. The statistical evidence is contrary to this conclusion, which is based on the writings and discussions of ecologists and environmentalists and advocates for zero population growth. There has not yet been time for the impact of this body of thought to show in the statistics. In 1967, only 3.1 percent of all wives fourteen to thirty-nine years of age expected to have no children when their families were completed.

2. Even before the positive drive to reduce the birthrate had been suggested, a decline in the birthrate had already set in. When the women of the early postwar generation began to have their babies in 1969, it rose again; but they were not

expected to have more children per marriage than their mothers' generation.

3. Veroff and Feld also rejected direct questioning about the effect of children on marriage because "pretests indicated that respondents uniformly said they were happy or satisfied with their parenthood when directly queried on this subject."

4. In one exception, childless wives rated their marital satisfaction lower than did mothers of up to three children; the researchers, Blood and Wolfe, interpreted this finding as cause rather than as effect. They concluded that "dissatisfied wives tend to expect either very few children (none or one) or an excessively large number."

5. It is interesting to note how trends in research interest follow the Zeitgeist. Before the era of the feminine mystique there was a considerable research literature on maternal rejection; it was recognized that parents—even mothers— did not always love their children. There was very little after that era. It has recently been resumed in a minor key in current interest in the battered baby syndrome.

6. Although more wives than husbands tended to report that children added to their happiness, Burgess and Wallin believed this to be a culturally induced difference.

7. In a study of women on assistance rolls, the average age at which the desertion of husbands occurred was at the age at which fourth parities occurred.

chapter five: marriage's past and its present future

1. In a recent book by fifteen authors, *The Family in Search of a Future, Alternate Models,* edited by Herbert A. Otto (New York: Appleton-Century, 1970), only three of the chapters were contributed by women.

chapter six: can any number play?

1. Here are the kinds of qualities specified in some advertisements: "Sincere, affectionate, handsome radical intellectual, twenty-nine, amateur translator, actor seeks mature, sensitive woman, twenty to thirty-five, to love and marry." We may add, parenthetically, that this is the only advertisement

out of twenty-six in this particular issue of the periodical, *The New York Review of Books,* in which marriage is mentioned. All eleven of the women and the remaining fourteen men specify other kinds of relationships. For example: "warm, stable, and honest relationship," "companionship," "sharing of books, music, food, occasional movies, and quiet evenings at home," "venturesome jaunts into Europe with object of fun and frolic," "intense relationship," and so on.

2. It is interesting that in the USSR, when young people were asked about the acceptability of computer matching, three-fourths answered affirmatively, and almost as many (70 percent) said that they would themselves be willing to participate. *Literaturnaya Gazeta* is quoted in *Parade Magazine* (October 3, 1971) as viewing computer mating as a public service, presumably to be offered by the state, since a "Socialist state bears a responsibility to facilitate the meeting of men and women who want to build families."

chapter seven: are some more equal than others?

1. Other components of the new companionate model of marriage, specified by Burgess and Locke but not relevant here, included a decline in romantic love, emancipation of youth, and the waning of the puritan taboo on sex.

2. In general, the tendency in statutory legislation is in the direction of equalizing the rights and liabilities of both spouses, either by adding to the wife's common-law rights and liabilities or by reducing those of the husband. Some jurisdictions impose the duty of support on a wife if the husband is unable to support himself.

3. The research studies on which this conclusion is based are: Paul Popenoe, "Can the Family Have Two Heads?" *Sociology and Social Research* 18 (September-October 1933): 12–17; Leonard Cottrell, Jr., unpublished study reported in E. W. Burgess and Leonard Cottrell, Jr., *Predicting Success or Failure in Marriage* (Englewood Cliffs, N.J.: Prentice-Hall, 1939); E. W. Burgess and Paul Wallin, *Engagement and Marriage* (Philadelphia, Pa.: J. B. Lippincott, 1953); Robert Winch, *Mate Selection* (New York: Harper, 1958); David M. Heer, "Dominance and the Working Wife," *Social Forces* (May 1958): 341–47; Lois Wladis Hoffman, "Parental Power Relations and the Division of

Household Tasks," *Marriage and Family Living* 22 (February 1960): 27–35; Robert O. Blood, Jr. and Donald M. Wolfe, *Husbands and Wives* (Glencoe, Ill.: Free Press, 1960); Robert O. Blood, "The Husband-Wife Relationship," in F. Ivan Nye and Lois W. Hoffman, eds., *The Employed Mother in America* (Chicago, Ill.: Rand McNally, 1963), pp. 282–305; Mirra Komarovsky, *Blue Collar Marriage* (New York: Random House, 1964), chapter 10; William A. Westley and Nathan B. Epstein, *Silent Majority* (San Francisco, Calif.: Jossey-Bass, 1969), chapter 6; Constantina Safilios-Rothschild, "The Study of Family Power Structure: A Review 1960–1969" *Journal of Marriage and the Family* 32 (November 1970): 539–53; Karen Renne, "Correlates of Dissatisfaction in Marriage," *Journal of Marriage and the Family* 32 (February 1970); Norman W. Bell and James L. Turk, "The Concept of Power: Some Observations on the Power of a Concept," paper presented at meetings of American Sociological Association, September 1970.

4. Everyone seems to know what we are talking about when we say that a man is henpecked or that a wife cannot call her soul her own, but there is little consensus among researchers when it comes to conceptualizing the situation. As a result, we are sunk in a semantic quagmire. Some researchers talk of power, some of dominance, some of predominance, some of prevalence, some of control, some of influence, some of leadership, some of super- and subordination, some of ideology. The terms are by no means equivalent, and although they all refer to phenomena we all recognize, they do not add up to a unidimensional, clearcut, measurable construct. The research studies are not, therefore, comparable, nor can their results be combined to delineate a trend. David M. Heer believes that when a husband attributes more influence to his wife than to himself, his reply must be accorded greater credence than the wife's because he is, so to speak, going against the cultural grain. It could, however, be just as cogently argued that, since the institutional bias is in favor of the husband, even minimal deviation on the part of the wife would seem much greater to the husband and he would tend to exaggerate it. The bias in favor of assigning greater power to the husband is especially strong in blue-collar marriages where, according to Veroff and Feld, the wife enjoys her power because it is covert. There have been three critical reviews of the concept of power in marriage, by Turk and Bell, Zelditch,

and Safilios-Rothschild. Morris Zelditch has summarized the situation like this:

> Problems ... arise ... from the current state of disorder in concepts and measures. ... In experimental studies, power can be taken to mean: (1) Who participates most in discussion? (2) Who had the ideas that were finally adopted by the family? (3) Who had the right to make the final decision, regardless of who originated the idea adopted? (4) Who received the most deference or agreement from whom? (5) Whose ideas were adopted if husband and wife initially disagreed? ... The problem arises partly from the absence of clear conceptualization of the process by which power is exercised, so that it is not clear how these concepts are related.

Zelditch also notes, as have other students of the subject, that egalitarianism is always overestimated (p. 702).

5. In 1933, for example, Popenoe found about two-fifths of his sample to be egalitarian; Westley and Epstein in 1969, a third; and Turk and Bell in 1970, again two-fifths.

6. When we speak of equal rights, we are on firmer ground; the rights of one person can and must be identical to the rights of another in order to be equal.

7. The results of these three studies may be summarized in the following schema:

SUMMARY OF THREE STUDIES ON THE EFFECT OF STRUCTURE ON
MARRIAGE, 1930s AND 1940s

	Husband-dominant	Egalitarian	Wife-dominant
Husband's score	low	high	intermediate
	low	high	high (happiness criterion)
Wife's score	low	intermediate	low
	low	high	low
	low (happiness criterion)	high	intermediate

Source: E. W. Burgess and Paul Wallin, *Engagement and Marriage*, p. 637. Aside from exceptions noted, all scores were based on an adjustment criterion. The studies were by Burgess and Cottrell, Lewis M. Terman, and Yichuang Lu.

8. By way of contrast, the mother-dominant families had grisly effects on children: the children were

> timid and withdrawn ... [and] lack self-discipline and industry and show serious psychopathological symptoms. ... The mother-dominant type emerges as the most serious pathological type. The

children from mother-dominant families face great difficulties in finding their own identity and individuality.

chapter eight: "other things being equal"; but *are* they?

1. For those astonished by this statement, the evidence is presented here. There have been no large-scale studies of a total population sample since Kinsey published his material in 1953. Most of the studies since that time have been of college students. On the basis of the Kinsey data, researchers have concluded that the great sexual revolution with respect to premarital sexual relations among women occurred in the 1920s; the proportion who had engaged in premarital sexual relations did not seem to increase after that until the 1960s. For the women Kinsey was reporting on, among those who married at the age of twenty or earlier—including about half of all married women—47 percent had had premarital sexual relations. Among those who married between twenty-one and twenty-five, including almost all of the remaining half, 42 percent had had premarital sexual relations. Only among the relatively few who had married at the age of twenty-eight to thirty, was the proportion more than half. In the 1960s, on the basis of evidence from samples of college students, there was apparently another upsurge in the proportion of women who engaged in premarital sexual relations, so that the proportion of women born in the 1950s entering marriage as virgins may be less than 50 percent. Researchers are careful to note that for the most part the premarital sexual relations have been only with future husbands. The current pattern of premarital sexual relations is probably changing.

2. Girls born in 1950 were twenty in 1970. But there were more of them than there were of twenty-two-year-old men for them to marry because the birthrate was higher in the year they were born, 1950, than it had been in 1948, the year their future husbands were born. They had to wait, therefore, until men of the increased number born in 1951 or 1952 became 22, in 1973 or 1974. It is this situation which is called the "marriage squeeze."

3. "It is erroneously believed," Peter Laslett tells us, "that [the family group in the preindustrial world] was large because it contained whole groups of kinsfolk living together. The impression seems to be that sons and daughters stayed with their parents after marriage and had their children

there: therefore the family group must often have been multigenerational. . . . It is also said that there would also be joint families of another type, because two married couples would often find it more convenient to share one household, just as perhaps they shared one plot of land. . . . But . . . families were *not* large. . . . [The rule was as follows:] No two married couples or more went to make up a family group; whether parents and children, brothers and sisters, employers and servants or married couples associated only for convenience. When a son got married he left the family . . . and started a family of his own. If he was not in a position to do this, then he could not get married, nor could his sister unless the man who was to take her for his bride was also in a position to start a new family." The old image of the so-called Grossfamilie, in which several generations of kinsfolk lived together as one big, happy family, was a mirage, a myth. If there ever were such multigeneration families they were rare.

4. The proportion of young adults eighteen to twenty-four in households who were classified by the census as children of a family head dropped from 50 percent in 1940 to only 36 percent in 1960. And the average number of children eighteen to twenty-four per family declined from .25 in 1940 to just half that size, .13 in 1960. In 1940 there were no family members eighteen years of age and over who were not in the household; by 1985 it is estimated that three out of ten families will have only one family member eighteen years of age and over in the household. We have here a statistical representation of the "generation gap."

5. When the People's Republic of China took its great leap forward in 1958, the general plan called for separate village dormitories for men and women. Provision was made for husbands and wives to have some time alone together, but by and large each sex was to live a segregated life. Such a style of living proved uncongenial to most of the people. It was abandoned before it actually began. But husbands and wives, Lucy Jen Huang tells us, may still live in widely separated regional areas.

chapter nine: male prophets and prophecies

1. Kenneth Boulding: "One's general impression . . . is that in spite of the agitation and apparently revolutionary upheaval

among college young people, and a certain dangerous polarization in our society between the long-haired privileged cavaliers and the hard-hatted roundheads, the forces making for structural stability in American society are so strong that it should continue for quite a while. . . . I doubt even if the form of the household will change very much in spite of a great deal of excitement and agitation in regard to communes, new forms of family living, etc." ("The Family Segment of the National Economy," *Journal of Home Economics* 62 [September 1970]: 454).

2. It is remarkable how little input has been made by women in blueprinting the future of marriage. In a recent book by fifteen authors, *The Family in Search of a Future, Alternate Models* (New York: Appleton-Century, 1970), edited by Herbert A. Otto, only three of the chapters were contributed by women.

3. This is the characterization by Yole G. Sills of a special category of science fiction to distinguish it from the older science fiction which rested more on projections of the hard sciences.

4. Noyes is here showing a male bias. When young women from five colleges and universities were asked in a *Playboy*-sponsored poll if they thought it possible to be satisfied with just one man for an entire life, 82 to 98 percent replied affirmatively (from an unsigned survey report, "Close-up: Five Schools," *Playboy* [September 1969]: 220).

5. In 1881, the Oneida Community abandoned its form of communism and became a joint stock company, Oneida Community, Limited.

6. Herbert A. Otto finds four basic reasons for the failures of communes: (1) disagreement over household chores or work; (2) interpersonal conflicts, especially jealousy; (3) lack of a strong economic base; and (4) the hostility of surrounding communities. ("Has Monogamy Failed?" *Saturday Review* [April 25, 1970]: 25.)

7. In one community in the Northwest, described by Sara Davidson, children were behaving like children elsewhere, and troubling their parents in the same ways. "There are three teen-agers at the farm—all girls—and all have tried running away to the city. One was arrested for shop-lifting, another was picked up in a crash pad with seven men. Steve says, 'We have just as much trouble with our kids as straight, middle-class parents do. I'd like to talk to people in other communities and find out how they handle their teen-agers. Maybe we could send ours there.' Stash says, 'Or

bring teen-age boys here.' The women at the farm have
started to joke uneasily that their sons will become uptight
businessmen and their daughters will be suburban housewives. . . . Sylvia says, 'Our way of life is an overreaction to
something, and our kids will probably overreact to us. It's
absurd. Kids run away from this, and all the runaways
from the city come here' " (Sara Davidson, "Open Land:
Getting Back to the Communal Garden," *Harper's* [June
1970]: 99).
8. A survey published in the July 1970 issue of *Psychology
Today* found twice as many husbands as wives (41 and 22
percent respectively) interested in mate swapping.

chapter twelve: toting it all up

1. Nor does the relative equality of numbers of males and females demand monogamy. In some societies, the rich can
afford several wives, the poor only one, if even that.

afterword

1. The fate of this book was symbolically significant. It was a
last vestige of the first cycle of twentieth-century feminism,
and it became a casualty of war. The plates were melted
down for war matériel. It will be reissued, however, by
Russell and Russell in 1973.
2. A representative of the New University Conference, Martin
Nicolaus, seized the microphone at the meetings of the
American Sociological Association in 1968 to accuse
sociologists of selecting their research projects to fit the
needs of the power structure, of putting their skills, talents,
and know-how at the service of the "rulers."

references

If references and bibliographies remind you of textbooks and you threw yours away when you left school, the avalanche of references that follows here may turn you off. At any rate, they call for an explanation if not for an apology.

This book differs from most books on the subject of marriage in that it is based almost exclusively on the findings of sociological research. I have therefore taken seriously one reviewer's charge in connection with another book that "it is inexcusable to omit the documentation that would permit an objective evaluation by the reader." The references are here because so much of the material presented is contrary to the conventional wisdom and folk clichés, and I feared that without thorough documentation it would be rejected, as it has been so often when presented orally to groups. I have marshaled the research in order to forestall time-consuming and unfruitful rebuttal by resistant readers who may cite one study that controverts all the others. For it is, indeed, true that one can often find a study somewhere that shows whatever it is you want to have proved. If the data themselves do not, their interpretation can. I know that marshaling research will not convince the unconvinceable, but I have felt as William James did that it should be possible for "those who desire this dreadful literature ... [to] find it."

Further, I am a sociologist, by definition a timid person. I am pegged to tables, charts, and documents, and my tether is short. A stern, faceless, nonpermissive, nonindulgent confrere looks over my shoulder as I write, demanding even before the sentence is finished that I document it with research facts and figures. Intimidated, I do, or at least try to. I am also a woman, and feel much braver when I can feel the research support at my back. Every statement of fact can be found somewhere in the following references.

Still I wish to make it clear that I do not gloss over the weakness of all this research. Much of it is poorly conceptualized, much superficial. Some of its limitations for gauging the future inhere in (1) the preconceptions of the researchers; some in (2) the effect of the research situation itself on the results achieved; some in (3) the nature of the samples studied; some in (4) the timing of the research; and some in (5) the cultural biases of the culture in which it took place.

preconceptions

In recent years researchers in the social and behavioral sciences have themselves been flabbergasted to learn how, despite all the safeguards built into their procedures, their own preconceptions and biases influence if they do not actually determine their results. A generation ago, a critic of some work on learning in rats pointed out that the way an experimenter held his animals could affect their behavior, helping the "gentled" strains of rats to learn faster than others and thus buttressing the researcher's theory of the inheritance of acquired characters. Another study showed how intimately the ideology of a scientist was related to his scientific findings.

Such unwitting biases have been especially noticeable in research on marriage. People with conventional backgrounds have found, for example, that premarital sexual relations have an adverse effect on marriage; less conventional researchers have not. When L. M. Terman described the happily married woman, he drew a picture of the archetypical Victorian hausfrau. And almost without exception, researchers with a psychoanalytic bent have found only harmful effects when a marriage did not fit their conception of husband-wife relations. Thus almost every kind of pathology—schizophrenia, alcoholism, criminality —has been traced to a home in which there was a weak father and a powerful mother.

the research situation

Not until recently have actual experiments been devised to show how subtly the research situation affects the results. Both psychologists and psychiatrists elicit from their human subjects the responses the subjects think they want. In the laboratory, "the Good Subject tries to comply with what he sees as the experimenter's scientific desires. . . . He will act to elicit the social approval he wants." We know that subjects in psychological and social-science research tend to give expected replies or replies that please the researcher. Women are so accustomed to maintaining the front of a happy marriage that they do so even if it is only for the researcher. In the clinic, the psychiatrist elicits the responses that fit his biases. When the patient presents information that does not fit his biases, he shows boredom; when the patient presents information that fits his biases, he shows great interest. In effect, he punishes with low attention the patient or subject for producing unwelcome data, and rewards him or her with attention for producing welcome data.

samples

Most research on marriage is based on samples, and a very considerable part of it on middle-class marriages, especially the most available—those of students and other accessible people, who tend to be middle class. This, for reasons spelled out in the Introduction, I do not count a defect too serious in discussing the future of marriage. Although there are wide differences in marriage among the several classes, the trend is in the direction of more years of schooling, more white-collar kinds of work, and higher incomes, the basic criteria of social class used in most studies. The upper-middle class are more articulate about marriage, the young are the most vocal in their analyses. These upper-middle-class young, in fact, constitute the best clue to the future of marriage.

The omission of samples of black marriage does call for an apology. This book is about the future of marriage in the white population not because the future of marriage in the black population is not equally worthy of study but because no one book can get it *all* together. I hope someone will soon tell us about the future of black marriage also.

timing

Much research suffers from the Walter Cronkite syndrome: "And that's the way it is, Thursday, February 29, 19XX."

Thursday, February 29, 19XX, perhaps. But next week? next month? or, for that matter, even Friday, March 1? Findings of research of the 1950s may no longer apply in the 1970s. Still, much research is presented as though the way it found things today is the way things "really" are, not only today but every day. Actually, there is hardly anything more perishable than today's news or today's research. The pictures we have of marriage and the family today are likely to be out of date by the time the data on which they are based have been processed —almost certainly by the time they have been interpreted and published. We are, as W. F. Ogburn once noted, like the dodo bird which flies backward to see where it has been. We know fairly well where we used to be, but relatively little about where we actually are today, and hardly at all where we will be tomorrow.

Just one example, borrowed from chapter 8, may suffice to show how tricky projecting the future on the basis of past research can be. We know that in the past marital stability has been positively associated with education. Since an increasing proportion of the population goes to college, one should be able to anticipate increasing stability in marriage. However, this is not so at all. We know from a CBS survey of young people that the most radical today are college students. We know that along with an increasing proportion of college educated, the divorce rate, after several years of decline and stabilization, is also going up. The relationship between education and marital stability reported by the researchers was the way it was last week; it may not be the way it is today. All past research has shown that, with some exceptions, marital stability was also related to income—the lower the income lower, in general, the level of stability. The logical conclusion would be that to improve marital stability one should increase income. However, at least for families on assistance rolls, increasing income does not necessarily improve marital stability. The Walter Cronkite syndrome gives one pause about projecting the future from the present.

cultural biases

That an all-pervasive male bias has dominated research not only on marriage but also on women and the relations between the sexes constitutes a serious limitation. We learn from historical research how men have conceived of the nature of the relationship as it was and how it should, in their view, be.

Only now are we researching history afresh to recover from oblivion the story of women. We will have a much better balanced understanding of marriage when this male bias has been overcome.

So much for the limitations of the research on which this book is based, embedded in the following references. They are serious, but not fatal. None of the major points made in this book rides on any one study. The evidence for the pathogenic nature of the occupation of housewife does not rest on any one study, nor the evidence for the effect of children on marriage; nor the evidence on egalitarianism in marriage; nor the evidence on any of the other themes. It is the general direction of the research findings that is finally so convincing. To me, at any rate—and, especially for the future of marriage, to others, I hope, as well.

---

introduction

Bell, Robert R. *Premarital Sex in a Changing Society*. Englewood Cliffs, N.J.: Prentice-Hall, 1966: 58.

————, and Buerkle, Jack. "Mother and Daughter Attitudes to Premarital Sexual Behavior," *Marriage and Family Living* 23 (November 1961): 340–42.

————, and Chaskes, Jay B. "Premarital Sexual Experience among Coeds, 1958 and 1968." *Journal of Marriage and the Family* 32 (February 1970): 81–84.

Burgess, E. W., and Wallin, Paul. *Engagement and Marriage*. Philadelphia, Pa.: J. B. Lippincott, 1953: 331.

Child, Irvin L. *Italian or American? The Second-Generation Conflict*. New Haven, Conn.: Yale University Press, 1943: 96–98, 108–10.

Freud, Sigmund. *Civilization and Its Discontents*. New York: Doubleday Anchor Books, 1958.

Gans, Herbert J. *The Urban Villagers*. New York: Free Press, 1962: 38–39, 51, 69–71.

Glick, Paul C., and Parke, Robert, Jr. "New Approaches in Studying the Life Cycle of the Family." *Demography* 2 (1965): 190, 191.

Kinsey, A. C. et al. *Sexual Behavior in the Human Female*. Philadelphia, Pa.: W. B. Saunders, 1953: Table 79, p. 337.

Komarovsky, Mirra. *Blue-Collar Marriage*. New York: Random House, 1964.

Lopata, Helena. *Occupation Housewife*. New York: Oxford University Press, 1971.

Marcuse, Herbert. *Eros and Civilization*. Boston, Mass.: Beacon Press, 1955.

Mills, C. Wright, and Gerth, H. H., eds. *From Max Weber: Essays in Sociology*. New York: Oxford University Press, 1958: 64.

Nisbet, Robert. "The Year 2000 and All That." *Commentary*. June 1968: 60–66.

Rainwater, Lee; Coleman, Richard; and Handel, Gerald. *Workingman's Wife*. Dobb's Ferry, N.Y.: Oceana Publications, Inc., 1959.

Shostak, Arthur B. "Working Class Americans at Home: Changing Expectations of Manhood." Paper read at Rutgers University Conference on the Working Class in the 1970s, October 1971.

Terman, Lewis M., et al. *Psychological Factors in Marital Happiness*. New York: McGraw-Hill, 1938: 321.

Toffler, Alvin. *Future Shock*. New York: Random House, 1970: chapter 11.

Weber, Max. *From Max Weber: Essays in Sociology*. New York: Oxford University Press, 1958: 327.

chapter one: the two marriages

Bell, Norman. *See* Turk, James L.

Bernard, Jessie. *American Family Behavior*. New York: Harper, 1942; New York: Russell and Russell, in press.

————. *Remarriage, A Study of Marriage*. New York: Dryden Press, 1956; New York: Russell and Russell, 1971.

————. *The Sex Game*. Englewood Cliffs, N.J.: Prentice-Hall, 1968; New York: Atheneum, 1972.

————. *Women and the Public Interest, An Essay on Policy and Protest*. Chicago, Ill.: Aldine-Atherton, 1971.

Brown, George W., and Ritter, Michael. "The Measurement of Family Activities and Relationships." *Human Relations* 19 (August 1966): 241–63.

Cheraskin, E., and Ringsdorf, W. M. "Familial Factors in Psychic Adjustment." *Journal of the American Geriatric Society* 17 (June 1969): 609–11.

1 Cor. 14:35; 1 Cor. 11:3.

De Tocqueville, Alexis. *Democracy in America*. New York: J. and H. G. Langley, 1840.

Elinson, Jack. *See* Haberman, Paul W.

Eph. 5:22–24.

Feld, Sheila. *See* Veroff, Joseph.

Feldman, Harold. *Development of the Husband-Wife Relationship.* Ithaca, N.Y.: Cornell University Press, 1967.

Feldman, Harold. *See* Rollins, Boyd C.

Ferber, Robert. "On the Reliability of Purchase Influence Studies." *Journal of Marketing* 19 (January 1955): 225–32.

Gen. 1, 2, and 3.

Gover, R. *One Hundred Dollar Misunderstanding.* New York: Grove Press, 1962.

Granbois, Donald H., and Willett, Ronald P. "Equivalence of Family Role Measures Based on Husband and Wife Data." *Journal of Marriage and the Family* 32 (February 1970).

Haberman, Paul W., and Elinson, Jack. "Family Income Reported in Surveys: Husbands versus Wives." *Journal of Marketing Research* 4 (May 1967): 191–94.

Heer, David M. "Husband and Wife Perceptions of Family Power Structure." *Marriage and Family Living* 24 (February 1962): 67.

Hoffman, Dean K. *See* Kenkel, W. F.

Kenkel, W. F., and Hoffman, Dean K. "Real and Conceived Roles in Family Decision Making." *Marriage and Family Living* 18 (November 1956): 314.

Kinsey, A. C., et al. *Sexual Behavior in the Human Male.* Philadelphia, Pa.: W. B. Saunders, 1948.

Lerner, Alan Jay. "I Remember It Well." From *Gigi.*

Maccoby, Eleanor E. "Woman's Intellect." In Seymour M. Farber and Roger H. L. Wilson, *The Potential of Woman.* New York: McGraw-Hill, 1963: 29.

Michels, Roberto. "Authority." *Encyclopedia of the Social Sciences.* New York: Macmillan, 1933: Vol. 2, p. 319.

Morrison, Denton E. *See* Wilkening, E. A.

Olson, David H. "The Measurement of Family Power by Self-Report and Behavioral Methods." *Journal of Marriage and the Family* 31 (August 1969): 549.

Ringsdorf, W. M. *See* Cheraskin, E.

Ritter, Michael. *See* Brown, George W.

Rollins, Boyd C., and Feldman, Harold. "Marital Satisfaction over the Family Life Cycle." *Journal of Marriage and the Family* 32 (February 1970): 24.

Safilios-Rochschild, Constantina. "Family Sociology or Wives' Family Sociology? A Cross-Cultural Examination of Decision-Making." *Journal of Marriage and the Family* 31 (May 1969).

————. "The Study of Family Power Structure: A Review 1960–1969." Ibid. 32 (November 1970): 539–52.

Scanzoni, John. "A Note on the Sufficiency of Wife Responses in Family Research." *Pacific Sociological Review*. Fall 1965: 12.

Schulder, Diane B. "Does the Law Oppress Women?" in Robin Morgan, ed. *Sisterhood Is Powerful*. New York: Vintage Books, 1970: 147.

1 Tim. 2:11.

Turk, James L., and Bell, Norman. "The Measurement of Family Behavior: What They Perceive, What They Report, What We Observe." Paper read at meeting of American Sociological Association, September 1970.

Veroff, Joseph, and Feld, Sheila. *Marriage and Work in America*. New York: Van Nostrand-Reinhold, 1970: 120–21.

Wilkening, E. A., and Morrison, Denton E. "A Comparison of Husband-Wife Responses Concerning Who Makes Farm and Home Decisions." *Journal of Marriage and the Family* 25 (August 1963): 351.

Willett, Ronald P. *See* Granbois, Donald H.

Wolgast, Elizabeth. "Do Husbands or Wives Make the Purchasing Decisions?" *Journal of Marketing* 23 (October 1958): 151–58.

Zelditch, Morris. "Family, Marriage, and Kinship." In Robert E. L. Faris, *Handbook of Modern Sociology*. Chicago, Ill.: Rand McNally, 1964).

chapter two: the husband's marriage

Athanasiou, Robert, et al. "Sex." *Psychology Today* 4 (July 1970): 43.

Bailar, John C., III. *See* King, Haitung.

Bartlett, John. *Famous Quotations*, 14th ed. Boston, Mass.: Little, Brown, 1968.

Bernard, Jessie. "Infidelity: Some Moral and Social Issues." In Jules H. Masserman, ed. *The Psychodynamics of Work and Marriage*. Vol. 16, 1970: 99–126.

———. "One Role, Two Roles, Shared Roles." *Issues in Industrial Society*. Vol. 2 (January 1970): 21–28.

Blau, Peter M., and Duncan, Otis Dudley. *The American Occupational Structure*. New York: John Wiley, 1967: 357.

Bradburn, Norman M. *The Structure of Psychological Well-Being*. Chicago, Ill.: Aldine, 1969: 149.

Bradburn, Norman M., and Caplowitz, David. *Report on Happiness*. Chicago, Ill.: Aldine, 1965: 9.

Burgess, E. W., and Wallin, Paul. *Engagement and Marriage*. Philadelphia, Pa.: J. B. Lippincott, 1953: 663.

Butler, Robert N. "Aspects of Survival and Adaptation in Human Aging." *American Journal of Psychiatry* 123 (April 1967): 1233–43.

Caplowitz, David. *See* Bradburn, Norman M.

Carter, Hugh, and Glick, Paul. *Marriage and Divorce: A Social and Economic Study*. Cambridge, Mass.: Harvard University Press, 1970: 348.

Clark, Walter. *See* Knupfer, Genevieve.

Duncan, Otis Dudley. *See* Blau, Peter.

Durkheim, Emile. *Suicide*. Trans. by J. A. Spaulding and George Simpson. New York: Free Press, 1951: 271.

Feld, Sheila. *See* Veroff, Joseph.

Glick, Paul C. "First Marriages and Remarriages." *American Sociological Review* 14 (December 1949): 727.

———. "Marriage, Socio-Economic Status and Health." In *World Views of Population Problems*. Hungarian Academy of Sciences, 1968: 135.

———. "Marital Stability as a Social Indicator." *Social Biology* 16 (September 1969): 158–66.

———. and Norton, Arthur J. "Frequency, Duration, and Probability of Marriage and Divorce." Mimeographed, 1970: Table 5.

"Hearts That Yearn." *Medical Journal of Australia*. May 3, 1969: 922.

Johnson, Ralph E. "Some Correlates of Extramarital Coitus." *Journal of Marriage and the Family* 32 (August 1970): 451.

King, Haitung, and Bailar, John C., III. "The Health of the Clergy: Review of Demographic Literature." *Demography* 6 (February 1969): 34–35.

Kinsey, A. C., et al. *Sexual Behavior in the Human Male*. Philadelphia, Pa.: W. B. Saunders, 1948: 585.

Klausner, Samuel Z., ed. *Why Men Take Chances*. New York: Doubleday, 1968.

Knupfer, Genevieve; Clark, Walter; and Room, Robin. "The Mental Health of the Unmarried." *American Journal of Psychiatry* 122 (February 1966): 842.

Lee, Russell V. Paper given at California Conference on Marriage, February 1964.

Maddison, David. "The Relevance of Conjugal Bereavement for Preventive Psychiatry." *British Journal of Medical Psychiatry* 41 (June 1968): 223–33.

———. "The Consequences of Conjugal Bereavement." *Nursing Times*. January 9, 1969: 50–52.

Marx, John, and Spray, S. Lee. "Marital Status and Occupational Success among Mental Health Professionals." *Journal of Marriage and the Family* 32 (February 1970): 114.

National Center for Health Statistics, *Suicide in the United States 1950–1964*. Series 20, No. 5, Public Health Service, 1967.

Norton, Arthur J. *see* Glick, Paul.

Ødegard, Ørnulv. "Marriage and Mental Health." *ACTA Psychiatrica et Neurologica Scandinavica*. Supplement No. 80, Report on the 10th Congress of Scandinavian Psychiatrists. Stockholm, 1952: 153, 160–61.

Odin, Melita H. "The Fulfillment of Promise: 40-Year Follow-up of the Terman Gifted Group." *General Psychology Monographs* 77 (1968): 92.

Pollak, Otto. *The Criminality of Woman* (Philadelphia, Pa.: University of Pennsylvania Press, 1950): 108, 157.

Room, Robin. *See* Knupfer, Genevieve.

Routh, Harold V. "The Progress of Social Literature in Tudor Times." In A. W. Ward and A. R. Waller, eds. *The Cambridge History of English Literature*. New York: Macmillan, 1933: 100.

Spray, S. Lee. *See* Marx, John H.

Terman, Lewis M. *Psychological Factors in Marital Happiness*. New York: McGraw-Hill, 1938: 336.

U.S., Department of Labor, 1969. Women's Bureau. *1969 Handbook on Women Workers*: 32.

Veroff, Joseph, and Feld, Sheila. *Marriage and Work in America*. New York: Van Nostrand-Reinhold, 1970: 89.

Whyte, William H., Jr. *The Organization Man*. New York: Simon and Schuster, 1956: 258–63.

chapter three: the wife's marriage

Adams, Whitney. "Woman in Advertising." *The Vocal Majority*. (June 1971): 19–21.

Ariès, Philippe. *Centuries of Childhood, A Social History of Family Life*. New York: Knopf, 1962: 390 ff.

Bauman, Karl E. "Relationship Between Age at First Marriage, School Dropout, and Marital Instability: An Analysis of the Glick Effect." *Journal of Marriage and the Family* 29 (November 1967): 672–80.

Bernard, Jessie. *American Family Behavior*. New York: Harper, 1942; New York: Russell and Russell, in press.

———. *The Sex Game*. Englewood Cliffs, N.J.: Prentice-Hall, 1968; New York: Atheneum, 1972.

———. "The Paradox of the Happy Marriage." In Vivian Gornick and Barbara Moran, eds. *Women in Sexist Society*,

Studies in Power and Powerlessness. New York: Basic Books, 1971: 85–98.

Bradburn, Norman M. *The Structure of Psychological Well-Being*. Chicago, Ill.: Aldine, 1969: 168.

Broverman, Inge K., et al. "Sex-Role Stereotypes and Clinical Judgments of Mental Health." *Journal of Counseling and Clinical Psychology* 34 (February 1970): 6–7.

Burgess, E. W., and Wallin, Paul. *Engagement and Marriage*. Philadelphia, Pa.: J. B. Lippincott, 1953.

Burke, Lee, et al. "The Depressed Woman Returns, A Study of Posthospital Adjustment." *Archives of General Psychiatry* 16 (May 1967): 551, 511.

Burr, Wesley R. "Satisfaction with Various Aspects of Marriage over the Life Cycle." *Journal of Marriage and the Family* 32 (February 1970): 29–37.

Canby, Henry Seidel. *The Age of Confidence*. New York: Farrar and Rinehart, 1934: 174.

Cheraskin, E., and Ringdorf, W. M. "Familial Factors in Psychic Adjustment." *Journal of the American Geriatric Society* 17 (June 1969): 609–11.

Coolidge, Mary Roberts. *Why Women Are So*. New York: Holt, 1912: chapter 4.

De Tocqueville, Alexis. *Democracy in America*. New York: J. and H. G. Langley, 1840: 209–10.

Evans, John W. *See* Seeman, Melvin.

Feld, Sheila. *See* Gurin, Gerald.

Feld, Sheila. *See* Veroff, Joseph.

Feldman, Harold. *Development of the Husband-Wife Relationship*. Ithaca, N.Y.: Cornell University Press, 1965: 112.

Ferber, Andrew, et al. "Current Family Structure, Psychiatric Emergencies, and Patient Fate." *Archives of General Psychiatry* 16 (June 1967): 659–67.

Folsom, Joseph K. *The Family and Democratic Society*. New York: John Wiley, 1934: 432.

Foote, Nelson. "Matching of Husband and Wife in Phases of Development." *Transactions of the Third World Congress of Sociology* 4 (1956).

Gavron, Hannah. *The Captive Wife: Conflicts of Housebound Mothers*. London: Routledge and Kegan Paul, 1966.

Glick, Paul C. *American Families*. New York: John Wiley, 1957: 154.

———. "Marriage, Socio-Economic Status and Health." In *World Views of Population Problems*. Hungarian Academy of Sciences, 1968: 135.

Gurin, Gerald; Veroff, Joseph; and Feld, Sheila. *Americans*

View Their Mental Health. New York: Basic Books, 1960: 42, 72, 110, 190, 234–35.

Hamilton, G. V. *A Research on Marriage.* New York: Boni, 1929.

Hubback, Judith. *Wives Who Went to College.* London: William Heinemann, 1957.

Johnson, Winifred Burt, and Terman, Lewis M. "Personality Characteristics of Happily Married, Unhappily Married, and Divorced Persons." *Character and Personality* 3 (June 1935): 304–5.

Kafka, John S.; Ryder, Robert G.; and Olson, David H. "A Nonconventional Pattern within the Conventional Marriage Framework." Mimeograph, n.d., p. 10.

Kepecs, Joseph B. *See* Rice, David G.

Kinsey, Alfred C., et al. *Sexual Behavior in the Human Male.* Philadelphia, Pa.: W. B. Saunders, 1948: 298, 303.

Klemer, Richard H. "Factors of Personality and Experience Which Differentiate Single from Married Women." *Marriage and Family Living* 16 (February 1954): 44.

———. *Factors of Personality and Experience Which Differentiate Single from Married Women.* Doctoral dissertation, Florida State University, 1953.

Knupfer, Genevieve; Clark, Walter; and Room, Robin. "The Mental Health of the Unmarried." *American Journal of Psychiatry* 122 (February 1966): 844.

Komarovsky, Mirra. "Functional Analysis of Sex Roles." *American Sociological Review* 15 (August 1950): 508–16.

———. *Blue-Collar Marriage.* New York: Random House, 1964.

Locke, Harvey J. *Predicting Adjustment in Marriage: A Comparison of a Divorced and Happily Married Group.* New York: Holt, 1951: 68–69.

Lopata, Helena Z. *Occupation Housewife.* New York: Oxford University Press, 1971.

McMillan, Emile L. "Problem Build-up: A Description of Couples in Marriage Counseling." *The Family Coordinator* 18 (July 1969): 267.

Market Facts of Canada. Survey for Canadian Broadcasting Company. Toronto, January 1971.

Martinson, Floyd M. "Ego Deficiency as a Factor in Marriage." *American Sociological Review* 20 (April 1955): 161–64.

Merrimen, Eve. *After Nora Slammed the Door.* Cleveland, Ohio: World Publishing Co., 1964.

Nye, F. Ivan. "Marital Interaction." In F. Ivan Nye and Lois Wladis Hoffman, eds. *The Employed Mother in America.* Chicago, Ill.: Rand McNally, 1963: 263–81.

Olson, David H. *See* Kafka, John S.

Orden, Susan R., and Bradburn, Norman. "Dimensions of Marriage Happiness." *American Journal of Sociology* 73 (May 1968): 717.

Pollak, Otto. *The Criminality of Women*. Philadelphia, Pa.: University of Pennsylvania Press, 1950: 157.

Public Health Service, National Center for Health Statistics. *Selected Symptoms of Psychological Distress*. August 1970: 9.

Rainwater, Lee. *And the Poor Get Children*. Chicago. Ill.: Quadrangle Books, 1960: 67–69.

Renne, Karen S. "Correlates of Dissatisfaction in Marriage." *Journal of Marriage and the Family* 32 (February 1970).

Rice, David G., and Kepecs, Joseph G. "Patient Sex Differences and MMPI Changes—1958 to 1969." *Archives of General Psychiatry* 23 (August 1970): 185–192.

Riesman, David. Introduction to Jessie Bernard, *Academic Women*. Philadelphia, Pa.: The Pennsylvania State University Press, 1964: xxiv.

Ringsdorf, W. M. *See* Cheraskin, E.

Rollins, Boyd C., and Feldman, Harold. "Marital Satisfaction over the Family Life Cycle." *Journal of Marriage and the Family* 32 (February 1970): 20–28.

Ross, Dorothy Robinson. "The Story of the Top One Percent of the Women at Michigan State University." Unpublished study.

Rossi, Alice. "Transition to Parenthood." *Journal of Marriage and the Family* 30 (February 1968): 34.

Ryder, Robert G. *See* Kafka, John S.

Schiff, Thomas J. "Negotiating Reality: Notes on Power in the Assessment of Responsibility." *Social Problems* 16 (Summer 1968): 7–10.

Schlesinger, Arthur M. *Learning How to Behave, A Historical Study of American Etiquette Books*. New York: Macmillan, 1946: 25.

Schulder, Diane B. "Does the Law Oppress Women?" In Robin Morgan, ed. *Sisterhood Is Powerful*. New York: Vintage, 1970: 157–60.

Seeman, Melvin, and Evans, John W. "Alienation and Learning in a Hospital Setting." *American Sociological Review* 27 (December 1962): 772–82.

Sharp, Lawrence J., and Nye, F. Ivan. "Maternal Mental Health." In F. Ivan Nye and Lois Wladis Hoffman, eds., *The Employed Mother in America*. Chicago, Ill.: Rand McNally, 1963: 309–19.

Slater, Philip. "What Hath Spock Wrought?" *Washington Post*, March 1, 1970.

Stoller, Robert J. *Sex and Gender.* New York: Science House, 1968: 63.

Terman, Lewis M., and Wallin, Paul. "Marriage Prediction and Marital-Adjustment Tests." *American Sociological Review* 14 (August 1949): 502.

————. *See* Johnson, Winifred Burt.

Tharp, Roland G. "Psychological Patterning in Marriage." *Psychological Review* 60 (March 1963): 114.

United States Census, 1960: Marital Status: Tables 4, 5, 6.

Veroff, Joseph, and Feld, Sheila. *Marriage and Work in America.* New York: Van Nostrand-Reinhold, 1970: 70.

Williams, Robert. "Book Power to the Fore." *Washington Post,* May 16, 1970.

Willoughby, Raymond R. "The Relationship to Emotionality of Age, Sex, and Conjugal Condition." *American Journal of Sociology* 43 (March 1938): 920–31.

chapter four: their children

Bart, Pauline. "Mother Portnoy's Complaint." *Transaction* 8 (November–December 1970): 71.

Bell, Robert. *Marriage and Family Interaction.* Homewood, Ill.: Dorsey Press, 1963: 335.

Bernard, Jessie. *Remarriage, A Study of Marriage.* New York: Dryden Press, 1956; New York: Russell and Russell, 1971: 127.

————. "One Role, Two Roles, Shared Roles." *Issues in Industrial Society* 2 (January 1971): 21–28.

————. "Demographic Trends and Structural Outcomes." In James A. Peterson, ed. *Marriage and Family Counseling.* New York: Association Press, 1968: 44–109.

————. *Women and the Public Interest, A Essay on Policy and Protest.* Chicago, Ill.: Aldine-Atherton, 1971.

Blood, Robert O., and Wolfe, Donald M. *Husbands and Wives.* Glencoe, Ill.: Free Press, 1960.

Brenton, Myron. *The American Male.* New York: Coward-McCann, 1966: 136, 193–94.

Burgess, E. W., and Wallin, Paul. *Engagement and Marriage.* Philadelphia, Pa.: J. B. Lippincott, 1953: 707–8.

Burr, Wesley R. "Satisfaction with Various Aspects of Marriage over the Life Cycle: A Random Middle Class Sample." *Journal of Marriage and the Family* 32 (February 1970): 29–37.

Campbell, Frederick L. "Family Growth and Variation in

Family Role Structure." *Journal of Marriage and the Family* 32 (February 1970): 48.

Coleman, M. D., and Zwerling, I. "The Psychiatric Emergency Clinic." *American Journal of Psychiatry* 115 (May 1959): 980–4.

Dizard, Jan. *Social Change in the Family*. Chicago, Ill.: University of Chicago Press, 1968: chapter 2.

Feld, Sheila. *See* Veroff, Joseph.

Feldman, Harold. *Development of the Husband-Wife Relationship*." Ithaca, N.Y.: Cornell University Press, n.d.: 126–8.

Glick, Paul C. *American Families*. New York: John Wiley, 1957: 66.

———, and Parke, Robert, Jr. "New Approaches in Studying the Life Cycle of the Family." *Demography* 2 (1965): 190.

Government of Sweden. *The Status of Women in Sweden*. Report to the United Nations, 1968.

Hobbs, Daniel, Jr. "Transition to Parenthood." *Journal of Marriage and the Family* 30 (August 1968): 413–7.

Hoffman, Lois W. "Effects on Children: Summary and Discussion." In F. Ivan Nye and Lois W. Hoffman, eds. *The Employed Mother in America*. Chicago, Ill.: Rand McNally, 1963: 210.

Hollingsworth, Lita S. "Social Devices for Impelling Women to Bear and Rear Children." *American Journal of Sociology* 22 (July 1916): 19–29.

Hurley, Jack R. and Palonen, Donna. "Marital Satisfaction and Child Density among University Student Parents." *Journal of Marriage and the Family* 29 (August 1967): 483–4.

Jones, Beverly. *Toward a Female Liberation Movement*. Boston: New England Free Press, n.d.: 15.

Le Masters, E. E. "Parenthood as Crisis." *Journal of Marriage and the Family* 19 (November 1957): 353.

Lieberman, James E. "A Case for the Small Family." *Population Reference Bulletin* (April 1970): 2–3.

Lopata, Helena Znaniecki. *Occupation Housewife*. New York: Oxford University Press, 1971: chapter 4.

Luckey, Eleanor. "Children: A Factor in Marital Satisfaction." *Journal of Marriage and the Family* 32 (February 1970): 44.

Meltzer, H. "Age and Sex Differences in Workers' Perceptions of Happiness for Self and Others." *Journal of Genetic Psychology* 105 (1964): 1–11.

National Center for Health Statistics, "Interval between First Marriage and Legitimate First Birth, United States, 1964–

1966." *Monthly Vital Statistics Report Supplement,* March 27, 1970: 1.

Nye, F. Ivan. "Marital Interaction." In F. Ivan Nye and Lois W. Hoffman, eds. *The Employed Mother in America.* Chicago, Ill.: Rand McNally, 1963: 269–72, 323.

Orden, Susan R., and Bradburn, Norman M. "Dimensions of Marriage Happiness." *American Journal of Sociology* 73 (May 1968): 392–407.

Palonen, Donna P. *See* Hurley, Jack R.

Parke, Robert, Jr. "Changes in Household and Family Structure in the U.S.A." *Proceedings of the International Population Conference, London, 1969.* Vol. III: 2244–63.

Peck, E. *The Baby Trap.* New York: Bernard Geis, 1971.

Peterson, James A. *See* Bernard, Jessie.

Renne, Karen S. "Correlates of Dissatisfaction in Marriage." *Journal of Marriage and the Family* 32 (February 1970): 61.

Rollins, Boyd C., and Feldman, Harold. "Marital Satisfaction over the Family Life Cycle." *Journal of Marriage and the Family* 32 (February 1970): 20–28.

Rose, Arnold. "Factors Associated with the Life Satisfaction of Middle-Class, Middle-Aged Persons." *Marriage and Family Living* 17 (February 1955): 15–19.

Rossi, Alice. "Transition to Parenthood." *Journal of Marriage and the Family* 30 (February 1968): 26–39.

Srole, Leo, et al. *Mental Health in the Metropolis: The Midtown Manhattan Study.* New York: McGraw-Hill, 1962: 164.

Sumner, William Graham. *Folkways.* Boston, Mass.: Ginn, 1911, 309–10.

Toffler, Alvin. *Future Shock.* New York: Random House, 1970.

U.S. Bureau of the Census, "Marital Status and Family Status: March 1969." *Current Population Reports,* Series P–20, No. 198, March 1970, p. 1.

Veroff, Joseph, and Feld, Sheila. *Marriage and Work in America.* New York: Van Nostrand-Reinhold, 1970.

Wallin, Paul. *See* Burgess, E. W.

Wolfe, Donald M. *See* Blood, Robert O.

Zwerling, I. *See* Coleman, M. D.

chapter five: marriage's past and its present future

Bernard, Jessie. *American Family Behavior.* New York: Harper, 1942: 171–2; New York: Russell and Russell, in press.

————. *American Community Behavior*. New York: Holt, Rinehart & Winston, 1962: 406–8.

————. "Infidelity: Some Moral and Social Issues." In Jules Masserman ed. *The Psychodynamics of Work and Marriage*. Vol. 16 (1970): 99–126.

Burgess, E. W., and Wallin, Paul. *Engagement and Marriage*. Philadelphia, Pa.: J. B. Lippincott, 1953: 663–4.

Calhoun, A. C. *Social History of the American Family*. Vol. 1. *Colonial Period*. Glendale, Calif.: Arthur H. Clark, 1917: 25–26.

Christie, Lee S. *See* Wells, Theodora.

Constantine, Joan M. *See* Constantine, Larry L.

Constantine, Larry L., and Constantine, Joan M. "Multilateral Marriage: An Alternate Family Structure in Practice." Mimeographed, n.d.: 13.

Cuber, John F., and Harroff, Peggy. *The Significant Americans, A Study of Sexual Behavior among the Affluent*. New York: Appleton-Century-Crofts, 1965: chapter 8.

Darwin, Charles. *Descent of Man*. Vol. 2 (London, 1888): 394 ff.

Davis, Kingsley. *Human Society*. New York: Macmillan, 1949: Chapter 7.

Easton, B. S., and Robbins, H. C. *The Bond of Honour, A Marriage Handbook*. New York: Macmillan, 1938: 49.

Farber, Bernard. *Family: Organization and Interaction*. San Francisco, Calif.: Chandler, 1964: 106–9.

Fletcher, Joseph. "Love Is the Only Measure." *Commonweal* 83 (1966): 431.

Haroff, Peggy. *See* Cuber, John F.

Homer's *Iliad*, Book VI.

Hunt, Morton. *The Affair: A Portrait of Extramarital Love in Contemporary America*. Cleveland, Ohio: World Publishing Co., 1969.

Kafka, John S.; Ryder, Robert G.; and Olson, David H. "A Nonconventional Pattern within the Conventional Marriage Framework." Mimeographed, n.d.: 19.

Kazickas, Jurate. "As Long as We Both Shall Love." *Washington Post*. February 7, 1971.

Kinsey, A. C. et al. *Sexual Behavior in the Human Male*. Philadelphia, Pa.: W. B. Saunders, 1948: 591.

Kraditor, Aileen S., ed. *Up from the Pedestal*. Chicago, Ill.: Quadrangle Books, 1968.

Laslett, Peter. *The World We Have Lost*. London: Methuen, 1965.

Martin, Judith. "Sex: An Answer." *Washington Post*, June 15, 1970.

Medsger, Betty. "Presbyterians Study Liberal Attitude on Sex." *Ibid.* May 26, 1970.

————. "Lutherans Weigh Stand on Extramarital Unions." *Ibid.* July 2, 1970.

Neubeck, Gerhard, ed. *Extra-Marital Relations.* Englewood Cliffs, N.J.: Prentice-Hall, 1969.

Noonan, John T., Jr. "Intellectual and Demographic History." *Daedalus.* Spring 1968: 468.

Olson, David H. *See* Kafka, John S.

Orth, Penelope. Personal letter. August 17, 1969.

Peron, Jean. *Du Mariage et du Contrat de Mariage.* Paris: Fernand Sorlot, 1938: 30.

Radler, D. H. *See* Remmers, H. H.

Reiss, Ira L. *The Social Context of Premarital Sexual Permissiveness.* New York: Holt, Rinehart & Winston, 1967.

Remmers, H. H., and Radler, D. H. *The American Teenager.* Indianapolis, Ind.: Bobbs-Merrill, 1957.

Richard, Paul. "Dissolving a Marriage." *Washington Post.* November 6, 1969.

Robbins, H. C. *See* Easton, B. S.

Russell, Bertrand. *Marriage and Morals.* New York: Liveright, 1929.

Ryder, Robert G. *See* Kafka, John S.

1 Sam. 1: 22, 23.

Sapirstein, M. R. *Emotional Security.* New York: Crown Press, 1948: 174.

Schlatter, Richard Bulger. *The Social Ideas of Religious Leaders 1660–1668.* New York: Oxford University Press, 1940: 29–30.

Sewell, Mary Ann. "Variety Is Her Cup of Tea." *Washington Post.* September 8, 1967.

Sumner, William Graham. *Folkways.* Boston, Mass.: Ginn, 1906: 348–9.

Unsigned. "Psychology of Fear." *Parade.* October 5, 1969.

Van Hoffman, Nicholas. " 'Renewable' Marriage." *Washington Post.* June 12, 1970.

Wallin, Paul. *See* Burgess, E. W.

Washington *Evening Star.* February 26, 1971.

Washington Post. July 13, 1969.

Ibid. October 19, 1969.

Ibid. April 2, 1970.

Ibid. October 4, 1969.

Ibid. June 7, 1971.

Wells, Theodora, and Christie, Lee S. "Living Together, An Alternative to Marriage." *The Futurist* 4 (April 1970): 51.

Westermarck, Edward. *The History of Human Marriage*. New York: Allerton, 1922. Vol. I: 334.

Whipple, A.B.C. "Things I Bet You Didn't Know." *Atlantic Monthly*. February 1971: 116.

Whitehurst, Robert N. "The Unmalias on Campus." Paper presented at meetings of National Council Family Relations. October 1969.

Wischnitzer, Rachel Bernstein. "Ketubah." *Universal Jewish Encyclopedia*. Universal Jewish Encyclopedia, 1948. Vol. 6: 367–72.

Yankelovich, Daniel, Inc. *Generations Apart*. A study of the generation gap conducted for CBS News (Columbia Broadcasting System, Inc., 1969).

chapter six: can any number play?

Bergler, Edmund. *Divorce Won't Help*. New York: Harper, 1948: 11.

Bernard, Jessie. *Remarriage, A Study of Marriage*. New York: Russell and Russell, 1971.

Calhoun, Arthur W. *A Social History of the American Family*. Vol. I. Glendale, Calif., A. H. Clarke, 1917: 168.

Dizard, Jan. *Social Change in the Family*. Chicago, Ill.: University of Chicago Press, 1968: 1.

Folsom, J. K. *The Family and Democratic Society*. New York: John Wiley, 1934: 479.

Foote, Nelson N. "Matching of Husband and Wife in Phases of Development." *Transactions of Third World Congress of Sociology*. 1956, Vol. 4: 29.

Glick, Paul C. "Permanence of Marriage." *Population Index*. October 1967.

Goldsen, Rose K., et al. *What College Students Think*. Princeton, N.J.: Van Nostrand, 1960: 85.

Kleinsrud, Judy. "Purchasing a House: A Matriarchal Move?" *New York Times*. September 5, 1967.

Kubie, Lawrence. "Psychoanalysis and Marriage, Practical and Theoretical Issues." In Victor W. Eisenstein, ed. *Neurotic Interaction in Marriage*. New York: Basic Books, 1956.

Loewy, Raymond. *Homes and Housing*. William Smith, 1967.

Laslett, Peter. *The World We Have Lost*. London: Methuen, 1965.

Milford, Nancy. *Zelda: A Biography*. New York: Harper and Row, 1970.

Mittelmann, Bela. "Analyses of Reciprocal Neurotic Patterns in

Family Relationships." In Victor W. Eisenstein, ed. *Neurotic Interaction in Marriage*. New York: Basic Books, 1956: 81–100.

Noonan, John T. "Intellectual and Demographic History." *Daedalus*. Spring 1968.

Russell, Bertrand. *Man and Morals*. New York: Liveright, 1929: 135–6.

Ryder, Robert G. "A Marriage Topography Derived from Unstructured Interviews." Mimeographed, n.d.

Schlatter, Richard Bulger. *The Social Ideas of Religious Leaders 1660–1688*. Stanford, Calif.: Stanford University Press, 1940: 16–18.

Spengler, Joseph J. "Demographic Factors and Early Modern Economic Development." *Daedalus*. Spring 1968: 433–46.

Tharp, Roland G. "Psychological Patterning in Marriage." *Psychological Bulletin* 60 (March 1963): 97–117.

Thrupp, Sylvia L. *The Merchant Class of Medieval London, 1300–1500*. Chicago, Ill.: University of Chicago Press, 1948: 193, 196.

U. S. Bureau of the Census. "Marital Status and Family Status: March 1970." *Current Population Reports*, Series P–20, No. 212, February 1, 1971, Table 1: 9.

Van De Walle, Etienne. "Marriage and Marital Fertility." *Daedalus*. Spring 1968: 490.

Van Haute-Minet, Michele. "Analyse Longitudinale de la Nuptialité des Célibataires et du Divorce." Paper presented at meetings of Congress of the International Union for the Study of Population, London, September 1969: 11.

Winch, Robert. *Mate Selection*. New York: Harper, 1958.

Wrigley, E. A. *Population and History*. New York: McGraw-Hill, 1969: 119.

Zelditch, Morris, Jr. "Family, Marriage, and Kinship." In Robert E. L. Faris, ed. *Handbook of Modern Sociology*. Chicago, Ill.: Rand McNally, 1964: 688–94.

chapter seven: are some more equal than others?

Bell, Norman, and Turk, James L. "The Concept of Power: Some Observations on the Power of a Concept." Paper presented at meetings of American Sociological Association, September 1970.

Belliveau, Fred, and Richter, Lin. *Understanding Human Sexual Inadequacy*. New York: Bantam, 1970: 146.

Bernard, Jessie. *American Family Behavior*. New York: Harper, 1942; New York: Russell and Russell, in press.

————. *The Sex Game*. Englewood Cliffs, N.J.: Prentice Hall, 1968; New York: Atheneum, 1972.

————. *Women and the Public Interest, An Essay on Policy and Protest*. Chicago, Ill.: Aldine-Atherton, 1971.

Blood, Robert O., and Wolfe, Donald M. *Husbands and Wives*. Glencoe, Ill.: Free Press, 1960.

Brown, Malcolm. Quoted in *Newsweek*. September 21, 1971: 66.

Burgess, E. W., and Cottrell, Leonard, Jr. Unpublished study reported in E. W. Burgess and Leonard Cottrell, Jr. *Predicting Success or Failure in Marriage*. Englewood Cliffs, N.J.: Prentice-Hall, 1953.

————, and Locke, Harvey J. *The Family*. New York: American Book Co., 1945.

————, and Wallin, Paul. *Engagement and Marriage*. Philadelphia, Pa.: J. B. Lippincott, 1953.

Centers, Richard; Raven, Bertram; and Rodrigues, Aroldo: "Conjugal Power Structure: A Re-examination." *American Sociological Review* 36 (April 1971): 264–78.

Cottrell, Leonard, Jr. *See* Burgess, E. W.

Densmore, Dana. "Against Liberals." *Journal of Female Liberation* 2 (February 1969): 63.

————. "Without You and Within You." *Ibid.* 4 (April 1970): 50.

DuBois, Cora. *People of Alors*. Minneapolis: University of Minnesota Press, 1944: 112.

Dunbar, Roxanne. "Sexual Liberation." *Journal of Female Liberation* 3 (November 1969): 49–56.

Epstein, Nathan B. *See* Westley, William A.

Feld, Sheila. *See* Veroff, Joseph.

Feldman, Harold. *Development of the Husband-Wife Relationship*. Ithaca, N.Y.: Cornell University Press, 1965: 115.

Friedenberg, Edgar Z. "Southern Discomfort." *New York Review of Books*. September 2, 1971: 8.

Gordon, Michael, and Shankweiler, Penelope J. "Different Equals Less: Female Sexuality in Recent Marriage Manuals." *Journal of Marriage and the Family* 33 (August 1971): 459–66.

Gould, Robert E. "Single Girls and Sex." *Sexual Behavior*. October 1971: 26–34.

Heer, David M. "Dominance and the Working Wife." *Social Forces*. May 1958: 341–7.

Herzog, Elizabeth. *See* Zborowski, Mark.

Hill, Reuben. *See* Waller, Willard.

Hoffman, Lois W. "Parental Power Relations and the Division of Household Tasks." In Hoffman, Lois W., and Nye, F. Ivan. *The Employed Mother in America.* Chicago, Ill.: Rand McNally, 1963: 215–30.

Hurlbut, John B. *See* Vernier, Chester G.

Kinsey, A. C., et al. *Sexual Behavior in the Human Male.* Philadelphia, Pa.: W. B. Saunders, 1948: 199.

Kirkpatrick, Clifford. *The Family as Process and Institution.* New York: Ronald, 1955: chapter 7.

Klein, Viola. *The Feminine Character.* New York: International Universities Press, 1948.

Komarovsky, Mirra. *Blue-Collar Marriage.* New York: Random House, 1964: chapter 10.

Locke, Harvey J. *See* Burgess, E. W.

Lu, Yi-chuang. Unpublished study referred to in Burgess and Wallin, *op. cit.*: 637.

Maccoby, Eleanor E. Summary of research in aggression, in *Development of Sex Differences.* Stanford, Calif.: Stanford University Press, 1966: 323–6.

Maslow, A. H. "Dominance, Personality, and Social Behavior in Women." *Journal of Social Psychology* 10 (February 1939): 3–39.

———. "Self-esteem (Dominance Feeling) and Sexuality in Women." Ibid. 16 (1942): 259–94.

Mead, Margaret. Quoted in *Washington Post.* November 26, 1969.

Messinger, Sheldon L. Comments at meetings of Society for Study of Social Problems, August 1971.

Millett, Kate. *Sexual Politics.* New York: Doubleday, 1970.

Mowrer, Ernest. *The Family, Its Organization and Disorganization.* Chicago, Ill.: University of Chicago Press, 1932: 98.

Neubeck, Gerhard. "The Dimensions of Extra in Extramarital Relations." In Gerhard Neubeck, ed. *Extramarital Relations.* Englewood Cliffs, N.J.: Prentice-Hall, 1970: 12–24.

Nye, F. Ivan. "Marital Interaction." In Lois W. Hoffman and F. Ivan Nye, *The Employed Mother in America.* Chicago, Ill.: Rand McNally, 1963: 263–82.

Plutarch. *Selected Lives and Essays.* Trans. by Louise Ropes Loomis. New York: Walter J. Black, Vol. 2: 311.

Poloma, Margaret M. "The Myth of the Egalitarian Family: Familial Roles and the Professionally Employed Wife." Paper presented at meetings of American Sociological Association, September 1970.

Popenoe, Paul. "Can the Family Have Two Heads?" *Sociology and Social Research* 18 (September–October 1933): 12–17.

Raven, Reuben. *See* Centers, Richard.

Renne, Karen. "Correlates of Dissatisfaction in Marriage." *Journal of Marriage and the Family* 32 (February 1970): 50.

Richter, Lin. *See* Belliveau, Fred.

Rodrigues, Aroldo. *See* Centers, Richard.

Safilios-Rothschild, Constantina. "The Study of Family Power Structure: A Review 1960–1969." *Journal of Marriage and the Family* 32 (November 1970): 539–53.

Schapira, Isaac. *Married Life in an African Tribe*. London: Faber and Faber, 1939: 276–84.

Seidenberg, Robert. "Is Sex Without Sexism Possible?" *Sexual Behavior* 2 (January 1972): 46–48, 57–62.

Seward, Georgene H. *Sex and the Social Order*. New York: McGraw-Hill, 1946.

Shankweiler, Penelope. *See* Gordon, Michael.

Slater, Philip E. "What Hath Spock Wrought?—Freed Children, Chained Moms." *Washington Post*. March 1, 1970.

Swingers Life. Vol. 5, No. 2, 1970.

Terman, Lewis M. *Psychological Factors in Marital Happiness*. New York: McGraw-Hill, 1938.

Tharp, Roland. "Psychological Patterning in Marriage." *Psychological Bulletin* 60 (March 1963): 97–117.

Turk, James L. *See* Bell, Norman.

Udry, J. Richard. "Sex and Family Life." *Annals of the American Academy of Political and Social Science* 376 (March 1968): 29.

Unsigned. "Highlights of Masters and Johnson's Therapy Techniques." *Medical Aspects of Human Sexuality* 4 (July 1970): 37.

Vernier, Chester G., and Hurlbut, John B. *American Family Laws*. Vol. 3 *Husbands and Wives* (1935): 24.

Veroff, Joseph, and Feld, Sheila. *Marriage and Work in America*. New York: Van Nostrand-Reinhold, 1970.

Waller, Willard, and Hill, Reuben. *The Family, A Dynamic Interpretation*. New York: The Dryden Press, 1951.

Wallin, Paul. *See* Burgess, E. W.

Westley, William A., and Epstein, Nathan B. *Silent Majority*. San Francisco, Calif.: Jossey-Bass, 1969.

Winch, Robert. *Mate Selection*. New York: Harper, 1958.

Winick, Charles. "The Beige Epoch: Depolarization of Sex Roles in America." *Medical Aspects of Human Sexuality* 3 (February 1969).

Wolfe, Donald M. "Power and Authority in the Family." In D. Cartwright, ed. *Studies in Social Power*. Ann Arbor, Mich.: University of Michigan Press, 1959.

———. *See* Blood, Robert O., Jr.

Women's Bureau, *1969 Handbook on Women Workers.* U. S. Government Printing Office, 1969: 23 ff.

Wyse, Lois. In interview in *Washington Post.* November 15, 1970. Mrs. Wyse was the author of *Mrs. Success,* a book about modern Lady Macbeths who were tired of trying to achieve satisfaction of their achievement motivation by way of their husbands.

Zborowski, Mark, and Herzog, Elizabeth. *Life Is with People, The Culture of the Shtetl.* New York: Schocken Books, 1952: 131–2.

Zelditch, Morris, Jr. "Family, Marriage, and Kinship." In Robert E. L. Faris, ed. *Handbook of Modern Sociology.* Chicago, Ill.: Rand McNally, 1964: 680–730.

chapter eight: "other things being equal"; but are they?

Ariès, Phillipe. "Wills and Tombs: The Rise of Modern Family Feeling." *New Society.* September 25, 1969: 475.

Bell, Inge Powell. "The Double Standard." *Transaction.* (November-December 1970): 75–80.

Bell, Robert, and Chaskes, Jay B. "Premarital Sexual Experience among Coeds, 1958 and 1968." *Journal of Marriage and the Family* 32 (February 1970): 81–84.

Bergler, Edmund. *Divorce Won't Help.* New York: Harper, 1948: 11.

Bernard, Jessie. *American Family Behavior.* New York: Harper, 1942: 285–6; New York: Russell and Russell, in press.

––––––. *Social Problems at Midcentury.* New York: Holt, Rinehart & Winston, 1957: chapter 14.

––––––. "Education as a Demographic Variable." *International Population Conference* Vol. 3, London, 1969: 1876–90.

––––––. "Present Demographic Trends and Structural Outcomes in Family Life Today." In James A. Peterson, ed. *Marriage and Family Counseling, Perspective and Prospect.* New York: Association Press, 1968: 60–70.

––––––. "No News, but New Ideas." In Paul Bohannan, ed. *Divorce and After.* New York: Doubleday, 1970: 3–28.

––––––. *Women and the Public Interest, An Essay on Policy and Protest.* Chicago, Ill.: Aldine-Atherton, 1971.

Bernstein, Carl. "Communes, A New Way of Life in District." *Washington Post.* July 6, 1969.

Cleckley, Hervey. *The Mask of Sanity, An Attempt to Clarif Some Issues about the So-called Psychopathic Personality* St. Louis, Mo.: Mosby, 1955.

Current Digest of the Soviet Press, "Are Betrothals Necessary Today?" 20 (December 4, 1968): 13. Reproduced from letter to *Komsomolskaya Pravda*. November 17, 1968.

Dominian, Jack. *Marital Breakdown*. London: Pelican, 1968: 159.

Dunbar, Roxanne, and Gizzard, Vernon. *Students and Revolution*. Cambridge, Mass. Mimeograph, n.d.

Feld, Sheila. *See* Veroff, Joseph.

Glick, Paul. *American Families*. New York: John Wiley, 1957: 154.

———. "Population and Family Formation." Paper presented at the 44th Annual Agricultural Outlook Conference, November 15, 1966: 9.

———. "Permanence of Marriage." *Population Index*. October 1967.

———, and Norton, Arthur J. "Probabilities of Marriage, Divorce, Widowhood, and Remarriage." Paper read at meetings of the Population Association of America, Atlanta, Ga., April 1970: Table 2.

———. *See* Parke, Robert, Jr.

———. *See* Saveland, Walter.

Goldsmith, Roxanne, "Megafamily: Meaningful Togetherness." *Washington Post*. June 28, 1970.

Gizzard, Vernon. *See* Dunbar, Roxanne.

Hagerty, Everett L. "The Hippie Commune in Relation to the American Family." Paper presented at meetings of National Council on Family Relations (October 1969).

Huang, Lucy Jen. *The Impact of the Commune on the Chinese Family*. General Electric Company, Santa Barbara, Calif. (December 1962): 37.

Kennedy, M. S. "Whatever Happened to . . .?" *Potomac Magazine*. September 19, 1971.

Kinsey, A. C., et al. *Sexual Behavior in the Human Male*. Philadelphia, Pa.: W. B. Saunders, 1948: 586–7.

Komarovsky, Mirra. *Blue-Collar Marriage*. New York: Random House, 1964.

Laslett, Peter. *The World We Have Lost*. London: Methuen, 1965: 2–3.

Nam, Charles B. "Changes in the Relative Status Level of Workers in the United States, 1950–1960." *Social Forces* 47 (December 1968): 166.

National Center for Health Statistics, "Births, Marriages, Divorces, and Deaths for June 1971." August 25, 1971: 1.

Norton, Arthur J. *See* Glick, Paul.

Otto, Herbert A. "Has Monogamy Failed?" *Saturday Review*. April 25, 1970: 24.

Parke, Robert, Jr. "Age at Marriage and Subsequent Marital

Experience." Paper at Population Association of America, April 1965: 7.

————. "Changes in Household and Family Structure in the USA." *International Population Conference*, Vol. 3 (London, 1969): 2244–63.

————, and Glick, Paul C. "Prospective Changes in Marriage and the Family." *Journal of Marriage and the Family* 29 (May 1967): 256.

Parkes, Alan S. "Social Effects on Sexual Function." *Impact of Science on Society* 18 (October–December 1968): 274.

Piepponen, Paave. "Age and Marriage." Paper presented at London Conference of International Union of Population, 1969: 8.

Ryder, Norman B. "The Time Series of Fertility in the United States." *International Population Conference* Vol. 2 (London, 1969): 597.

Saveland, Walter, and Glick, Paul C. "First-Marriage Decrement Tables by Color and Sex for the United States in 1958–1960," *Demography* 6 (August 1969): 243.

Sorokin, Pitirim. *Social and Cultural Dynamics*. Vol. 4. New York: Harper, 1937: 776.

Sussman, Marvin B., ed. *Sourcebook in Marriage and the Family*. Boston, Mass.: Houghton Mifflin, 1968: chapter 3.

Terman, Lewis M., and Wallin, Paul. "Marriage Prediction and Marital-Adjustment Tests." *American Sociological Review* 14 (August 1949): 497–504.

Thompson, J. H. "Households and Family Structure in the United Kingdom." *International Population Conference* Vol. 3 (London, 1969): 2271–82.

Thrupp, Sylvia. *The Merchant Class of Medieval London 1300–1500*. Chicago Ill.: University of Chicago Press, 1948: 196.

U.S. Bureau of the Census, *Population, 1960: Age at First Marriage*. Table 17.

————. "Marital Status and Family Status, March 1969." Series P–20, No. 198, March 25, 1970: 1.

————. *Current Population Reports*, Series P–25, No. 394, June 6, 1968: 4.

Veroff, Joseph, and Feld, Sheila. *Marriage and Work in America*. New York: Van Nostrand-Reinhold, 1970.

Wallin, Paul. *See* Terman, Lewis M.

Watson, John B. Quoted in Chicago *Tribune*. March 6, 1927: 1.

Wrigley, E. A. *Population and History*. World University Library, 1969: 100, 105, 103.

Yablonsky, Lewis. *The Tunnel Back: Synonon*. New York: Macmillan, 1965.

Yankelovich, Daniel, Inc., *Generations Apart*. A study of the generation gap conducted for CBS News (Columbia Broadcasting System, Inc., 1969).

Zimmerman, Carle C. *The Family and Civilization*. New York: Harper, 1947: 796.

chapter nine: male prophets and prophecies

Bartell, Gilbert D. *Group Sex*. New York: Wyden, 1971.

Barth, Alan. "A State License to Have Children?" *Washington Post*. February 24, 1969.

Bernstein, Carl. "Communes, A New Way of Life in District." *Washington Post*. July 6, 1969.

Boulding, Kenneth. "The Family Segment of the National Economy." *Journal of Home Economics* 62 (September 1970): 447–54.

Constantine, Joan. *See* Constantine, Larry.

Constantine, Larry, and Constantine, Joan. "Multilateral Marriage: Alternate Family Structure in Practice." Mimeograph, September 12, 1969.

————. "Where Is Marriage Going?" *The Futurist* (April 1970): 46.

Ellison, Harlan, ed. *Dangerous Visions No. 3*. Berkeley Public Corporation, 1969.

Farson, Richard E., et al. *The Future of the Family*. Family Service Association of America, 1969: 55–76.

Glick, Paul C., and Norton, Arthur J. "Probabilities of Marriage, Divorce, Widowhood, and Remarriage." Paper presented at Population Association of America meetings, April 1970.

Grold, L. James. "Swinging: Sexual Freedom or Neurotic Escapism?" *American Journal of Psychiatry* 127 (October 1970): 521–3.

Holloway, Mark. *Heavens on Earth*. New York: Dover Publications, 1966.

Kenkel, William. "Marriage and the Family in Modern Science Fiction." *Journal of Marriage and the Family* 31 (February 1969): 14.

McKain, Walter C. *Retirement Marriage*. Storrs, Conn.: Storrs Agricultural Experiment Stations, 1968: 36–37.

Matthews, Tim. "A Featherweight Utopia without Buttons or Clocks." *Washington Post*. September 28, 1969.

Negley, Glenn, and Patrick, J. Max. *The Quest for Utopia*. New York: Henry Schuman, 1952.

Norton, Arthur J. *See* Glick, Paul.

Noyes, John Humphrey. *History of American Socialisms.* New York: Dover Publications, 1966.

Orleans, Myron, and Wolfson, Florence. "The Future of the Family." *The Futurist.* April 1970.

Patrick, J. Max. *See* Negley, Glenn.

Perrot, Roy. "Film-makers' Utopia." *Washington Post.* August 4, 1969.

Remsberg, Bonnie. *See* Remsberg, Charles.

Remsberg, Charles, and Remsberg, Bonnie. "Weird Harold and the First National Swingers' Convention." *Esquire.* December 1970: 189 ff.

Rossi, Peter. Cited in *Psychology Today.* March 1971: 20.

Sills, Yole G. "Social Science Fiction." *International Encyclopedia of the Social Sciences.* New York: Macmillan, Free Press, 1968. Vol. 14: 473–82.

Skinner, B. F. *Walden Two.* New York: Macmillan, 1948.

———. "The Design of Experimental Communities." *International Encyclopedia of the Social Sciences.* New York: Macmillan, Free Press, 1968. Vol. 16: 271–5.

Smith, James R. and Smith, Lynn G. "Co-Marital Sex and the Sexual Freedom Movement." *Journal of Sex Research* 6 (May 1970).

Smith, Lynn G. *See* Smith, James R.

Sturgeon, Theodore. "If All Men Are Brothers Would You Let One Marry Your Sister?" In Harlan Ellison, ed. *Dangerous Visions No. 3.* Berkeley Public Corporation, 1969: 6–55.

Symonds, Carolyn. "A Pilot Study of the Peripheral Behavior of Sexual Mate Swappers." Unpublished master's thesis, University of California, Riverside, Calif., 1967.

Toffler, Alvin. *Future Shock.* New York: Random House, 1970.

Unsigned editorial. *Journal of Female Liberation* 2 (February 1969): 8.

Unsigned survey report. *Psychology Today.* July 1970.

Varni, Charles A. "An Explanatory Study of Wife Swapping." Unpublished master's thesis, San Diego State College, 1970.

Wolfson, Florence. *See* Orleans, Myron.

chapter ten: female prophets and prophecies

Ansley, Fran. "Functions of the Theory and Practice of Male Chauvinism." *Female Liberation Newsletter.* Vol. 1, No. 1, n.d., p. 5.

Bernard, Jessie, "The Fourth Revolution." *Journal of Social Issues* 22 (April 1966): 76–87.

——. "One Role, Two Roles, Shared Roles." *Issues in Industrial Society*. Vol. 2 (1971): 21–28.

——. *Women and the Public Interest, An Essay on Policy and Protest*. Chicago, Ill.: Aldine-Atherton, 1971.

Bernstein, Judi; Morton, Peggy; Seese, Linda; and Wood, Myrna. *Sisters, Brothers, Lovers . . . Listen. . . .* Boston: New England Press, n.d.: 4.

Bross, Barbara. "How to Love Like a Real Woman." *Cosmopolitan*. June 1969.

Brown, Helen Gurley. *Sex and the Single Girl*. New York: Pocket Books, 1965.

Brown, Judith. *Toward a Female Liberation Movement*, Part II. New England Free Press, 1968.

Brownmiller, Susan. "Sisterhood Is Powerful." *New York Times Magazine*. March 15, 1970: 140.

Burton, Gabrielle. *I'm Running Away from Home But I'm Not Allowed to Cross the Street*. Pittsburgh: Feminist Press, 1972.

Densmore, Dana. "On Celibacy." *Journal of Female Liberation* 1 (November 1968): 22–25.

——. "Against Liberals." Ibid. 2 (February 1969): 63.

——. "The Quaker." Ibid. 2 (February 1969): 84.

——. "Chivalry—The Iron Hand in the Velvet Glove." Ibid. 3 (November 1969).

Dudar, Helen. "Women's Lib: The War on 'Sexism.' " *Newsweek*. March 23, 1970.

Dunbar, Roxanne. "The Man and Woman Thing." *Journal of Female Liberation* 2 (February 1969): 35.

——, and Gizzard, Vernon. *Students and Revolution*. Cambridge, Mass., mimeograph, n.d.

Farson, Richard, et al. *The Future of the Family*. New York: Family Service Association of America, 1969: 60.

Firestone, Shulamith. "Love." *Notes from the Second Year: Women's Liberation*. (1970).

——. *The Dialectic of Sex*. New York: William Morrow, 1970.

Giele, Janet. "History of Women's Groups in the United States." Paper at American Sociological Association, August 1971.

Gizzard, Vernon. *See* Dunbar, Roxanne.

Hill, Reuben. *See* Waller, Willard.

Hornig, Roberta. "See Aunt Debbie . . . First-Grade Symbol of Swinging Single." *Washington Evening Star*. March 28, 1970.

Jones, Beverly. *Toward a Female Liberation Movement*, Part I. New England Free Press, 1968.

Kearon, Pamela. "Man-Hating." *Notes from the Second Year: Women's Liberation* (1970).

Komarovsky, Mirra. *Blue-Collar Marriage.* New York: Random House, 1964: chapter 9.

Langhorst, Hilary. "A Final Word." *Journal of Female Liberation* 3 (November 1969): 114–6.

Leghorn, Lisa. "All or Nothing." Ibid.: 86.

Limpus, Laurel. *Liberation of Women, Sexual Expression, and the Family.* New England Free Press, n.d.: 61.

Mead, Margaret. "Marriage in Two Steps." *Redbook Magazine.* July 1966.

Morton, Peggy. *See* Bernstein, Judi.

O'Donnell, Ellen. "On Celibacy." *Journal of Female Liberation* 1 (November 1968): 14.

———. "Let Me Eat Cake!" Ibid.: 35.

Platt, John R. "Child Care Communities: Units for Better Urban Living." *The Urban Review* 3. (April 1969): 17–19.

Plutarch, *Selected Lives and Essays.* Trans. by Louise Ropes Loomis. New York: Walter J. Black, 1951: 316.

Reiss, Ira. L. *The Social Context of Premarital Sexual Permissiveness.* New York: Holt, Rinehart & Winston, 1967.

Scudder, Vida. *On Journey.* New York: Dutton, 1937: 212 ff.

Seese, Linda. *See* Bernstein, Judi.

Terry, Marilyn. "The Psychological Commune." *Journal of Female Liberation* 1 (November 1968): 60–61.

Unsigned. "Alternatives." *Off Our Backs.* May 16, 1970.

Unsigned editorial. *Journal of Female Liberation* 2 (February 1969): 9.

Unsigned editorial. *Women, A Journal of Liberation.* 1 (Winter 1970): 81.

Vidal, Gore. "Number One." *New York Review of Books.* June 4, 1970: 14.

Waller, Willard, and Hill, Reuben. *The Family, A Dynamic Interpretation.* New York: Dryden Press, 1951: 326.

Warrior, Betsy. "Man as an Obsolete Life Form." *Journal of Female Liberation* 2 (February 1969): 77–80.

Wells, Theodora, and Christie, Lee S. "Living Together, An Alternative to Marriage." *The Futurist* 4 (April 1970): 50–51.

Wood, Myrna. *See* Bernstein, Judi.

"Women Rap about Sex." *New York Notes from the First Year.* June 1968: 23–26.

Zielke, Harmut. Quoted in *Newsweek.* July 20, 1970: 76.

chapter eleven: the shared-role pattern

Bernard, Jessie. "Changing Family Lifestyles: One Role, Two Roles, Shared Roles." *Issues in Industrial Society* 2 (January 1971): 21–28.

————. *Women and the Public Interest, An Essay on Policy and Protest.* Chicago, Ill.: Aldine-Atherton, 1971: chapter 5.

Bradburn, Norman M. *See* Orden, Susan.

Brown, E. H. Phelps, and Browne, M. H. "Hours of Work." *International Encyclopedia of the Social Sciences.* Vol. 8. New York: Macmillan, Free Press, 1968: 487–90.

Browne, M. H. *See* Brown, E. H. Phelps.

Brownmiller, Susan. "Sisterhood Is Powerful." *New York Times Magazine.* March 15, 1970: 140.

Chute, David. "4-Day Week Seen as Possible Key to Improving Quality Control." *Washington Post.* March 7, 1971.

Feld, Sheila. "Feelings of Adjustment." In Lois W. Hoffman and F. Ivan Nye, eds. *The Employed Mother in America.* Chicago, Ill.: Rand McNally, 1963: 331–52.

Government of Sweden. *The Status of Women in Sweden.* A Report to the United Nations, 1968.

Grønseth, Erik. "The Dysfunctionality of the Husband Provider Role in Industrialized Societies." Paper prepared for the Seventh World Congress of Sociology, Varna, Bulgaria, 1970.

Hoffman, Lois W. "Division of Household Tasks." In Lois W. Hoffman and F. Ivan Nye, eds. *The Employed Mother in America.* Chicago. Ill.: Rand McNally, 1963: 215–30.

Jaffe, A. J. "Labor Force Definitions and Measurement." *International Encyclopedia of the Social Sciences.* Vol. 8. New York: Macmillan, Fress Press, 1968: 471.

Kennedy, M. S. "Whatever Happened to Joe and Casey and B. J. and Phil and Bob and Arlene and Jennifer and Carol and Hedy and Nan?" *Potomac Magazine.* September 19, 1971.

Komarovsky, Mirra. *Blue-Collar Marriage.* New York: Random House, 1964: chapter 3.

Leder, Kit. "Women in Communes." *Women, A Journal of Liberation* 1 (Fall 1969): 34.

Lueloff, Jorie. "...and Father Stayed Home." *Woman's Day* (August 1971): 53 ff.

Mainardi, Pat. "The Politics of Housework." *The Quicksilver Times* Supplement (October 16, 1969): 16–17. (This paper has been widely circulated in mimeographed form. It is included also in Robin Morgan, ed. *Sisterhood Is Powerful.* New York: Vintage, 1970: 447–54.)

North, Sandie. "The 50/50 Marriage: Is This What Women Want?" *Look Magazine,* October 5, 1971: 57–61.

Nye, F. Ivan. "Personal Satisfactions." In Lois W. Hoffman and F. Ivan Nye, eds. *The Employed Mother in America.* Chicago, Ill.: Rand McNally, 1963: 320–30.

————. "Marital Interaction." Ibid.: 263–81.

Oettinger, Louise. "Swedish View of Women." *Washington Post.* June 9, 1970.

Orden, Susan, and Bradburn, Norman M. "Working Wives and Marriage Happiness." *American Journal of Sociology* 74 (January 1969): 392–407.

Parade Magazine. December 27, 1970.

Peterson, Virginia. Release dated August 1970, by The Advocates, WGBH/KCET, Boston, Mass.

Poor, Riva. *4 Days, 40 Hours: Reporting a Revolution in Work and Leisure.* Boston: Bursk and Poor, 1970.

————. "A 3-Day Weekend Ahead?" *Washington Post.* September 5, 1971.

Renne, Karen. "Correlates of Marital Dissatisfaction in Marriage." *Journal of Marriage and the Family* 32 (February 1970): 54–67.

Rowan, Hobart. "Labor's Drift to 4-Day Week Is Inevitable." *Washington Post.* February 28, 1971.

Sexton, Patricia Cayo, *The Feminized Male.* New York: Random House, 1969.

Sharpe, Lawrence J., and Nye, F. Ivan. "Maternal Mental Health." In Lois W. Hoffman and F. Ivan Nye, eds. *The Employed Mother in America.* Chicago, Ill.: Rand McNally, 1963: 309–19.

Talbot, Stanley. *Time Magazine.* November 10, 1952: 109.

U.S. Department of Labor, Women's Bureau, *1969 Handbook on Women Workers* (1969): 49.

Washington Post, November 7, 1971.

chapter twelve: toting it all up

Bernard, Jessie. "No News, but New Ideas." In Paul Bohannan, ed. *Divorce and After.* New York: Doubleday, 1970: 3–28.

————. "Jealousy in Marriage." *Medical Aspects of Human Sexuality* 5 (April 1971): 200–15.

Bettelheim, Bruno. *Children of the Dream.* New York: Macmillan, 1969.

Davis, Kingsley. *Human Society*. New York: Macmillan, 1947: chapter 7.

Farson, Richard. "How Could Anything That Feels So Bad Be So Good?" *Saturday Review*. September 6, 1969: 20.

Freud, Sigmund. *Civilization and Its Discontents*. New York: Doubleday Anchor, 1958.

Goode, W. J. *World Revolution and Family Patterns*. New York: Free Press, 1963: 366–80.

Huxley, Aldous. *Brave New World*. New York: Harper, 1946.

Keniston, Kenneth. *The Uncommitted, Alienated Youth in American Society*. New York: Delta Books, 1965.

Marcuse, Herbert. *Eros and Civilization, A Philosophical Inquiry into Freud*. Boston, Mass.: Beacon Press, 1966.

Miller, Daniel R., and Swanson, Guy E. *The Changing American Parent*. New York: John Wiley, 1958.

Ogburn, W. F. *Social Change*. New York: B. W. Huebsch, 1922: 244.

Orwell, George. *1984*. New York: Harcourt, Brace, 1949.

Swanson, Guy E. *See* Miller, Daniel R.

Unsigned letter. *Psychology Today*. October 1969: 62.

Westermarck, Edward. *The History of Human Marriage*. Allerton, 1922: chapter 8. (First edition, 1891.)

afterword

1. Hochschild, Arlie, "Another Idol of Social Science." *Transaction*. November-December 1970: 13–14.

index

ABOUT THE AUTHOR

DR. JESSIE BERNARD, widely known for her research and scholarship in the fields of family and community organization, is professor emerita of sociology at Penn State University. Dr. Bernard is the author of *American Family Behavior*, *Academic Women*, and *The Sex Game*, among other titles. She makes her home in Washington, D.C.

We Deliver!
And So Do These Bestsellers.

RELAX!

SIT DOWN
and Catch Up On Your Reading!

☐	THE BELL JAR by Sylvia Plath	(6400—$1.75)
☐	HER by Anonymous	(6669—$1.50)
☐	THE EXORCIST by William Peter Blatty	(7200—$1.75)
☐	THE DAY OF THE JACKAL by Frederick Forsyth	(7377—$1.75)
☐	SHEILA LEVINE IS DEAD AND LIVING IN NEW YORK by Gail Parent	(7633—$1.50)
☐	THE ODESSA FILE by Frederick Forsyth	(7744—$1.75)
☐	THE HARRAD EXPERIMENT by Robert Rimmer	(7950—$1.50)
☐	THE LOVE MACHINE by Jacqueline Susann	(7970—$1.75)
☐	ONCE IS NOT ENOUGH by Jacqueline Susann	(8000—$1.95)
☐	SERPICO by Peter Maas	(8244—$1.75)
☐	THE FIFTH ESTATE by Robin Moore	(8333—$1.75)
☐	THE MANNINGS by Fred Mustard Stewart	(8400—$1.95)
☐	BURR by Gore Vidal	(8484—$1.95)
☐	JAWS by Peter Benchley	(8500—$1.95)
☐	THE BEGGARS ARE COMING by Mary Loos	(8540—$1.75)

Buy them at your local bookstore or use this handy coupon for ordering:

Bantam Books. Inc.. Dept. FBB. 414 East Golf Road. Des Plaines. Ill. 60016

Please send me the books I have checked above. I am enclosing $_____$ (please add 35¢ to cover postage and handling). Send check or money order —no cash or C.O.D.'s please.

Mr/Mrs/Miss_____

Address_____

City_____State/Zip_____

FBB—2/75

Please allow three weeks for delivery. This offer expires 2/76.

Bantam
On Psychology

- [ ] THE FIFTY-MINUTE HOUR, Robert Lindner — 4388 • .95
- [ ] PSYCHOANALYSIS AND RELIGION, Erich Fromm — 5558 • .95
- [ ] BLACK RAGE, William H. Grier, M.D. and Price M. Cobbs, M.D. — 6881 • $1.25
- [ ] BREAKING FREE, Nathaniel Branden — 7002 • $1.25
- [ ] PSYCHO-CYBERNETICS AND SELF-FULFILLMENT, Maxwell Maltz, M.D. — 7286 • $1.50
- [ ] IN AND OUT THE GARBAGE PAIL, Fritz Perls — 7299 • $1.65
- [ ] GOING CRAZY: THE RADICAL THERAPY OF R. D. LAING, Dr. Hendrik Ruitenbeek, ed. — 7352 • $1.65
- [ ] THE DISOWNED SELF, Nathaniel Branden — 7502 • $1.50
- [ ] THE MIND GAME: WITCHDOCTORS AND PSYCHIATRISTS, E. Fuller Torrey — 7657 • $1.50
- [ ] WHAT DO YOU SAY AFTER YOU SAY HELLO? Eric Berne, M.D. — 7711 • $1.95
- [ ] NUTRITION AND YOUR MIND: The Psychochemical Response, George Watson — 7793 • $1.95
- [ ] THE PSYCHOLOGY OF SELF-ESTEEM: A New Concept of Man's Psychological Nature, Nathaniel Branden — 7862 • $1.50
- [ ] GESTALT THERAPY VERBATIM, Fritz Perls — 8022 • $1.95
- [ ] AWARENESS: exploring, experimenting, experiencing, John O. Stevens — 8053 • $1.95
- [ ] STRANGERS TO THEMSELVES: Readings on Mental Illness, Gene and Barbara Stanford, eds. — 8267 • $1.25
- [ ] PSYCHOSOURCES, A Psychology Resource Catalog, Evelyn Shapiro, ed. — 8501 • $5.00

Buy them at your local bookstore or use this handy coupon for ordering:

Bantam Books, Inc., Dept. ME, 414 East Golf Road, Des Plaines, Ill. 60016

Please send me the books I have checked above. I am enclosing $_____
(please add 35¢ to cover postage and handling). Send check or money order
—no cash or C.O.D.'s please.

Mr/Mrs/Miss_____

Address_____

City_____State/Zip_____

ME—3/75

Please allow three weeks for delivery. This offer expires 3/76.

Bantam Book Catalog

It lists over a thousand money-saving best-sellers originally priced from $3.75 to $15.00 —bestsellers that are yours now for as little as 50¢ to $2.95!

The catalog gives you a great opportunity to build your own private library at huge savings!

So don't delay any longer—send us your name and address and 10¢ (to help defray postage and handling costs).

6879-SB
5-21